The
Belles of
New England

LOWELL OFFERING

December, 1845.

"*Is Saul also among the prophets?*"

A REPOSITORY
OF ORIGINAL ARTICLES, WRITTEN BY
"FACTORY GIRLS."

LOWELL MISSES CURTIS & FARLEY.
Boston: Jordan & Wiley, 121
Washington street.
1845.

The Belles of New England

The Women of the Textile Mills
and the Families Whose
Wealth They Wove

WILLIAM MORAN

THOMAS DUNNE BOOKS
St. Martin's Press ♏ New York

THOMAS DUNNE BOOKS.
An imprint of St. Martin's Press.

www.stmartins.com

Design by Kathryn Parise

Endpapers: The Amoskeag Mills collected portraits of the men and women who traveled to Manchester to work for the company. (Courtesy of the Manchester Historic Association)
Frontispiece: The *Offering* was one of the first workers' publications in the country. (Courtesy of the American Textile History Museum, Lowell, Massachusetts)
Excerpt from "A Lone Striker" from *The Poetry of Robert Frost* edited by Edward Connery Lathem, © 1964 by Lesley Frost Ballantine, copyright 1936 by Robert Frost, © 1969 by Henry Holt and Co. Reprinted by permission of Henry Holt and Company, LLC.
Excerpt from the poem "Parlez-vous?" by Paul Marion is reprinted by permission of the author and Loom Press. Copyright © 1985 by Paul Marion.

LIBRARY OF CONGRESS CATALOGING-IN-PUBLICATION DATA
Moran, William, 1934-
    The belles of New England : the women of the textile mills and the families whose wealth they wove / William Moran.
        p. cm.
    Includes bibliographical references (p. 267) and index (p. 277).
    ISBN: 0-312-32600-9   ISBN: 978-0-312-32600-5
    1. Women and textile workers—New England—History. 2. Textile industry—New England—History. 3. Industrialists—New England—History. 4. Family-owned business enterprises—New England—History. 5. Rich people—New England—History. 6. Social classes—New England—History. I. Title.

HD6073.T42 U56 2002
338.4'7677'0097409034—dc21

2002068378

D 10 9 8 7 6 5

For Nancy, Lisa, and Beth

CONTENTS

‐‐‐—◦◦●◦◦—

CONTENTS

ACKNOWLEDGMENTS

This book could not have been written without the help of the people acknowledged here. I am grateful to Roy Rowan, a distinguished journalist who opened the doors to the world of book publishing for me. My agent, Myra Manning, led me through the doors, and was a tower of strength, determination, and optimism. Marcia Markland, my editor at Thomas Dunne Books/St. Martin's Press, and Cynthia Merman, my copy editor, guided this work to publication with insight and skill.

I owe special thanks to Clifton N. Burrowes, Jr., and Robert Pierpoint, who read early versions of the manuscript and guided me away from grammatical and editorial troubles. Whatever errors survived subsequent revisions are mine alone.

Louise Sandberg of the Special Collections desks at the Lawrence, Massachusetts, Public Library, read the chapter on the 1912 Lawrence strike and made helpful suggestions. She generously shared her knowledge of the city's industrial history. Claire Sheridan, librarian at the American Textile History Museum in nearby Lowell, was of invaluable help throughout the preparation of this book, as was Pat Jaysane of the Immigrant City Archives in Lawrence.

My thanks also to Jane E. Duggan, Willian Faucon, and Eugene Zepp

ACKNOWLEDGMENTS

of the Boston Public Library; Nicole Hayes and Christine Riggle of the Baker Library, Harvard Business School; Tom Featherstone of the Walter P. Reuther Library at Wayne State University, Detroit; Randy Manella and Catharina Slautterback of the Boston Athenaeum; Dan Walsh, curator at the Lowell National Historical Park; Penelope Rosemont, George H. Kerr Publishing Co., Chicago; Julie Herrada and Mark A. Chaffee of the Special Collections Library, University of Michigan; Mary Riley, librarian, and Kerry A. O'Brien, assistant dean of faculty, Bates College, Lewiston, Maine; Martha Mayo of the Center for Lowell History; Leslie A. Morris, curator of manuscripts, and Emily C. Walhout of the Reading Room, Houghton Library at the Harvard University; Eileen O'Brien, curator of library collections, Manchester (N.H.) Historic Association; Ken Skulski and Mary Armitage of the Immigrant City Archives in Lawrence; Patricia J. Albright, Mount Holyoke College Archives; James M. Jacobs, director, Immaculate Conception Cemetery in Lawrence; and for their help along the way, Ray Brady, James Houtrides, Myra MacPherson, Ardis Cameron, Meghan Stern, and Beth Moran. Finally, I thank Thomas Dunne for believing in this book.

The Belles of New England

I am going home where I shall not be obliged to rise so early in the morning, nor be dragged about by the factory bell, nor confined in a close noisy room from morning to night. I shall not stay here. . . . Up before day, at the clang of a bell and out of the mill by the clang of the bell—into the mill and at work in obedience to that ding-dong of a bell—just as though we were so many living machines.

—"The Spirit of Discontent" in the *Lowell Offering*. Author unknown.

1

A Place in the Universe

The young women who lived in northern New England in the early nineteenth century seemed destined to play a passive role in American history. They spent confining lives on isolated family farms and in tranquil rural villages. They helped with the farm chores or earned their keep as house servants for prosperous neighbors and assumed that eventually they would have a home of their own. That was what society expected of them. Marriage prospects were limited; the most likely candidates were young men who also worked on the farms. So women of purpose felt the shackles of mediocrity give way when the news began spreading in 1814: A cotton mill had just opened on the Charles River in Waltham, Massachusetts, near Boston, and it needed workers—women workers.

Newspapers published stories about the new enterprise, and travelers passing through told of seeing the busy factory. They said the mill provided wonderful benefits for the workers, including comfortable boardinghouses, a library, and evenings of lectures and music. And surely more mills like it would soon be built. The women already working in the Waltham mill wrote back home to rhapsodize about their good fortune.

They told of earning cash for the first time in their lives, of being on their own, of being free.

The mill was the creation of Francis Cabot Lowell, a Boston merchant whose decision to become a manufacturer was to affect the lives of millions of people through many generations. After Waltham, and after Lowell's death, his associates built a new textile city along the Merrimack River in Massachusetts and named it Lowell in his honor. Ten miles north, they built Lawrence. In New Hampshire, they created the mill cities of Manchester and Nashua. In Maine, thousands of looms hummed in factories that sprang up in the farm towns of the Saco River Valley.

Francis Cabot Lowell had conceived of the country's first complete factory to transform cotton bales into finished cloth. He hired unskilled "operatives" to tend machines that spun thread out of cotton, and skilled weavers to guide the thread through looms, creating finished fabrics. These women were among the first workers of the American Industrial Revolution. They were pioneers in the struggle for women's equal pay and equal rights in the workplace. They lost many of their battles, but they never surrendered to injustice. They helped give birth to the American labor movement, and they made history.

The Yankee farm women were the first wave of mill workers. At the very time they left the mills in large numbers, in the 1840s, Ireland was devastated by a potato famine, and Irish immigrants came into the mills. At the very time the Irish left the looms for better opportunities in America, Quebec farm families gave up the struggle to subsist on their worn-out land, and French Canadians took up new lives in the New England mill cities. In ensuing decades they were joined by immigrants from Europe who heeded the call of the mill bells. For some people, the jobs offered hope. For others, the work led to ruined health, drudgery, and despair. But with all their travails, the mill workers bequeathed to New England a rich diversity of languages, religions, and cultural traditions that are still evident in hundreds of neighborhoods where their descendants live.

Tourists who travel to New England glimpse with fleeting interest the many mills still standing but now mostly empty. Once, the mills proudly roared with industrial tumult, and the roar was heard in every home, store, schoolhouse, and shop. The factory cacophony proclaimed that there was economic vitality in the town, jobs for the people, and hope for the future. Now the old redbrick buildings with their mute bell towers are crumbling vestiges of a vanished way of life. A few of them contain museums memorializing the roles that the textile workers played in American industry. Some of them house trendy shops, restaurants, condominiums, and small industries, including textile firms. Mostly they are a hulking, gloomy presence standing in silence as if ashamed that they symbolize broken promises. They have no apparent relevance to the people who speed by them on highways, or even to those who live today in their shadows. Yet millions of Americans count someone in their families who in the past century operated screeching machinery in these buildings for twelve to fourteen hours a day, six days a week, until their bodies wore out.

At first, hundreds of young women stood at the looms and other machines that Francis Cabot Lowell built. Then thousands migrated to the new mill cities. Friends and neighbors gathered in village centers to join families in bidding good-bye as stagecoaches carried the women away. Women who could not afford the coach fare mounted the family horse and clung to a father or brother as they rode to the factory doors. The poorest of them packed a bag and walked over the hills and into the valleys of New England to apply for jobs at the factory gates.

The new mill system demanded social adjustments of everyone. There had never been such a structured manufacturing system in the country. There had never been such large numbers of young women living away from their families in American cities. Managers and workers alike had to figure out how to make the textile industry succeed. The first mill women had known hard work on their family farms but had never answered to a formal boss until they took orders from overseers in the mills. Most of the men who became overseers had never before been responsible for so many workers.

When the women began speaking up for themselves on work issues, they shocked the bosses and the public. Women were discouraged from creating a public fuss about anything. People remembered Thomas Jefferson's statement, made only a few decades earlier, that "the tender breasts of ladies were not formed for political convulsion." The mill women marched onto the American stage while New England Puritans still subscribed to John Calvin's sixteenth-century dictum: "Let the woman be satisfied with her state of subjection, and not take it amiss that she is made inferior to the more distinguished sex."

It was the sons who received the best education or the best trade apprenticeships. It was the sons who inherited the family farm. In the eyes of the law, a woman was not capable of spending her own money in a responsible way—and certainly not someone else's. Before 1840, a woman could not be the treasurer of her social club unless a male sponsor agreed to assume responsibility for her financial decisions. Women did not have the vote and they could not practice law, medicine, or any other profession. Almost all of them were dependent on men for their inferior existence. Their secondhand status suited Lyman Beecher, a prominent Calvinist clergyman of the time. He endorsed a resolution at a religious conference providing that "in social meetings of men and women for religious worship, females are not to pray." His daughters shrugged off his primitive view and inspired American women to strive for equality. Isabella Beecher Hooker worked in the suffragist movement, Catharine Beecher pioneered in women's education, and Harriet Beecher Stowe was the first American woman to achieve world fame as an author. The farm women heading for the new mills paid no heed, either, to those who would deny them a full role in society.

Soon, the mills were dependent on women, who became an important part of the American economy. In turn the women earned great rewards. "The thought that I am living on no one is a happy one, indeed," Ann Swett Appleton wrote to her sister after getting a job in a New Hampshire mill.

Ann Swett Appleton had fled to the mill from a broken family; her mother was in a mental institution and her father had turned to alcohol. Women worked at her side for their own reasons. Some were unmarried and could no longer abide the charity of relatives, some were runaway wives who used false names to get their jobs so they could vanish in the new industrial cities and start new lives. There were indigent widows who wanted to be something better than a maid or seamstress. A mill worker wrote that among the women who lived in her boardinghouse was one who had fled from a miserly father; he had told her to leave home and fend for herself. Another could no longer tolerate the grim life imposed on her by a strict, religious mother. Another had been abused in several homes where she had worked as a servant.

"The cotton factory was a great opening to these lonely and dependent women," wrote Harriet Hanson Robinson in *Loom and Spindle,* her account of life among the mill workers of Lowell in the 1830s. "From a condition approaching pauperism they were at once placed above want; they could earn money, and spend it as they pleased; and could gratify their tastes and desires without restraint, and without rendering an account to anybody. At last they had found a place in the universe; they were no longer obliged to finish out their faded lives mere burdens to male relatives."

Some who entered the mills acted on noble impulses. Laura Nichols of East Haddam, Connecticut, was a teenager when she went to work in a cotton mill in Moodus, near her home. She yearned for an education, but her parents, with four other children, had come on hard times. Years later she told her own children in a memoir that while sacrificing for her family she had never stopped thinking of the future. "I had no hope of riches," she wrote, "but felt there was something better within my reach and I must have it or die in the attempt. I began to realize that my future would be largely what I made of it, that my destiny was, as it were, in my own hands."

In the western Massachusetts town of Adams, Daniel Anthony built a small textile mill soon after the Waltham factory opened, and he, too, hired young women to work for him. Members of his family boarded the workers in their homes and conducted evening classes for them. His eleven-year-old daughter, Susan B. Anthony, admired the skill of a woman weaver and tried to persuade her father to promote the woman to overseer, a job traditionally held by men. The father refused, and Susan became a witness to the secondary role of women in American society.

Most of the men who went into the mills earned more pay than the women. Mechanics arrived with handmade tool chests. Machinists came to keep the looms in working order. Skilled dye workers emigrated from the textile centers of England to create American calico prints. Irish laborers came to build the mills, dams, and canal systems that carried water power to the mill machines. There was work for everyone who wanted a job. A thousand mills rose along the rivers of New England. By 1850, when Laura Nichols went to work in the Moodus mill, there were one hundred thousand mill workers in New England.

Day and night they produced the woven cloth that Americans needed from cradle to grave: fabrics for infant wear, bedspreads and tablecloths, dresses and suits, wedding gowns and formal wear, work clothes for everyone, hospital frocks, and silk linings for caskets.

Mills in the old whaling town of New Bedford turned out Wamsutta sheets and pillowcases. "We Weave the World's Worsteds," the Lawrence woolen mills boasted. In Lewiston, Maine, the Bates mills proudly proclaimed that their bedspreads were "Loomed to be Heirloomed." The Shelton Looms in Connecticut dressed society women in sheer negligees. The mills of Biddeford, Maine, wove "Lady Pepperell" blankets and towels for millions of American homes.

When America went to war, mill workers produced the wool for the blue uniforms that dressed the Union army at Gettysburg and Antietam, the doughboys' khaki during World War I, and the navy whites and army olive drabs of World War II. When Americans first went west, they loaded their Conestoga wagons and prairie schooners with jeans woven in the mills of Lowell and Lawrence. Pioneer women who made clothes for their families bought bolts of brightly colored calicos at frontier stores, but not without first asking, "Will it wash?" The calicos from New England mills held their colors through many washings. One of Francis Cabot Lowell's partners, Nathan Appleton, visited mills in Belgium and saw the manufacturing of fine lace. His New England mill workers were soon weaving lace curtains so efficiently that American women could afford a touch of class in their homes. When women peeled off their frumpy cotton hosiery for the last time, the mills wove the silk for more alluring stockings. When Jazz Age revelers threw out their petticoats, the mills produced filmy fabrics, and bold young flappers danced the 1920s away in knee-length dresses. Americans could choose from a dazzling variety of garments on the racks of Bonwit Teller in New York, Marshall Field in Chicago, Neiman-Marcus in Dallas, and Filene's of Boston. Rural customers shopped in small-town clothing stores and from the catalogs of Montgomery Ward and Sears, Roebuck.

In the early days of the industry, clipper ships loaded with New England finished cloth sailed to market ports on the Red Sea and the Indian Ocean. The most recognizable trademarks carried over the Pacific to Shanghai and Singapore were the symbols of American-made textiles. The image of a dragon imprinted on cloth signified that it was produced in the Pepperell Mill in Biddeford. An Indian head with three feathers told the world that the cloth was made in Nashua, New Hampshire. American merchant John Cushing wrote in 1830 that in China, "from the Emperor to the laborer," everyone wore clothing made of cotton produced in New England. Cushing correctly predicted that the American mills would dominate the Asian market. Two decades later a British reporter in India wrote, "American cotton manufacturers are already clothing our own Indian army." The mills had commercial customers, too, in Africa, Argentina, Brazil, Chile, Mexico, and Turkey. The looms of New England ran faster and faster to meet the demand. The mill women worked faster and harder to keep up. The mill owners made fortunes, even as social critics scorned them for exploiting their workers and abolitionists condemned them for using cotton picked by slaves.

The new industrialism inspired writers and poets. Harriet Farley, who edited a workers' magazine in the 1840s, wrote of the Lowell mills: "One of the most beautiful sights we have ever witnessed was . . . when all these factories were lighted up for the evening's labor. The uniform and brilliant illumination, with the lights again gleaming up from the calm Merrimack, the brightness of the city beyond, the clear blue sky above, from which the sparkling stars were sending down their glittering beams into the glassy waters of the river, all combined to form a spectacle, which might almost lead an observer to believe that our hard-working, matter-of-fact city had been transformed into a fairy land." The poet John Greenleaf Whittier saw Lowell as "a city springing up, like the enchanted palaces of the Arabian tales, as it were in a single night—stretching far and wide its chaos of brick masonry and painted shingles." Whittier, who lived in nearby Haverhill, was enchanted by the mill women, and his words helped form the public's favorable opinion of them. "Acres of

7

girlhood, beauty reckoned by the square rod," he wrote. "The young, the graceful . . . Who shall sneer at your calling? Who shall count your vocation otherwise than noble and ennobling?"

Whittier came to realize that the mills demanded much of the women. Many of the workers became ill and had to return home. Others left with maimed bodies. Some were scalped when their hair was caught up in machinery; some lost arms, hands, and fingers that were mangled by the speeding belts and gears that drove the machines.

Visitors who toured the mills never heard the screams of the injured and did not perceive the darker aspects of the workers' lives. Davy Crockett visited the Lowell mills in 1834, two years before he was to die at the Alamo. "I went in among the young girls and talked with many of them," Crockett was quoted as saying. "Not one expressed herself as tired of her employment, or oppressed with work; all talked well, and looked healthy." Charles Dickens hated the oppression of workers in the English textile mills of his time and also went to Lowell to see for himself: "Out of so large a number of females, many of whom were only then just verging upon womanhood, it may be reasonably supposed that some were delicate and fragile in appearance; no doubt there were. But I solemnly declare, that from all the crowd I saw in the different factories that day, I cannot recall or separate one young face that gave me a painful impression; not one young girl whom, assuming it to be a matter of necessity that she should gain her daily bread by the labour of her hands, I would have removed from those works if I had the power."

Most of the women worked long enough to save money to help pay off the mortgage on the family farm. Some put their brothers through Harvard and Yale and Amherst. Some put aside money for their weddings. Some started new lives on the expanding Western frontier. Some walked out of the mills and into the schools of higher education that were the first to admit women. When Mary Lyon, the founder of Mount Holyoke College, opened the doors of her "female seminary" in South Hadley, Massachusetts, in 1837, she announced, "It is for this class principally, who are the bone and sinew and the glory of our nation that we have engaged in this undertaking."

Laura Nichols held fast to her goal of leaving the mill in Connecticut to seek a better life. When she had managed to save fifty dollars she said good-bye to her family, took a parting glance at the beautiful old homes in East Haddam on the Connecticut River, and headed for Mary Lyon's school. "Steamboat to Hartford, railroad to Springfield . . . and stage to South Hadley was the way of travel," she wrote in her family memoir. "It was the first time I had ever been beyond Hartford. Can you imagine my emotion when the Seminary first dawned upon my view: a moment of joyous transport was that." She graduated from Mount Holyoke with the Class of 1854. Like countless other mill women, she became a teacher. Eventually, as Laura Nichols Bridgman, she and her minister husband went to Africa as missionaries.

It is unlikely that her overseer missed Laura Nichols when she left the mill. Plenty of other women, starting their own lives, would have been eager to replace her because history was on the side of the mill owners. There would always be replacements—people from the unyielding farmland of Ireland and Quebec, from the butchery of European wars, from the despair of mountain villages in Greece and Hungary, from the political repression and religious persecution of Poland and Russia, from the smoky textile cities of Germany and Belgium, from the islands of poverty in Portugal, from the misty highlands of Scotland, and from the sun-soaked hills of Italy and Lebanon. The immigrants came to do the hard work that was expected of them. They endured the bigotry of native New Englanders and struggled to save their cultural heritage. When their children ached with hunger, they struck for fair wages and humane working conditions, even as their priests tried to discourage them from challenging authority. Early in the twentieth century, they finally revolted against the mill owners' barbaric exploitation and turned for help to radical labor agitators. When they did that, police and company goons stood in their path, and National Guard machine guns took aim at them. But immigrants kept seeking jobs in the mills because they yearned to live in America. Factory gates from Maine to Connecticut continued to swing open in the predawn darkness to welcome their labor. After World War II, the mill owners coveted bigger profits in the South. They relinquished responsibility for the New England communities so dependent on them and closed the mill gates forever in the faces of their workers.

2

The Glory of the Nation

When the first women workers arrived in the new mill cities in the 1820s and 1830s, they marveled at the biggest buildings they had ever seen. These were the immense cotton factories, longer than a village lane, where they would spend so much time. The women chatted with country twangs and looked out of place in their homespun clothes, often hand-me-downs. They had whimsical names like Jerusha and Hepsabeth, Prudence and Patience, Leafy and Florilla.

The first thing they did after payday was go shopping. They were raised to observe Protestant tenets that commanded them to strive for salvation in another world. But working women with hard-earned cash in hand decided that life was meant to be enjoyed, too. Earthly delights enchanted them. In the new mill city of Lowell, they swept into the stores to buy satin capes, silks, and laces at Willoughby & Hill's on Central Street; fine hats in Mrs. A. A. Coburn's Silk and Straw Millinery at the corner of Merrimack and Kirk streets; boots and shoes at the American House Block; and books and stationery at B. C. Sargent in the City Hall building. The boldest of them smoked Egyptian cigarettes. The afflicted found relief with Ayer's Pills, a vegetable cathartic (dose from two to ten). The store counters brimmed with tortoiseshell combs, costume jew elry, and cosmetics for young women who had never before applied rouge to their alabaster cheeks.

After a few weeks in the city, the women did not look "country" anymore. People called them "factory girls" and "factory queens," titles they bore with pride. Factory-girl romance stories became a staple of magazines.

"I tell you Sarah, I feel pretty ambitious," Ann Swett Appleton wrote to her sister after getting a mill job in Manchester, New Hampshire. Referring to her overseer, she reported, "Yesterday forenoon Mr. Sage says Ann you may step out here and get your pay. He paid me four dollars for two weeks work. What do you think of that!"

Harriett Hanson Robinson remembered the excitement of young women like Ann Swett Appleton as they came to realize that others were willing to pay them for their labor: "After the first payday came, and they felt the jingle of silver in their pockets, their bowed heads were lifted, their necks seemed braced with steel, they looked you in the face, sang blithely among their looms and frames, and walked with elastic step to and from work."

They belonged to a class of women the nation idolized. "It is difficult to imagine any creature more attractive than an American beauty between the ages of fifteen and eighteen," James Fenimore Cooper acclaimed. "There is something in the bloom, delicacy, and innocence of one of these young things that reminds you of the conceptions which poets and painters have taken of angels."

Michel Chevalier, a visiting lawyer from France, was struck by the chivalrous manners of the new urban societies that protected young women from men who might take advantage of them. "What amongst us [Frenchmen] would pass for a youthful imprudence or a pretty trick is severely frowned upon . . . particularly by the Americans of New England," Chevalier wrote. It did not surprise him that farm families allowed their daughters to pursue new lives far from home because "they are under the safeguard of the public faith." A mill executive told Chevalier that among the thousands of young women in Lowell, there were only three known cases of pregnancy and that in each case, the parties involved married immediately and "we have no cases of actual bastardy."

In Dover, New Hampshire, mill owners boasted in 1835 that "there has never been a case of bastardy in Dover." Despite management's obvious desire to suggest social stability in the mill towns, there is no accurate information on the number of such incidents because women usually returned to their families to deal with private matters.

The fate of young women in factory towns was on the minds of many. A workers' magazine, *The Factory Girl's Garland,* gave mill women in the Exeter, New Hampshire, area much to think about: "Young ladies, when you are surrounded by dashing men . . . when the tones of love and the words of compliment float out together . . . when a daring hand is pressing yours, or your delicate tresses are lifted by him who you fancy loves you, when the moonlight invites to trusting, and the stars seem to breathe out innocence, listen with caution to the words you hear."

When the mill women strolled through the shopping districts, young bachelors tipped their hats to them. To the women, life must have been more exhilarating than in the old hometown; to the vastly outnumbered men, the mill cities must have seemed like paradise. Nathaniel Hawthorne thought many of the women would "mate themselves with the pride of drawing rooms and literary circles."

The women missed their families, their many other relatives, and their friends. They worried about those they left behind because everyone constantly faced life-threatening diseases including dysentery, typhoid, tuberculosis, and diphtheria.

The families knew that the mills offered their daughters the chance for a better life, and parents encouraged them to stay on the job. Eben Jennison, a farmer in Charleston, Maine, wrote to his daughter in Lowell to say that times were tough on his rocky soil: "If you should be blessed with your health and are contented I think you will do better where you are than you could here." Going back home raised the dire prospect of a lifetime on the farm, and as *The Atlantic Monthly* observed: "The most intelligent and most enterprising of the farmers' daughters become school teachers, or tenders of shops, or factory girls. They . . . will, nine times in ten, marry a mechanic in preference to a farmer. They know that marrying a farmer is a very serious business. They remember their worn-out mothers."

In Derry, New Hampshire, Eliza Adams, one of eight children, left the family farm for Lowell. She found shelter in a boardinghouse owned by the Lawrence Manufacturing Company. The next morning she checked in at the Lawrence Mill for a job assignment. She was twenty-six years old. Unlike most of her coworkers, Eliza Adams, for her own reasons, delayed plans for marriage or further education and spent decades in the mills. Eventually, her independent life brought her rich personal rewards.

The call of the mills lured Mary Paul, who was fifteen when she left Bridgewater, Vermont. As she set out for Lowell, she told her father, "I think it would be much better for me than to stay here." It took years for her to find what she wanted out of life, but like most of her coworkers, she succeeded in doing so.

Sometimes it seemed that whole towns in farm areas were abandoned by young women. In 1831, a Massachusetts newspaper, the *Dedham Patriot*, reported that "a valuable cargo, consisting of fifty females, was recently imported into this state from Down East [Maine] by one of the Boston packets. Twenty of this number were consigned to Mann's factory at Franklin and the remaining thirty were sent to Lowell and Nashua."

While the women worked, their fortunes were inextricably bound to their employers, and their good fortune was that the Boston capitalists who were the first mill owners were men of social conscience. When Francis Cabot Lowell planned his first mill in Waltham, he knew that in addition to building a manufacturing enterprise, he was bringing about great social change. He had seen, both in England and in southern New England, the exploitation of textile workers and remembered it with horror. He conceived a system to avoid such abuses. He would not only provide jobs for his women workers, he would take care of them, too.

The policy of watching out for workers on and off the job seems to some, in retrospect, to be the creation of paternalistic fussbudgets. Yet the original motivation clearly was to make manufacturing a civilized enterprise based on a belief in the dignity of workers, especially the dignity of the young women whom Lowell and his associates recruited to join their enterprise. The women shared with the owners common bonds of language, place, religious heritage, and reverence for family

14

members who had fought for independence just four decades earlier. These workers were first-generation daughters of the American Revolution.

"Here was in New England a fund of labor, well educated and virtuous," said Lowell's business partner, Nathan Appleton. "It was not perceived how a profitable employment has any tendency to deteriorate the character ... under these circumstances, the daughters of respectable farmers were readily induced to come into these mills for a temporary period."

Francis Cabot Lowell had thought that the women should work in the mills for only three years or so, then move on to further their education, marry, or find new careers. He did not want thousands of women to become economically dependent on the mills all their working lives. He set their wages at two dollars a week above a small charge for their housing and meals. The pay seemed fair to the workers; two dollars a week in the early nineteenth century was enough to buy clothes and other essentials, send some money home, and build up a savings account.

The Boston merchants who founded the city of Lowell built a huge complex of mills on the banks of the Merrimack River. They planned well for the arrival of thousands of women workers. The owners' on-site agent, Kirk Boott, contrived a social order to serve a whole new population that, almost overnight, occupied the country's biggest industrial center. Boott built mills, housing for the women, parks, schools, a church, and almost everything else the community needed. He beautified the city with shade trees and emerald-green malls. He built the Merrimack Hotel, which provided visiting mill directors and salesmen with luxury rooms, fine cuisine, and the best of wines. He built a grand home, a Greek Revival mansion, in the middle of town.

Lowell was the city of the future, the wonder of the nation. A contemporary politician thought the nation's first planned industrial community would "be remembered till the long lapse of ages and the vicissitudes of fortune shall reduce all of America to oblivion and decay." Michel Chevalier found in Lowell "the peaceful hum of an industrious population, whose movements are regulated like clockwork." He was more reserved about the future. Lowell, he wrote, "is decent, neat and peaceful. Will it always be so? Will it be so [for] long? It would be rash to affirm it."

When the women arrived in town with their trunks and bandboxes, they discovered that there was a price for corporate paternalism. While the mills expressed concern for the workers' welfare, they also dictated how the workers would conduct themselves off the job. The women were expected to live in company boardinghouses. Boott hired mature women to run the boardinghouses and to inform the mill managers when problems arose. These women, often widows, were called "keepers," and the best of them became the most important figures in the lives of their homesick boarders. They did the cooking, kept an eye on the health of their charges, saw to it that they went to church on Sunday, and played the role of mother when needed. "The price of such a woman, indeed, is *above rubies*," wrote Harriet Farley, editor of a mill workers' magazine.

Sometimes newcomers to the crowded city had to scramble for shelter. Charlotte Hilbourne recounted her problems on the night she arrived in Lowell to begin work at a mill corporation. She went to several of the corporation's boardinghouses, but all were filled up. "Wherever there was a vacancy or spare corner in a bed, there I must locate," she wrote. "At last a vacancy was discovered, the only vacancy on the corporation." Her place of rest was "a narrow bed appropriated by me and a fat, blowzy maiden" from New Hampshire.

The houses had six to seven bedrooms, three beds to a room, two women to a bed. In the spacious dining room, the keeper served heaping dishes rich in calories and starches. A second dining table was set up in the parlor. A sitting room offered the only privacy for women when they entertained gentlemen callers or visiting relatives.

In the evenings, peddlers came by to sell candy, shoes, books, newspapers, and flattery. The mill women, like some of the Boston elite, enjoyed dabbling in phrenology. Phrenologists analyzed their personalities—for a fee, of course—by examining the skull for its shapes and protuberances. A skeptical woman worker wrote that the phrenologists' real role was "to pander to the vanity of those who are ready to believe they are possessed of every virtue and talent under the sun, because the *phrenologist* tells them so." Evenings also brought the women together for song at the parlor piano. There was no drinking, no smoking of Egyptian cigarettes (not in the presence of the keeper, anyway), no cursing, and no staying out after evening curfew. The boardinghouse door was locked for the night at ten P.M. Out of the women's heavily supervised existence came a lasting benefit: Their common experiences in the corporation homes and in the mills created a sense of solidarity that would soon manifest itself in struggles for better pay and better working conditions. Together the women would wage public battles never before witnessed in the country.

Dr. John O. Green of Lowell checked up on the women's health and worried about their frenzied work schedule. The big meal of the day was served at noon, but the mills allowed only a half hour for the meal break. The women rushed home from the mills, wolfed down their food, and raced back to work. Green noted that there was "scarcely any rest for the commencement of a healthy digestion." A worker complained, "They don't give us time for *manners*."

There was no indoor plumbing. In warm weather and cold, the women used a privy or outhouse in the backyard, just as they had done at home. The mills paid neighboring farmers to haul off the sewage at night. Some privies contaminated the wells that were the source of drinking water; the fear of a cholera outbreak was always present.

Visits to public bathhouses were only occasional. Evidence of the women's stay in Lowell reflects the difficulty of maintaining personal cleanliness. Historical archaeologists digging at boardinghouse sites have found containers and jars that once held cosmetics and cologne. A report on the digs stated, "these small luxuries were probably prized possessions that aided personal hygiene. They would have helped disguise the odors and irregularities of complexion that might result from infrequent bathing."

The women were tired after long hours on the job, but some of them attended evening lectures by such notable Americans as John Quincy Adams, Ralph Waldo Emerson, and Henry David Thoreau. They also spent evenings at the "Self Improvement Circles" they organized, discussing classical literature and reading aloud from their own writings.

Most of them had never advanced beyond the eighth grade, but they were determined to learn.

Professor A. P. Peabody of Harvard, who traveled to Lowell to speak before them, remembered: "When the lecturer entered, almost every girl had a book in her hand and was intent upon it. When he rose, the book was laid aside and paper and pencil taken instead. . . . I have never seen anywhere so assiduous note-taking. No, not even in a college class, as in that assembly of young women, laboring for their subsistence."

Historian Van Wyck Brooks wrote of them: "They subscribed to the British reviews. They had classes in German; they all seemed to know *Paradise Lost* by heart and talked about Wordsworth . . . in the intervals of changing bobbins on the looms." They formed debating clubs, charitable associations, and missionary societies. In Saco, Maine, the York Mill workers transformed the cultural life of the town by establishing the Saco Athenaeum, the Beethoven Society, and the Saco Lyceum.

The workers shared information about the new colleges and seminaries opening for women, including Mary Lyon's in South Hadley, Catharine Beecher's in Hartford, and Emma Willard's in Troy, New York. Many attended these schools after leaving the mills. "Gain, and not bread, is the object of their pursuit," observed a Lowell mill agent.

They were raised by churchgoing families, and most of them held to their faith in the mill cities. Some taught Sunday school along with mill supervisors. They attended revival meetings and subscribed to religious magazines. Some joined the temperance movement. They rebelled when Kirk Boott ordered them to attend the church he had built near their boardinghouses. "As Kirk Boott was an Episcopalian," wrote a sardonic John Coolidge, "the church was naturally of the same persuasion, and as Christianity does not recognize a St. Kirk, the parish was perforce dubbed St. Anne's in honor of the agent's wife." Boott required the women to pay a modest pew fee at St. Anne's, but in the face of their resistance he stopped the practice. Within a few years, other denominations built churches for the women. Harmony was restored, and everyone returned to the business of manufacturing.

In mill towns across New England, early-morning factory bells summoned the men and women to work. The streets were filled with people walking to the mills and crossing canals on footbridges that led them to the mill yard. Townspeople still in their beds could hear the young women singing. By the light of the moon, the workers glanced at the canal's water level. A high level told them that plenty of power was available to turn the mill wheel and run the machines; a low level meant a scarcity of power, temporary mill shutdowns, and layoffs.

The bells aroused the mill towns from slumber, rang when work started, rang to begin and end mealtimes, and rang to signal the close of the workday. Some bosses tried to squeeze more work out of their employees by sounding the last bell a few minutes later than official quitting time. "This is unprincipled conduct," a newspaper said in an editorial scolding the cheating managers. Workers raised money to place public clocks in town squares and church steeples to verify the time kept by the mills.

The workers had large parties two times a year that sent subtle messages to the owners and to the public that the mill environment was not healthy. The celebrating centered on the whale-oil lamps placed near machinery in the fall and winter because of the early darkness. The oil fumes spread a stench throughout the buildings. When spring and its late sunsets arrived, the lamps were blown out for the last time and put aside for a few months. The relieved mill hands staged huge "blowing out" parties to celebrate. A history of Biddeford, Maine, tells of a grand ball in Central Hall that "began at 8:30 in the evening, broke off at midnight for refreshments across the street at the Biddeford House, and then resumed to go on till sunrise—and time to go into the mill for work." When the lamps returned in the fall, the workers, resigned to endure the stench for another season, partied again to mark the time for "lighting up." The quaint custom continued until gas illumination replaced the whale-oil lamps in the 1850s.

Women had no idea what their specific job assignments would be when they reported to the mill for the first time, but they knew at once that this was a place of order and discipline. Rules and regulations were posted on the walls. For both men and women the number-one rule was: "No persons can be employed by the Company whose known habits are or shall be dissolute, indolent, dishonest, or intemperate, or who habitually absent themselves from public worship and violate the Sabbath, or who may be addicted to gambling of any kind." Hannah Josephson, in *Golden Threads*, an account of early mill days, wrote: "This moral poppycock might have been insulting to the self-respecting girls of New England had they not been accustomed to hearing such pompous platitudes from their earliest years.... As if habits of industry had not been drilled into them by primers and parents and preachers!"

Most of the women accepted the regulations governing their personal lives. "It was a rigid code of morality under which we lived," recalled Lucy Larcom about her experiences in the Lowell mills. "Nobody complained about it, however, and we were doubtless better off for its strictness." Thomas Dublin found that "though regulation in practice was never quite as harsh as it appeared in print, managers adopted a strict paternalism they assumed was needed to control the newly independent women. They constructed a social system acceptable to a rural public often antagonistic to urban life, thereby protecting Lowell's population and assuring a steady stream of new recruits into the mills."

Men did the heavy work; they wrestled the five hundred-pound cotton bales into sheds adjoining the mill, cut away the bale bindings, and operated machines that shook the cotton free of dirt and leaves. The snowy cotton was delivered to the mill where other machines operated by men untangled and straightened the fibers into parallel lines until they became dense strands. On the second floor the women took over, tending the spinning machines that transformed the cotton strands into yarn, or thread. When the thread broke, they quickly tied it in a small smooth knot with a rapid finger movement. As a young man, poet Robert Frost spent two years working in a Lawrence mill and saw the dazzling motion of hands on threads:

> And if one broke by any chance,
> The spinner saw it at a glance.
> The spinner still was there to spin.
> That's where the human still came in.
> Her deft hand showed with finger rings
> Among the harplike spread of strings.

She caught the pieces end to end
And, with a touch that never missed,
Not so much tied as made them blend.

The thread was spooled onto bobbins; when the bobbins were filled, workers took them off the spinning machine and replaced them with empty ones. This simple task was assigned to the greenest recruits and, in some mills, to children. Full bobbins were delivered to the fourth and fifth floors and loaded into the shuttles of the looms. Skilled weavers stood at the looms. Like the spinners, they developed a delicate touch to draw the thread through the loom, an operation they repeated thousands of times during a shift, producing mile after mile of fabric. Men performed the next step in production, manipulating huge print machines that applied dyes to the cloth in many colors and patterns. In the finishing room, women inspected the cloth for defects, an exacting task that in time diminished eyesight. Finally, others folded the textiles for shipping all over the world to manufacturers of products for wear and for the home.

A few women took one look at the mills, clasped their ears against the screeching of hundreds of machines, felt the trembling of the floor-boards under their feet, covered their faces from the flying lint, saw coworkers faint in the factory heat, and quit on the first day. But most felt compelled to live with the noise, the repetitive tasks, and the regimentation, and they stayed on.

Except for meal breaks, the howl of the machinery never stopped during the entire workday of twelve or thirteen or fourteen hours. "You know that people learn to sleep with the thunder of Niagara in their ears," one of the women wrote. "And the cotton mill is no worse, though you wonder that we do not have to hold our breath in such a noise." Lucy Larcom told how she survived: "In the sweet June weather I would lean far out the window, and try not to hear the unceasing clash of sound inside.... I discovered, too, that I could so accustom myself to the noise that it became like a silence to me. And I defied the machinery to make me its slave. Its incessant discords could not drown out the music of my thoughts if I would let them fly high enough."

The women pasted scraps of poetry on their machines and on the walls. They placed flowerpots on the windowsills. In moments of rest, they drank in the words of Shelley and Keats to nourish their torpid minds; they gazed at geraniums and daisies to freshen their fatigued eyes.

Sarah Bagley, who worked in the mills before she became a leader of labor-reform efforts, recalled that it was difficult to converse in the bedlam of the mill, "but aside from the talking, where can you find a more pleasant place for contemplation? There all the powers of the mind are made active by our animating exercise, and having but one kind of labor to perform, we need not give all our thoughts to that, but leave them measurably free for reflection on other matters."

Bagley and thousands of other women soon came to see that their compact with the mill owners was made at the cost of their health and, in some cases, their lives. The Boston capitalists had pledged to deal honorably with their employees, but as the years passed a new generation of managers placed no limits on how much work would be demanded of them; there was inattention to industrial safety and to a clean work environment. Those issues would not be resolved for more than a century, but the women in the New England mills took the first steps in America's long journey toward labor reform.

One of the women wrote: "The daughter leaves the farm, it is said, a plump, rosey-cheeked, strong and laughing girl, and in one year comes back to [her family] better clad, 'tis true, and with refined manners and money for the discharge of their little debts and for the supply of their little wants—but alas, how changed!...This is a dark picture, but there are even darker realities, and these in no inconsiderable numbers."

Plant managers nailed the windows shut to achieve the high humidity needed to keep threads pliable so that breakage would be minimized and the looms would not have to be stopped as often for thread repairs. The humidity caused respiratory ailments, including tuberculosis and influenza. Cotton lint filled the workrooms "as snow falls in winter," one worker said, and people were covered with it head to toe. Women used snuff to limit the amount of lint they inhaled; men chewed tobacco. Weavers breathed in lint when they sucked thread through the eye of the foot-long wooden shuttles that fed the thread to the looms. They called their lip motion the "kiss of death." A doctor who attended mill workers reported: "I have been called to cases where I suspected this to be the cause of trouble in the stomach. After getting an emetic, they have in some cases vomited little balls of cotton." The "kiss of death" lasted in the mills for decades, until the invention of self-threading shuttles. Lung illnesses remained a plague in the mills for many years, and the textile workers were among the first Americans to be diagnosed with "brown lung" or byssinosis, which impairs lung capacity, causing coughing and shortness of breath. Eventually, 70 percent of the early mill workers died of respiratory diseases; the comparable figure for Massachusetts farmers at the time was 4 percent.

As demanding as the factory jobs were, the women were no strangers to hard work. They had done chores in their rural homes from the time they were children. They knew how to raise crops and livestock, how to cook, and how to nurse the sick. They could make clothing and soap and candles. They helped their family farms to survive. They knew privation. When they went to work in the mills, "The conscientious among them took as much pride in spinning a smooth thread . . . or in making good cloth, as they would have done if the material had been for their own wearing," wrote Harriet Hanson Robinson. "And thus was practiced long before it was preached, that principle of true political economy—the just relation, the mutual interest, that ought to exist between employers and employed." And, of course, a good spinner was a woman of independent means, as one of them wrote:

> *Despite the toil we all agree,*
> *Out of the mill or in,*
> *Dependent on others we ne'er will be*
> *As long as we're able to spin.*

When the bells tolled and the shift ended, the women, their heads aching, their ears ringing, and their feet sore and swollen, shut down their machines, descended dusty staircases, crossed the mill yard in the evening darkness, and walked through the company gate and back into fresh air. The streets resounded with the talk and laughter of thousands of workers heading to their boardinghouses a few blocks away. When summer evenings offered beautiful sunsets, the women gathered on the streets where they lived to share a rare communion with nature. The silence was broken only by their softly spoken conversation and their coughing.

The most important public issue for the women, as for the rest of the country, was slavery. The women were troubled by the knowledge that the cotton they processed, the very source of their livelihood, was picked by fellow human beings held in bondage. To make matters worse, the women were required to weave what was described at the time as "negro cloth," a coarse yarn used to make work clothes for the slaves. From spinning machine to spinning machine, from loom to loom, they passed around the abolitionist poetry of John Greenleaf Whittier:

> *Speed on the light to those who dwell*
> *In Slavery's land of woe and sin,*
> *And through the blackness of that Hell*
> *Let Heaven's own light break in.*

Year after year the women signed petitions demanding an end to slavery; they joined antislavery societies and contributed money to the cause. Many of them considered abolition more important than the beginning of their own labor movement.

When Senator Jeremiah Clemens of Alabama asserted that "the Southern slaves were better off than the Northern operatives," mill worker Clementine Averill wrote a letter from Lowell to the *New York Tribune* charging that he was not fit to hold public office. "Are we torn from our friends and kindred, sold and driven about like cattle, chained and whipped, and not allowed to speak one word in self-defence?" she asked.

Lucy Larcom wrote that "if the vote of the mill girls had been taken, it would doubtless have been unanimous on the antislavery side." Years after her work in the mills, she composed lines that reflected the feelings of most of her coworkers:

When I've thought what soil the cotton-plant
We weave is rooted in, what waters it—
The blood of souls in bondage—I have felt
That I was sinning against the light to stay
And turn the accursed fibre into cloth.

Yet the whole existence of the New England textile mills in the years preceding the Civil War depended on an uninterrupted cotton supply. The workers, the mill owners, and every business in every mill city were economically bound to the Southern plantation owners and their slaves. Business went on, the textile industry continued to grow, and slavery increasingly vexed the national conscience.

By the early 1830s, the Boston investors, with Kirk Boott as their on-site supervisor, had built nineteen mills in Lowell alone. In just ten years the population of the city reached twelve thousand, and almost half the people worked in the mills. There was similar growth in the rest of New England. The vision of Francis Cabot Lowell had been realized: Manufacturing had brought great wealth to the investors and prosperity to the region. Lowell's founding partner was pleased with his profits and with his workers. "The superior capabilities of these girls exemplified Nathan Appleton's ideal of a manufacturing community and gave him a sense of pride in his accomplishments," wrote a biographer.

Appleton and the other mill owners enjoyed a cheerful song about their workers:

O sing me a song of the Factory Girl
So merry and glad and free—
The bloom on her cheeks, of health it speaks!—
O a happy creature is she!

She tends the loom, she watches the spindle,
And cheerfully talketh away;
Mid the din of wheels, how her bright eyes kindle!
O a happy creature is she!

THE BELLES OF NEW ENGLAND

O sing me a song of the Factory Girl!
  Link not her name with the SLAVES.–
  She is brave and free as the old elm tree,
    That over her homestead waves.

There were many expressions of pride in the mill women. Banks printed paper currency with engravings depicting them at their looms. The Lowell mill owners invited President Andrew Jackson to see the workers and staged a spectacle in his honor. The owners belonged to the conservative Whig party and disliked Jackson's Democratic, prolabor policies, but realized that a presidential visit was, for the industry, a valuable public relations event. Jackson took time out during the festivities to ask questions about wages, hours, and production. But mostly, this was to be a celebration. Militia units paraded past Jackson's reviewing stand to the beat of drums. Citizens and schoolchildren marched by to salute him. Then came the stars of the parade, two thousand five hundred women from the mills. Costumers had outfitted them in beautiful dresses and sashes, and each of them carried a parasol. Jackson was escorted past a mile-long line of the young women, who offered him smiles and applause and fresh bouquets. He was in his glory. The tough old general declared: "Very pretty women, by the Eternal!"

When the mill women went home to visit, their sophisticated style impressed their rural neighbors, too. They had read more books, listened to more classical music, and done more to expand their horizons than just about anyone in town. Occasionally there was stuffy reaction to their working lives. A New Hampshire newspaper declared that "the ambition of woman should be to beautify and adorn the domestic circle." Instead, the paper lamented, she has settled for the "quasi-slavery of a cotton factory." A writer in Vermont worried about "a propensity among those in ordinary circumstances to ape the rich, and also a false taste, by which some of our country misses attempt to heighten the charms of their persons by excessive ornament in dress." Charles Dickens disagreed. "They were all well dressed," Dickens commented, "but not to my thinking above their condition; for I like to see the humbler classes of society careful of their dress and appearance, and even, if they please, decorated with such little trinkets as come within the compass of their means."

With all their newfound success, the women were not always sure of themselves. In a study of letters they wrote during their years in the mills, Thomas Dublin found that they were sometimes perplexed about the right thing to do concerning their families and their own future. Mary Paul wrote to her aging father back in Vermont, "I hope sometime to be able to do something for you and sometimes feel ashamed that I have not before this." In Clinton, Massachusetts, a mill worker remembered only as Lucy Ann wanted to attend Oberlin College in Ohio, founded in 1833 and open to both men and women. She wrote to a cousin: "I have earned enough to school me awhile, & have not I a right to do so, or must I go home, like a dutiful girl, place the money in father's hands, & then there goes all my hard earnings.... But if I go to Oberlin I take comfort & forget all those long wearisome mill days & perhaps I prepare myself for usefulness in this life." Whether Lucy Ann resolved her conflicts of personal freedom, duty, and aspiration is unknown.

Sarah Metcalf, whose mother seemed to want her to return home, wrote back to say she would hold on to her Lowell job a little longer because "I am making three dollars a week, and three and a half a week, and [the overseer] says he will do as well by me all winter long if I stay.... I can probably lay up fifty dollars besides having my teeth fixed, and getting my next summer's clothes."

Ann Swett Appleton never lost her compass and never forgot the plight of her mother, who was living her final years in a mental institution. In a letter to her sister Sarah, Ann wrote, "I went out and bought our poor mother a dress yesterday and I never can spend my earnings better to my satisfaction and I mean as far as lies in my power to keep her well clad and comfortable."

Although their jobs made personal accomplishments possible, the long hours the women worked, and the worsening conditions in the mills, began to breed resentment. Weavers in Pawtucket, Rhode Island, staged the first strike by American women in 1824 when eight mills in the town jointly announced a longer workweek. It was the first time that workers saw the mill managers use their power to act in concert against them. With support from the public, the women prevailed and won a compromise agreement with the mills. Other workers did not fare as well. In 1828, textile workers in Paterson, New Jersey, struck for a ten-hour day. State officials sent in the militia, and the fight for reduced work hours was lost. With the new wealth of the industrialists, wrote Caroline Ware in an early history of the mills, came "a control over the lives of working men and over the resources of the nation. . . . It was this power which came from industry and from the corporate form of organization which made of the capitalist a giant in the community whom others served and feared."

Workers everywhere in the country's new industries labored for low wages, unable to overcome owners of factories, mines, and foundries who rarely yielded to pleas for better working conditions and for a living wage. The worst fears of socially conscious citizens were realized as poverty and slums blighted industrial centers. Jefferson had feared such a turn of events, too. "The mob of great cities," he wrote, "add just so much to the support of pure government as sores do to the strength of the human body. When we get piled upon one another in large cities, as in Europe, we shall become corrupt as in Europe, and go to eating one another as they do there."

The women in New England were not familiar with the militant strike tactics used by workers in other parts of the country, but they did stage "turnouts," walking away from their jobs in unison to protest management decisions. In 1828, labor trouble broke out among the women workers at the Cocheco cotton mill in Dover, New Hampshire, and the local newspaper criticized their militancy. The criticism was no surprise to the women because many newspapers of the time sided with the mill owners during such disputes. "A general turnout of the girls employed in the cotton factories in this town to the number of 600 or 800 took place on Friday last, on account of some imaginary grievance," the Dover *Enquirer* told its readers. "It has, we believe, *turned out* to their cost, as well as disgrace." The newspaper clucked that women should not air their grievances in public. "The girls, on leaving the factory yard formed a procession of nearly half a mile in length, and marched through the town with martial music," the *Enquirer* reporter wrote. "The whole presented one of the most disgusting scenes ever witnessed." The *National Gazette* in Philadelphia was less harsh but more sarcastic: "The late strike and grand public march of the female operatives in New Hampshire exhibit the Yankee sex in a new and unexpected light. By-and-by the governor may have to call out the militia to prevent a gynecocracy." It was another futile strike, but the Dover workers through the years continued to be among the most militant in New England.

Orestes A. Brownson, a radical reformer of the time, was among the first to ask the public to think about conditions in the mills and the price of industrial progress. "The operatives are well-dressed, and we are told, well paid," Brownson wrote. "They are said to be healthy, contented and happy. This is the fair side of the picture; the side exhibited to distinguished visitors." Brownson contended that most of the mill women "wear out their health, spirits and morals without becoming one whit better off than when they commenced labor."

Worker dissension spread through the mills of Massachusetts, New Hampshire, and Maine during a series of depressions in the 1830s and 1840s. The mills imposed a pay cut or simply closed when they were losing money, and the workers had to go back home until operations started up again. In 1834, the owners reduced wages 15 percent. Management also ordered the boardinghouse keepers to pack eight women to a room instead of six. Hundreds of women in Lowell walked off the job. Management refused to budge, and within a few days the women had no choice but to go back to work. They returned with a different view of mill life. In the early years, they had considered the mill owners to be benevolent coadventurers in the new industry. Now, the women knew, those days were over.

The trouble spread to nearby Lawrence, where mill agent William Austin informed his Boston office, "This afternoon we have paid off several of these Amazons & presume they will leave town on Monday." The Lawrence women lost their strike, too. In Nashua, where the mills imposed similar pay cuts, management persuaded the women not to strike on grounds that if they stayed on the job "it will be worthy of your patriotism."

Agent James F. Curtis told the women in the Cocheco mills of Dover that their pay also would be cut by 15 percent and that they had to give two weeks' notice before leaving their jobs. He warned them not to strike because "riotous combinations answer no good purpose and only lower in the public estimation a class otherwise respectable." Eight hundred women brushed aside his argument and walked out. For the first time, they used public relations to further their cause. They placed a newspaper advertisement declaring that the mill owners intended "to reduce the females in their employ to that state of dependence on them in which they openly, as they now do secretly, abuse and insult them by calling them 'slaves.' "

The women held mass rallies. They asked why the men in the mill, including the overseers and Curtis himself, were not taking a pay cut. They answered their own question: Management thought the only pay reductions that would succeed were those imposed on women. The Dover women invented new ways of achieving worker solidarity. They pooled their money to support workers who wanted to return home during the strike, and formed a committee to share strike strategy and information with women in other mill towns.

Agent Curtis, under attack from the women and from the public, which supported the strikers, dug in his heels. He informed all new job applicants at the mill that they had to sign agreements pledging not to join any labor organization. Furthermore, they had to accept, as a condition of employment, the wages management decided to pay, even if the wages were subsequently lowered. This was one of the country's first labor agreements, later called yellow-dog contracts, in which the employer held all the power and the workers none.

Curtis typified the tough new managers who ran the Boston-owned mills. Robert Whitehouse, a Dover historian, wrote: "Curtis was a strange and alien addition to the community, for he possessed none of the qualities that make a successful and popular business man. He was educated for the Navy, he sailed the Seven Seas, he was trained to quick execution of orders . . . he seemed to regard Dover people as so many underlings on one of Uncle Sam's warships. He knew the whims of sailors but failed to understand the . . . prattle and foolishness, moods and grievances, jealousies and suspicions of a cotton-mill's operatives. . . . It is an unsolved mystery why those Boston directors of the Cocheco Manufacturing Company put such a man here to superintend their mills. He was a flat failure."

Curtis quit as the mill agent shortly after the strike to become superintendent of the Boston and Worcester Railroad. While riding one of his trains he stuck his head out a window to check rail conditions. His head hit a post that was erected too close to the tracks and he was decapitated. When the news arrived in the Dover mills, the women cheered.

Lucy Larcom maintained that most of the women did not support strikes; they preferred to return home during labor disputes rather than take part in a public display in the streets. But she also wrote that "the mistaken impression went abroad that a paradise of work had at last been found. Romantic young women came from a distance with rose-colored pictures in their minds of labor turned to pastime, which were doomed to be sadly blurred by disappointment."

The women pressed on with demands for fairer treatment despite their numerous setbacks, and with each new strike and each new setback they became more effective. In 1836, fifteen hundred of them walked out again in Lowell because management imposed a 5 percent increase in boardinghouse fees. Walkouts occurred in Dover and in Chicopee, Massachusetts, over the same issue. This time, the women formed the Factory Girls Association, and a member declared, "As our fathers resisted until blood the lordly avarice of the British ministry, so we, their daughters, will never wear the yoke which has been prepared for us."

This time the women used persuasion to cripple mill operations. They targeted sections of the mills that were the most crucial to production and encouraged uncommitted workers to join the turnout. Two weeks after the strike began, only 20 percent of the women returned to work. It was a remarkable achievement for strike leaders who had no real union. Management took notice of their growing militancy, if not their power. A Lowell mill boss reported that they "manifest *good spunk*." Still, the higher boarding fees remained in place, the Factory Girls Association disintegrated, and within a few weeks the women returned to their jobs, defeated again.

The aging mill owners in Boston grasped at the steady dividends they awarded themselves and their stockholders and let slip away the credo of social responsibility for the workers they employed and for the communities where they built their mills. They had little interest in new technology except when it could save money on labor costs. Over the decades they allowed the mills to become obsolete. They grew careless about the quality of corporate housing for their employees and uncaring about the growth of slums near their mills.

Public attention increasingly focused on the conditions of the mill workers. The *New-York Weekly Tribune* editorialized, "Girls of fifteen to eighteen or twenty should be most carefully shielded from the life-long evils which result from excessively severe or protracted toil, not only for their own sakes but in view of their duty and destiny as the future wives and mothers of the nation."

A Boston newspaper reported that in Lowell, some mill women had venereal disease and some worked in brothels. A doctor at Lowell Hospital filed a complaint about the "manifest disregard of cleanliness," poor ventilation, and overcrowded conditions in the boardinghouses. Another medical survey found that from 1840 to 1849, half of the approximately sixteen hundred patients at the city hospital had been treated for typhoid fever and that the main cause was poor ventilation in the mills. Yet another doctor reported to the American Medical Association after touring the mills, "There is not a state's prison or house of correction in New England where the hours of labor are so long, the hours for meals so short, and the ventilation so much neglected as in the cotton mills with which I am acquainted."

Henry David Thoreau visited the mills, too. "I cannot believe that our factory system is the best mode by which men may get clothing," he wrote. "The condition of the operatives is becoming every day more like that of the English, and it cannot be wondered at . . . since the principal object is, not that mankind may be well and honestly clad, but unquestionably, that the corporations may be enriched."

Henry Miles, a Lowell minister, was a defender of the mill owners, and addressed the health issues in a book about mill life. "That there is sickness among the seven thousand factory girls of Lowell, cases of prostration of strength, and incapacity to bear the fatigues of confinement and toil, it would, of course, be absurd to deny," Miles wrote. But he argued that the basic cause of illness was that some of the women were not taking care of themselves. As for a majority of them, "a walk throughout the mills must convince one, by the generally healthy and robust appearance of the girls, that their condition is not inferior, in this respect, to other working classes of their sex. Certainly, if multitudes of them went home to sicken and die, equal multitudes of their sisters and neighbors would not be very eager to take the fatal stations which are deserted." What Miles did not say was that by the time he was writing, in the mid-1840s, most of the women coming into the mills were from destitute backgrounds and were desperate for work.

Miles surveyed some of the boardinghouses and included reports from their keepers, who, like their charges, were employees of the mills. He quoted one keeper as filling out a report this way: "Have kept a boardinghouse on the Boott [mill corporation] for nine years; have thirty-four boarders now; have had as many as five hundred in all; probably a fifth of those have been married; there has been no death in my house; three have gone home sick, and one of these died in a few months . . . two have been dismissed for bad conduct; never have had much sickness, and it is three years since a physician has been in the house; perhaps have had, in the nine years, twelve cases [of sickness] lasting a week."

A second keeper's report was similar in content and phrasing, suggesting that Miles offered the keepers editorial guidance: "Have kept a boardinghouse on the Lawrence [Corporation] seven years; now have twenty-seven boarders; have had in all a hundred and twenty-five; twenty-seven of my girls have been married; two have died; eight gone home sick; three dismissed from the house; have never had much sickness; a dozen cases lasting a week."

Miles's several explanations for sickness among the women included the idea that "there is something in the monotony of a mill life which seems to beget a morbid hankering for little artificial stimulants of the appetite, and the tone of the stomach is frequently deranged by a foolish and expensive patronage of the confectioner." He provided no documentation for his curious assertion.

The workers in the mills believed that if anyone was going to look out for their interests it would have to be themselves. Some small strikes did bring victory. In 1845, women at the Dwight Corporation in Chicopee, Massachusetts, walked out to protest a wage cut. After the mill was idle for two days, managers asked the workers to return and gave them a raise of fifty cents a week.

Eliza Adams, who had journeyed to Lowell full of hope from the family farm in New Hampshire, was among those who embraced the principles of labor solidarity. In a poem she called "Lines Written on the Reduction of Wages in Lowell," she wrote:

> Shall we proud New England's daughters
> Bend our necks to wear the yoke
> When our fathers crossed the waters
> And tyrant chains of England broke . . .
>
> Let the common cause unite us
> Firm in purpose true in heart
> For oppression doth invite us
> Everyone to take her part.

In the early 1840s, the courts issued rulings favorable to organized labor. But creating an effective women's union was difficult because of the circumstances of the times. Hannah Josephson wrote that women trying to organize for better pay or improved working conditions were considered "morally reprehensible." They were also inexperienced negotiators. By their own choice, they were a transient workforce, staying in the mills only a few years. So when labor trouble first developed, none of them had been around long enough to acquire experience in negotiating with managers who were ferocious adversaries in bad times and closefisted even in good times. Despite all their disadvantages, Kathleen Barry wrote, this was a new generation of workers who were "already freer from the home than their mothers ever thought of being, and dared to act collectively for their sex."

The most strident of the women leaders was Sarah Bagley, who came to Lowell from Candia, New Hampshire, to work in the Hamilton Mill. She was one of the organizers of the Lowell Female Labor Reform Association in 1844, with branch chapters at the Amoskeag Mills in Manchester and in the mills of Waltham, Fall River, Dover, and Nashua. She gained prominence in the New England labor movement and spoke with great power at many women's conventions. She also took time to conduct night classes for mill women who wanted to continue their education.

Bagley was fired from her mill job after she became a labor leader, but that only gave her more time to use her gifts of oratory and organization. She began her battles on behalf of the workers during turbulent times. Susan B. Anthony was campaigning for the right of women to vote. Social reformers Horace Mann, in public education, and Dorothea Dix, in the treatment of the imprisoned and insane, were at the peak of their powers. Sojourner Truth was striving for the emancipation of slaves. Karl Marx and Frederich Engels were writing the *Communist Manifesto* with its call, "Workers of the world, unite!" Sarah Bagley was as significant as any of them to the women in the New England textile mills. More than anyone she opened their minds to the idea that they did not have to settle for secondhand lives.

"Is anyone such a fool as to suppose that out of six thousand factory girls in Lowell, sixty would be there if they could help it?" she wrote. "Whenever I raise the point that it is immoral to shut us up in a close room twelve hours a day in the most monotonous and tedious of employment I am told that we have come to the mills voluntarily and we can leave when we will. Voluntarily! . . . the whip which brings us to Lowell is *necessity*. We must have money; a father's debts are to be paid, an aged mother to be supported, a brother's ambition to be aided and so the factories are supplied. Is this to act from free will? . . . Is this freedom? To my mind it is slavery."

The Female Labor Reform Association elected Bagley president and adopted the motto "Try Again." Her goal was to win a ten-hour work day, a growing issue in the New England mills. Skilled workers and artisans in the rest of the country had won a ten-hour day years earlier, and federal workers had done so in 1840. Now, as the women declared in a ditty, it was their turn:

If I must wend my way
Uncheered by hope's sweet song
God grant that in the mills a day
May be but Ten Hours long.

From the start, the ten-hour day was unobtainable in an industry where managers demanded maximum production from the workers every precious second of every precious minute. Now Bagley was demanding the elimination of two and three *hours* from the workday. The manufacturers rejected the demand. One of them spoke of the women as if they were helpless wards of the industry: "The morals of the operatives will necessarily suffer if longer absent from the wholesome discipline of factory life, and leaving them thus to their will and liberty, without a warrant that this time will be well employed." It is doubtful that the manufacturer would have risked sharing his thoughts in the presence of the fiery Bagley.

Bagley visited prisons to study the work days of inmates. At the Massachusetts state prison she saw a splendid library used by convicts who had plenty of leisure time to read. "They work four hours less per day than the operatives of Lowell," she told a newspaper. At the New Hampshire state prison she found that the inmates also worked fewer hours. Taunting the capitalists she was battling, she told of meeting a distinguished-looking inmate who could have been mistaken for a mill owner because he was "respected without regard" for how he got rich. He was behind bars for forgery.

Thousand of workers in Lowell, led by Bagley, petitioned the Massachusetts legislature for more civilized working hours: *"We the undersigned peaceable, industrious and hardworking men and women of Lowell, in view of our condition—the evils already come upon us by toiling from thirteen to fourteen hours per day, confined in unhealthy apartments, exposed to the poisonous contagion of air . . . hastening us on through pain, disease and privation, down to a premature grave, pray the legislature to institute a ten-hour working day in all the factories of the state."*

Bagley led a group of women up Beacon Hill to the State House in Boston to speak at a hearing that was one of the first official investigations of labor conditions in America. The women were described as self-possessed and articulate as they testified about management abuses, but they failed to persuade the legislators. Referring to the woeful working conditions in the mills, the committee said, "We acknowledge all this, but we say, the remedy is not with us." The legislators told the women to deal directly with their bosses. "Labor is intelligent enough to make its own bargains, and look out for its own interests without any interference from us," the committee said. The women accused the legislators of acting in "cringing servility to corporate monopolies."

The workers responded to an indifferent legislature with political retribution. Although the women did not have the vote, the men in the mills did, and they used it on the women's behalf to defeat a Lowell member of the legislature, William Schouler, because he did not adequately support the women's struggle for reduced hours. The women thanked the voters "for consigning William Schouler to the obscurity he so justly deserves." With his defeat at the polls, Schouler may have been the first American politician to experience the collective wrath of women.

New Hampshire enacted a ten-hour law in 1847, but the mill owners found a way to circumvent the intent of the law: They simply fired everyone. Those who wanted their jobs back had to sign personal contracts that exempted them from the ten-hour provision, and this allowed the mills to work them for the same long hours as before. The New Hampshire workers staged mass protests all over the state, and less than half the women signed the contracts. The mills had to close until they could find enough women willing to work under the owners' conditions. By this time even Great Britain, home of William Blake's "dark Satanic Mills," had enacted a law to limit women's work to ten hours a day. Bowing to public pressure, New England states established an eleven-hour day in 1853. The ten-hour day was a lost cause in most of American industry until 1874. By then the Yankee women who had fought for it had long disappeared from the mills. It took decades more before the labor movement won the eight-hour day.

Through most of the years of conflict over working conditions in the mid-nineteenth century, the economy was robust, and the industry reaped profits. Still, management insisted on greater output, and the workers complained of the "speedup." Weavers who once tended one or two looms were now required to tend three or four. The mills did this each time the designers of spinning machines and looms built new labor-saving features into their products. The women argued that piling more work on them was unfair, especially when their pay, after deductions for room and board, went from $2.60 a week down to $2.23. Women shoe workers in Lynn, Massachusetts, were earning one or two dollars more than that.

The women were obdurate when it came to the wage issue. Their bosses, even bosses who sympathized with them, were just as stiff-necked about holding the line on the payroll. Samuel Rodman, treasurer of the New Bedford Steam Company, a textile mill, kept a log during the contentious summer of 1847:

July 9. Some trouble with the girls at the factory today on account of the wages. Six of them left. A. G. Snell [another company official] and I talked kindly to them, showed that wages paid here were still higher than in most establishments, and that the reduction was on our part the result of necessity and not of choice.

July 13. There is some trouble at the factory with the weavers, indicating dissatisfaction with the price per cut. On the whole, things look very discouraging there.

July 14. [after the weavers quit]. Conferred with some of the stockholders who united in the opinion that we should not yield to their demand and measures were taken to obtain others if they should hold out, but in the afternoon I was glad to learn they had returned on learning from the superintendent that no more would be paid.

Overseers in many textile mills were awarded bonuses when the women produced more; consequently, they drove the workers harder and harder. "The girls were afraid to stay away when they fell sick," Hannah Josephson said, "fearful of falling behind one another, as some of the newer overseers were brutal and tyrannical, and took advantage of their position to play favorites." Women were fired on overseers' charges of labor agitation, disobedience, lying, and misconduct. The mills established a quasi-military justice system to deal with insurrection. Workers who were "dishonorably discharged" were blackballed by the other mills in town. Some got around the problem by using aliases when applying for new jobs. If workers left voluntarily they had to secure a formal certificate of honorable discharge in order to get a job anywhere else. "Mine," wrote Harriet Hanson Robinson, "of which I am still quite proud, is dated the year of my marriage, and is as follows: 'HARRIET J. HANSON has been employed in the Boott Cotton Mills...and is honorably discharged. (Signed) J. F. TROTT.' "

Henry Miles cited entries from a Lowell company log of 1839 that recorded firings:

Jan. 3, Lydia, No. 1 spinning room, "obtained an honorable discharge by false pretenses. Her name has been sent round to the other Corporations as a thief and a liar."

Jan. 3, Harriet in the No. 4 spinning room and Judith in No. 5 weaving room, "discharged as worthless characters."

March 14, Ann, No. 2 spinning room, "discharged for reading in the mill."

The company log recorded one especially lawless day:

March 25, Harriet in No. 4 carding room, Laura in No. 4 spinning room, Ellen in No. 1 carding room and George from the repair shop, "all discharged for improper conduct."

Expressing unhappiness with the pay was enough to warrant firing. Other reasons, mill bosses said, included hysteria, levity, impudence, madness, and drunkenness. Charlotte Foster was dismissed by the Hamilton Mill on a charge that she was a "night walker." Mary Moses and

Lucy Richardson were fired for dancing in the spinning room of the mill. Elizabeth Wilson was let go by managers at the Hamilton because she was "a devil in petticoats." In a study of the mill's records, Carl Gersuny found that "no distinction was made between what workers did on company time and what they did on their own. Being 'reported' was grounds for dismissal even if the report had no bearing on work performance."

John Greenleaf Whittier observed the declining condition of the women he had idealized during their happier years. Now he saw them under attack and lost in a sea of industrial strife. He was no longer in awe of Lowell as the paragon of American industry. "There have been a good many foolish essays written upon the beauty and divinity of labor by those who have never known what it really is to earn one's livelihood by the sweat of the brow," the poet wrote. "Let such be silent."

The public's image of the women worsened as reports spread that there were problems in the mills. The women, upset by the reports, searched for ways to tell their side of the story and to communicate with each other. They wanted to share their experiences in the mills, their longing for home, and their love of literature. With the help of Abel Thomas, minister of the Second Universalist Church, they founded a magazine in 1840 that they called the *Lowell Offering*. Thomas was editor for the first two years, then turned over the operation to the workers, and the *Offering* became the first magazine in America wholly run by women. Harriet Farley from Claremont, New Hampshire, began editing the magazine in 1842. Whittier was an editorial adviser. The *Offering* became the most admired employee magazine in the country.

The contributors, observing contemporary conventions of modesty, usually signed pen names or initials to their poems, stories, and essays. Their subjects ranged from childhood memories of family life to their views of the workplace and women's role in industry. No one had ever read this kind of writing in America. More than fifty women wrote for the magazine over the five years of its existence, including Lucy Larcom and Sarah Bagley before she became an advocate for labor reform. Thousands of women in the mills all over New England read the magazine.

At first, the articles were glowing descriptions of life in the mill, but the tone of the essays soon changed. "Susan" wrote: "The girls here are not contented; and there is no disadvantage in their situation which they do not perceive as quickly, and lament as loudly, as the sternest opponents of the factory system do. They would scorn to say they were contented, if asked the question, for it would compromise their Yankee spirit—their pride, . . . independence, and love of 'freedom and equality' to say that they were *contented* with such a life as this."

Another writer for the *Offering* was Betsey Chamberlain, a widow who settled in Lowell with her three children. Chamberlain wrote a piece that touched on many of the issues bothering the workers. She recounted a factory girl's dream in which "A New Society" is created by the adoption of a set of resolutions, including:

> *Resolved*, That no member of this society shall exact more than eight hours of labor, out of every twenty-four, of any person in his or her employment.
>
> *Resolved*, That, as the laborer is worthy of his hire, the price for labor shall be sufficient to enable the working people to pay a proper attention to scientific and literary pursuits.
>
> *Resolved*, That the wages of females shall be equal to the wages of males, that they may be enabled to maintain proper independence of character, and virtuous deportment.
>
> *Resolved*, That industry, virtue and knowledge, (not wealth and titles,) shall be the standard of respectability for this society.

But then, Betsey Chamberlain wrote, the factory girl awoke to find it was only a dream.

Another worker publication, more blunt in its criticism, soon came on the scene. *The Voice of Industry* told the public that the mill system was "one of slow and legal assassination." The paper was cofounded by Sarah Bagley, and her militancy was a presence on every page. "This talk about the continued prosperity, happy condition, and future independence of the producing class of this country, as a class, is all fiction, moonshine," the *Voice* declared. "There is at this very moment a great strife between capital and labor, and capital is fast gaining the mastery." The *Voice* charged that the continuing conflict robbed the women of their health. It said that the skeletal system of young women who were just coming into full development and strength was traumatized by long hours of physical exertion. The result often was scrofula, or tuberculosis of the lymphatic glands, and spinal ailments. The *Voice* confronted mill owner Abbott Lawrence in its pages, hurling verbal daggers at him in an open letter. The paper condemned him for tolerating overcrowding in boardinghouses that were infested with rats and bloodsucking bedbugs: "Your factory system is worse by far than that of Europe," the paper told Lawrence. "You furnish your operatives with no more healthy sleeping-apartments than the cellars and garrets of the English poor.... You shut up your operatives two or three hours longer a day in your factory prisons than is done in Europe.... You compel them to stand so long at the machinery ... that varicose veins ... swelling of the feet and limbs, and prolapsus uter, diseases that end only with [death], are not rare but common occurrences."

A worker signing her poem as "Pheney" submitted these lines to the *Voice:*

> And amidst the clashing noise and din
> Of the ever beating loom,
> Stood a fair young girl with throbbing brow,
> Working her way to the tomb.

If words could kill, the *Voice* might have achieved at least some reforms. But Abbott Lawrence, unscathed by mere words, did not change anything.

Women slaves in the cotton states suffered some of the same ailments as the New England mill women, including scrofula and prolapsus uter. They were plagued with spontaneous abortions, stillbirths, and death in childbirth. They contracted lung diseases, just as the women in the North did, and suffered an affliction exclusive to them: sore and infected fingers from picking cotton from sunrise to sunset, day after day, year after year.

Frederick Douglass and Sojourner Truth, among the few African Americans in a position to speak out on behalf of the slaves, saw their suffering; when Douglass became dispirited, Sojourner Truth sought to comfort him. "Frederick," she asked, "is God dead?"

The Yankee women continued their exodus from the mills. Some joined emigration societies that were taking people to the West to clear the forests and raise crops on soil that was richer than the rock-strewn land at home. The mills hired men to roam the countryside in horse-drawn wagons to find women desperate enough to work in the mills. The long, low "slavers" carried a dozen or more women and all their belongings and all their remaining hopes for the future. The mills paid the drivers a dollar for each woman they recruited, more if the woman came from such a long distance that it would be difficult for her to quit once she was in the mill city. So the drivers traveled to economically depressed rural areas in the northern tiers of Maine, New Hampshire, and Vermont for their human harvest, misleading the women about wages and working conditions. The women scrambled to escape from their bleak surroundings and so were easily misled. They climbed into the eerie-looking slaver wagons, not in joyous pursuit of adventure like the first mill women, but just to get a job and to survive. One driver who transported a Maine woman oversold the attractions of mill life. When the young woman arrived in Lowell, heard the racket of the mills and finally realized what her fate was to be, she demanded that the driver take her back home, and he did.

A Portland, Maine, newspaper decried the trade in human misery. "There are hundreds of young females shipped from this State every year to the factory prison-houses, like cattle, sheep and pigs sent to slaughter," the newspaper said, and their destiny was to labor in "the polluted and polluting manufacturing towns where they are prepared for a miserable life and a horrible death in the abodes of infamy."

As wage cuts continued, Irish immigrants began coming into the mills. For the Yankee women, the adventure in American industry was at an end. "You could not count on high-spirited and intelligent New England girls to accept such a drop in their standards tamely," Hannah Josephson wrote. "They were not deceived by the sanctimoniousness of corporate paternalism." In a final break with the past, the exhausted Yankee women quit the Self Improvement Circles. "A time came when the speedup threatened to drain them of all energy for intellectual pursuits after working hours," Josephson said. They "fought a dignified campaign to regain their old standards. Once this was lost, they did not renew the struggle. They simply retired from the scene."

As conditions worsened, the *Lowell Offering* came under increasing criticism for being too optimistic, and too friendly with the owners, while not speaking out enough on behalf of the workers. Bagley called editor Harriett Farley a "mouthpiece for the corporations." Farley contended that the best way to achieve better working conditions was to "do good by stealth," to persuade mill owners with civil language, not bombast. She denied that the magazine's contributors were the "poor, caged birds" their critics called them, "singing of the flowers which surround our prison bars, and apparently unconscious that those bars exist." To the end of her years as editor she maintained that position. "I have never felt disposed to croak or whine about my factory life," she said, "and have endeavored to impose a cheerful spirit into the little magazine I edit." With subscriptions falling off, the *Offering* put out its last issue in 1845.

Sarah Bagley mysteriously and suddenly dropped out of the labor movement and took a new turn in her life. She became among the first women telegraph operators in the country, opening the Lowell telegraph office in 1846. The Female Labor Reform Association she had led faded in significance. There is no substantial biographical information on this early pioneer in the struggle for women's rights. Writer Helena Wright said that Bagley "was a pivotal figure, representing the entry of women into the industrial work force in the United States, their attempts to join with men in the labor reform movement of the 1840s, and the ultimate failure of women's influence without a political power base. Bagley's problems and frustrations were symptomatic of those of all leaders rendered impotent by the circumstances of defeat. We can only admire what she was able to accomplish in spite of her position and wish that we knew more about the forces which shaped her life." Her struggles with management often ended in frustration, but Sarah Bagley ignited fires of labor rebellion that the mill owners never smothered.

As other women vanished from the mill cities, they also left behind scant details of their lives, except for their record as pioneers in American labor history. They were what Mary Lyon had hoped they would be—the bone and sinew and glory of the nation.

Mary Paul returned to her native Vermont and established a garment shop in Brattleboro. Then, perhaps because of hard experiences in the mills, she explored the possibilities of more equitable labor in a utopian community. She left after a year and eventually she married.

Some women fulfilled Nathaniel Hawthorne's prophecy and mated themselves "with the pride of drawing rooms and literary circles." They married mill executives and other professionals, and became society matrons in the towns where they had begun their working lives.

Other women took different paths out of Lowell. Harriett Farley gave up her literary career, married, and moved to New York City. Margaret Fuller became a sculptor in Boston. Eliza Jane Cate wrote eight books. Sarah Shedd saved her earnings as a mill worker and then as a teacher and left twenty five hundred dollars for the establishment of a library in her home town of Washington, New Hampshire.

Lucy Larcom, who had pasted poems on the wall near her workstation in the mill, never let the factory system consume her soul. Like so many of her coworkers, she knew there was something better, and when she revealed the thoughts that flooded her mind during her mill years, she seemed to speak for them all: "I felt that I belonged to the world, that there was something for me to do in it, though I had not yet found out what." She found her destiny as a writer and poet, and then as a teacher at the school that became Wheaton College near Boston.

Eliza Adams of Derry, New Hampshire, stayed in Lowell much longer than her coworkers. Then she moved to Ipswich, Massachusetts, so she could both work in a mill and study at the academy in town. She moved from mill to mill a few more years and finally had saved enough money to buy a farm in South Hadley, the town where Mary Lyon had established Mount Holyoke. She adopted three girls and as a single mother prospered on the farm.

When John Tyler was president, he, like Andrew Jackson, visited Lowell to learn about the remarkable New Englanders who had helped launch

America's Industrial Revolution. Eliza Adams was still living in the city, and she took time off from work to be among the thousands of people who went to the railroad station to see Tyler. But neither she nor any other factory women paraded before the president, as they had done for Jackson. Most of the Yankee-bred, rosy-cheeked, independent-minded young women were gone, leaving Irish immigrants to work in their place. It would not be good public relations for the mill owners to show President Tyler their new workforce. It would not be prudent to stage a parade of overworked, underpaid people who were not much better off than the wretches of the British mill system who had so horrified Francis Cabot Lowell.

3

The Lords of the Loom

Francis Cabot Lowell lived and worked in an environment steeped in American history. Everywhere he went in Boston, he followed in the paths of heroes. He passed the Old North Church from which Paul Revere received the lantern signal to make his midnight ride to warn the colonists that the British were coming. On his way to the banks and trading houses where he did business, Lowell passed the Old South Meeting House where the Sons of Liberty protested British-imposed taxation without representation and then marched to the harbor to stage the Boston Tea Party. He knew Faneuil Hall, where the founders of the country launched the American Revolution. He knew the Old Granary Burying Ground where patriots slept in the soil they made free. Boston gave to the country many revolutionaries. Among them was Francis Cabot Lowell himself, a father of the American Industrial Revolution.

When Lowell began thinking about entering the textile industry, he was just thirty-five years old. He had known only success, wealth, and prominence as a member of one of the oldest families in Massachusetts; the family traced its roots back to the eleventh century, when an ancestor fought under William the Conqueror. Lowell was born in Newburyport, Massachusetts, and reared in Boston. He entered Harvard at the age of fourteen and joined the hedonistic Porcellian Club. He was suspended from college for starting a bonfire in Harvard Yard but was readmitted. One of the few known personal details about him is that he tried to control an explosive temper by becoming a vegetarian. When his years as student and hell-raiser were over, he turned to the duties of business.

Lowell's only serious misfortune was frail health. His wife, Hannah, was prone to illness, too. Hoping that a change of surroundings would help them, they sailed for Great Britain in 1810 and were joined there by Nathan Appleton, Lowell's business acquaintance in Boston. Both men had sustained setbacks in their trading businesses when England and France went to war. President Thomas Jefferson imposed a trade embargo against the two countries until they recognized U.S. neutrality rights. To the great frustration of American merchants, the embargo lasted for fourteen months, shutting down ports along the East Coast. Clipper ships with no sailing orders stood idle in harbors from Portland, Maine, to Baltimore, Maryland. Grass grew on wharves that were falling apart from neglect. Warehouses were filled with rotting grain, tobacco, and other goods that had been destined for China, India, and Europe, and no manufactured goods were coming into the country from England or France.

Lowell pursued new ways to make money. The United States had many small factories, foundries, and mills that turned out tools and timber, clocks and shoes, firearms and fabrics. But there was a national desire for domestic industries big enough and strong enough to compete in price and quality with the pre-embargo flood of imports from the huge factories in Europe. Businessmen braced for the flood to resume once the embargo ended. George Gibb wrote that Lowell, "almost alone among his fellow Boston merchants, knew what was soon to come and what now must be done."

While Lowell was in England, he studied the British textile industry, the mightiest in the world. As a prominent Boston businessman, he had many contacts among the British textile men. They arranged for him to see what they allowed few foreigners to see: the operations of the mills of Lancashire, Birmingham, Manchester, and Leeds. He marveled at the machinery created by James Hargreaves, Richard Arkwright, and Samuel

Crompton that spun yarn with dazzling speed; most of all, Edmund Cartwright's power loom fascinated Lowell as it turned out finished cloth.

Lowell was spellbound by the genius of British technology, but he also
witnessed the brutality of the British system. While he was in England,
skilled textile workers revolted against labor-saving machines that threatened to eliminate their jobs. The workers were called Luddites after Ned
Ludd, an early participant in the protests. Luddites smashed the machines
and rioted in several mill cities. Company police shot some of them;
others were hanged.

Lowell saw children, as well as adults, seized from poorhouses and
forced to work. Others were recruited from the poverty-stricken masses
living in the streets. Factory owners circulated handbills that bore a chilling legend: "Men With Growing Families Wanted." Overseers wielding
lashes forced the mill workers to labor until they dropped from exhaustion. The only escape was the pauper's grave. Parliament held hearings
on the national scandal; some of the testimony of witness Elizabeth Bent-
ley concerned her years as a child laborer in a mill:

Q. What age are you?

A. *Twenty-three.*

Q. Where do you live?

A. *At Leeds.*

Q. What time did you begin work in the factory?

A. *When I was six years old.*

Q. What were your hours of work in that mill?

A. *From 3 in the morning till 9 at night.*

Q. Suppose you flagged a little, or were late, what would they do?

A. *Strap us.*

Q. Have you ever been strapped?

A. *Yes.*

Q. Severely?

A. *Yes.*

Q. You are considerably deformed in person as a consequence of this
   labor?

A. *Yes I am.*

Q. You were perfectly straight and healthy before you worked in a mill?

A. *Yes, I was as straight a little girl as ever went up and down town.*

Q. Where are you now?

A. *In the poorhouse.*

Two centuries earlier, Sir Edward Coke had told England during a court case that corporations "cannot commit treason, nor be outlawed, nor excommunicated, for they have no souls." Lowell became determined to instill in his corporation, if not soul, at least a sense of decency.

Despite what he saw in England, Lowell pursued all the knowledge he could as he toured the British mills. The government fiercely guarded the secrets of production; it banned the export of both textile machinery and the technology that would enable overseas competitors to design and make the machines. But as a business courtesy, the mill managers showed Lowell everything. They explained how the machines worked, how much human labor they saved, and how much wealth they created by transforming cotton from Brazil, India, and the British West Indies into finished fabrics.

Lowell was a brilliant mathematician with an extraordinary memory, useful talents for an industrial spy. After each mill tour, he went back to his vacation quarters, briefed Appleton for hours, and committed to memory everything he saw and heard. On his way back to Boston, his ship stopped at Halifax, Nova Scotia, where British customs officials searched his baggage. Then they searched it again. There were no writings, no drawings, no secrets of the British textile industry hidden away in his belongings, only in his mind.

Lowell built his mill in 1814 on the Charles River in Waltham, ten miles west of Boston. The site was at a waterfall that dropped perpendicularly twenty feet, then flowed down another half mile, dropping thirty-five more feet. There was enough kinetic energy in the flowing and falling water to turn the huge waterwheel installed at the base of the mill. As the wheel turned, it drove a system of gears and leather belts that powered the machines in the mill.

A gifted mechanic, Paul Moody, joined Lowell in Waltham. Moody, the son of a Newburyport sea captain, had a limited education, but by the time he was sixteen he had become a skilled weaver. What was more to his interest was how textile machinery worked. He and Lowell set out to design machines modeled on the ones Lowell had seen in England. Their goal was to process bales of cotton through a sequence of machines into finished cloth, all under one roof. They built one industrial marvel after another: machines to remove dirt and leaf from the cotton, then machines to draw out cotton bundles into strands, then machines to spin the strands into thread. Their greatest achievement was the design of a power loom to weave the thread into cloth. As with the Cartwright loom, this achievement would greatly reduce the labor needed to manufacture cloth. When the power loom was assembled, Lowell invited Appleton to have a look.

"I well recollect," Appleton wrote, "the state of admiration and satisfaction with which we sat by the hour, watching the beautiful movement of this new and wonderful machine, destined as it evidently was, to change the character of all textile industry."

The revolutionary design of the Waltham mill came two decades after Eli Whitney invented the cotton gin. The machine removed seed from cotton fiber fifty times faster than a slave could by hand. Whitney's invention made cotton a more profitable crop, and consequently Southern plantation owners expanded production as fast as they could. Cotton still had to be picked by hand, and with the increased demand created by Whitney's gin, many more slaves were needed in the fields.

Small textile factories were already operating in the United States by the time Lowell and Moody designed their machines. Samuel Slater, under the patronage of Providence merchant Moses Brown, built a factory in Pawtucket, Rhode Island, to spin cotton. Like Lowell, Slater had seen the British mills in operation and had surreptitiously carried away ideas for machinery designs. But Slater could not unlock the secret of the power loom. He had to contract out the weaving phase of production to women who worked in their homes or for independent shop owners. His factory delivered the cotton threads, the women manually operated their small looms, and after many hours of work they produced finished cloth. There were about three hundred small factories like Slater's, all of them lagging well behind the British mills in technology, and even farther behind Lowell's new mill in Waltham.

The way Slater ran his mills also influenced Lowell's decision to institute a paternal employment system. Slater had brought with him from England the view that anyone desperate enough to work in his mill would be hired. He employed entire families, including small children. No mill owned by Lowell and his associates did this, although some children did perform light tasks in some of their mills. Lowell's associates would have recoiled from recording an employee roster the way Slater did in one of his mills in 1816:

        1 family with 8 members working
        1 family with 7 members working
        2 families each with 5 members working
        4 families each with 4 members working
        5 families each with 3 members working

By 1830, more than half the mill workers in Rhode Island were children. Corporal punishment for lagging child workers was a common practice, administered in areas of the mills designated as whipping rooms. Slater's new competitors would have none of it.

Lowell formed the Boston Manufacturing Company with one hundred thousand dollars, some of it his own money. A contemporary said that many of Lowell's business associates "used all their influence to dissuade him from the pursuit of what they deemed a visionary and dangerous scheme." Some of them thought he was mad. The Cabot side of the family at first declined to take a risk in the new venture. Some capital came from Nathan Appleton and from Patrick Tracy Jackson, Lowell's brother-in-law. The rest was put up by the Boston elite that ran the banking, financial, insurance, and shipping interests on State Street. They became known as the Boston Associates, and, George Gibb wrote, they "hoped to find in the untried field of manufactures a medium for creating new wealth and perpetuating old dynasties." It all worked. In time the new company owned numerous mills in Massachusetts, New Hampshire, and Maine. Other investment groups built mills throughout New England.

In their heyday, the mills created fortunes for the founding families of the industry. The owners were often penurious in paying their workers but magnanimous in using their money to benefit great New England institutions. They wished, Van Wyck Brooks wrote, "to perpetuate their names and glorify their capital not only in the elegance of their mansions but also in churches, parks and public buildings, in professional chairs at Harvard College, in schools and asylums and hospitals." They were merchant-patricians, Brooks wrote, who regarded Boston as a holy city, and thought of Rome, Paris, and London as mere suburbs. Brooks added: "They meant to make Boston a model town. They meant to make New England a model region." They rejected the chilling Calvinism of their ancestors and joined the more liberal Unitarian and Episcopal denominations. The doctor-poet Oliver Wendell Holmes called them the Boston Brahmins, "a harmless, inoffensive, untitled aristocracy" bound through generations by business and marriage.

The Lowells and the Cabots were among the first American families to acquire great wealth. Their mansions in Boston made Beacon Street, Commonwealth Avenue, and Louisburg Square national landmarks. In ensuing decades, hundreds of their descendants grew up in these luxurious surroundings, among them the poet Amy Lowell:

> *My Grandpa lives in a wonderful house*
> *With a great many windows and doors,*
> *There are stairs that go up, and stairs that go down*
> *To such beautiful, slippery floors.*

Everything Francis Cabot Lowell set out to do he accomplished, but fortune dictated that he would not live to see the fabulous growth of the New England textile industry. Through the years after his return from England, through all the planning and designing and building of the Waltham mill, Lowell never recovered his health. Neither did Hannah Lowell. She died in 1815 when she was thirty-nine years old; he died two years later, at the age of forty-two. They left three sons and a daughter, whose descendants bear the Lowell and Cabot family names to this day.

It is not known what Lowell thought of his accomplishments or what plans he had for developing the industry he had created. He left no diaries or journals, apparently believing that his actions stood as his record. It is not even known what he looked like. There is no portrait of him, only a silhouette that suggests a resolute young man pursuing a great adventure. "He was," wrote Nathan Appleton, "the informing soul which gave direction and form" to the American textile industry.

In 1815, the first full year the Waltham mill was in production, sales totaled just $3,000. Within seven years sales reached $345,000. With improved efficiency in the mill, managers were able to bring down the price of fabrics and so expand their markets. Annual dividends ranged from 12 to 28 percent.

Lowell had chosen well when he invited Appleton and Patrick Tracy Jackson to be his partners. Appleton, born in New Ipswich, New Hampshire, was the son of Isaac Appleton III, who helped raise a militia that joined the Minute Men at Concord in 1775. Nathan was twenty-four when he took a business trip to Charleston, South Carolina, where he witnessed a slave auction. He wrote of "the horrid sight of the sale of human flesh" and of the spectacle of men, women, and children trembling on the auction block as they waited to see which bidder would be their new master "while the unfeeling auctioneer with cutting taunts and jeers is adding insult to injury." At the time, Appleton had no idea that much of his fortune would come from the sweat and blood and lives of slaves.

The mild-mannered Appleton was a brilliant banker and politician. By the time he met Lowell, writes Robert F. Dalzell Jr., in *Enterprising Elite,* "He may have been a man on the make, but he was also a man who already had it made." Appleton subscribed to Lowell's policy of treating workers well. Of all the industry's early leaders, Appleton was probably the most respected. "In fact, good conditions for and fair treatment of labor were moral issues with Appleton," Frances W. Gregory wrote in a biography. As a mill owner, he viewed the growth of industry as an opportunity for workers and, Gregory observed, "he alone among the promoters repeatedly described the utopian environment that he wanted and hoped to create.... He had a sense of mission to make the United States succeed and to make it a better place to work than England was."

Appleton shared his wealth with his daughter, Frances, and her husband, Henry Wadsworth Longfellow, giving them one hundred thousand dollars worth of stock in his mills. It was an immense fortune, ensuring Longfellow a comfortable life as a poet and professor of literature at Harvard. As with many aristocratic Boston families, the slavery issue threatened tranquility in the Appleton and Longfellow households. Longfellow, in polite disagreement with his father-in-law, was an abolitionist. He described slavery as "the feudal curse, whose whips and yokes insult humanity." Appleton, despite what he had seen at the Charleston slave auction, was a businessman to the core and supported slavery in the South because it benefited the textile industry.

Patrick Tracy Jackson, like Lowell, was born in Newburyport. Jackson had sailed the world on merchant ships, supervising trade conducted in foreign ports. His father served in the Continental Congress and in later years was treasurer of Harvard College. His grandfather Tracy came penniless to America from Ireland and became a rich and distinguished citizen of Newburyport. Jackson, whose blond hair, blue eyes, quick temper, and cheerfulness bespoke his Irish heritage, eventually settled in Boston as a leading merchant. When Lowell told him of his plan for a textile factory, Jackson did not hesitate to invest.

Together, Appleton and Jackson, as principals of the Boston Associates, oversaw the growth of their mills after Lowell's death. The Charles River at the Waltham factory site did not provide enough water power to serve the sort of operation Jackson conceived: a gigantic complex with many mills, a textile empire bigger than anything the United States had ever seen. So the Boston Associates searched for other potential sites in rural New England. They found what they wanted in the little farming town of East Chelmsford, Massachusetts, twenty-eight miles northwest of Boston, at the confluence of the Merrimack and Concord rivers.

East Chelmsford had been a favorite haunt of Henry David Thoreau, who described the swift-running Merrimack as "a silver cascade which falls all the way from the White Mountains to the sea." It was here in the Merrimack Valley that the giant mills would be built. The valley covered five thousand square miles of land and water. It stretched 134 miles from New Hampshire's Lake Winnipesaukee in the north, down through the sites of future mill cities and on to the Atlantic at Newburyport. Generations of people, native and European-born, were destined to live and work and die in this valley.

The Associates bought land from farmers in East Chelmsford, acquired rights to build canals, dams, and mills all along the Merrimack River in Massachusetts and New Hampshire, and set up the Merrimack Manufacturing Company. They transformed the marshy riverside meadows into the city of Lowell. Patrick Tracy Jackson built the Boston and Lowell Railroad so the mills could ship textiles to markets throughout the United States. At the invitation of the Associates, other investors bought mills in Lowell. One of them was Abbott Lawrence, who later built the textile city named for his family.

In the fall of 1824, production began in the Merrimack Mill, and before long there were thirty-three cotton factories in Lowell. The pristine river that Thoreau had known was now full of dams and canals that diverted the flow of water to the mill wheels that powered the machinery. Theodore Steinberg has described how chemicals from mill waste discolored and polluted the water with sulfuric acid, lime, and arsenic. Within three decades, Steinberg noted, this massive defilement of nature had almost destroyed fisheries that had abounded with salmon and bass.

The corporate structure set up by the Boston Associates gave the Merrimack Manufacturing Company control of both land and the mills' water power. Thomas Dublin wrote that the company "took charge of every aspect of establishing a new textile mill. It sold the land, leased the water rights, put up the mill buildings, outfitted them with machinery crafted in its machine shop, constructed canals and roads, and furnished housing for the workers." A visiting investor from Boston could see the many new mills where his money was at work for him. The mills were so intertwined that they shared top managers and directors, who in turn had the power to set wages at the same levels in all the factories, making it impossible for a worker to shop around for better pay.

Kirk Boott, who was designated to run the operation in Lowell, was born in Boston. His father, an English merchant who had settled in

America after the Revolution, sent young Kirk to England for his education at Rugby Academy and Sandhurst, the royal military school. Then he attended Harvard where, it is said, he concentrated on sowing an abundance of wild oats. As a British military officer he served under the duke of Wellington but resigned his commission when the United States and England went to war in 1812. Back home in Boston he went into the importing business and attracted the attention of Appleton and other mill owners. He was an imposing, decisive, and talented martinet. It was said of him that "Confucius would have recognized him as The Superior Man." He was the emperor of Lowell and everyone knew it.

Boott unified thousands of people of varying skills in the pursuit of profits. Whatever it took to make the mills the best they could be, he was determined to get it. He needed the finest calico printers in the world and went to England to hire them. The very best was John Dynely Prince of Lancashire. A history of the city of Lowell cites the legend that Boott asked Prince how much pay he expected. "Five thousand dollars a year," Prince replied. Boott told him that not even the governor of Massachusetts made that much money. "Well," Prince said, "can the governor of Massachusetts print?" Boott gave in, and Prince went to work for him. The laws protecting the secrets of British textile manufacturing were still in force, but skilled cloth printers, chemists, and engravers from England and Scotland found ways to sidestep them and followed Prince to Lowell. They lived in their own handsome housing complexes, called John Bull's Row and the Scotch Block, and were treated as the elite of the mill workers. With their arrival, Lowell mills were able to match the quality of machine-made textiles produced anywhere in the world.

Southerners feared the growing industrial might of the North exemplified by Lowell's success. They worried that their principal role was to supply cotton for the New England mills. They debated why they weren't manufacturing textiles or anything else on a significant scale, why almost everything they bought came from Northern factories, and why they relied so heavily on agriculture for their economic well-being. They had some small mills of their own where slaves and Southern whites worked together, but their output did not compare with the North's massive production levels. Commentators argued that industrial weakness brought shame on the South. "That we have cultivated cotton, cotton, cotton, and bought everything else, has long enough been our opprobrium," the Augusta, Georgia, *Courier* editorialized in 1827. There was growing Southern resentment of the Northern manufacturers and the protective tariffs that gave them a price advantage over imported goods. Seeds of rebellion sprouted in the Southern cotton fields.

The most vigorous advocate of the protective tariffs was Daniel Webster, who spoke often in the United States Senate on behalf of the Boston Associates. Webster was known around Boston and Washington as "Black Dan" because of his swarthy features. In *The Devil and Daniel Webster*, Stephen Vincent Benét described him as "a man with a mouth like a mastiff, a brow like a mountain, and eyes like burning anthracite." John F. Kennedy wrote of Webster in *Profiles in Courage:* "There could be no mistaking he was a great man—he looked like one, talked like one, was treated like one and insisted he was one."

Webster had one of the biggest law practices in the country and earned twenty thousand dollars a year, a substantial income for the time. The Boston Associates rewarded him with company stock and fees when he became their legal consultant. He loved the lavish life but made bad investments and had chronic money problems. To his dying day, he was dependent on the mill owners for his personal welfare; they contributed thousands of dollars so he could stay in public office and serve their interests.

The tariff conflict was debated in the Senate in 1830, with Robert Hayne of South Carolina declaring a new tariff null and void. Hayne argued that the federal government was merely a confederation of states, and that the states had the right to discard laws enacted by Congress. Webster argued against the doctrine of nullification. Under the Constitution, he contended, a congressional act was the law of the land. He warned that if states started setting aside acts of Congress, the result could be civil war. In a celebrated moment of his career he proclaimed: "Liberty and Union, now and forever, one and inseparable!" Webster won the debate, the tariffs stayed in place, and the Northern textile industry continued to flourish and grow.

Division deepened in New England over the slavery issue. Nathan

Appleton and other industry leaders usually opposed further extension of slavery as new states joined the Union but accepted its existence in the South. They belonged to the Whig party, which preceded the Republican party, and were called the "Cotton Whigs." They looked to the day when the slaves would eventually be emancipated by their owners and work as free people in Southern mills as well as on the cotton plantations.

Abolitionists, known as the "Conscience Whigs," wanted the slaves freed immediately, not eventually. Sometimes it was a dangerous position to take. John Greenleaf Whittier, a Quaker who believed that slavery was a sin, became the poet of the abolition movement. While he was the editor of a newspaper published by the Anti-Slavery Society, a mob attacked his office and set fire to the printing shop, but Whittier kept the paper going. Other proslavery mobs attacked him in Concord, New Hampshire, and in Boston.

"Let Southern oppressors tremble," declared abolitionist William Lloyd Garrison. "Let their secret abettors tremble—let all the enemies of the persecuted blacks tremble." When a proslavery mob in Boston attacked Garrison, Appleton showed no sympathy, dismissing him as a "fanatical monomaniac."

The abolition debate did not shake the plantation-factory alliance. "The wheels of the cotton factories revolved at a furious pace," Van Wyck Brooks wrote, "and the Southern slave drivers plied their whips to feed the Yankee mills with Southern cotton. The more the prosperity of New England came to depend on cotton, the closer the propertied classes drew to the Southern planters, with whom they felt obliged to ally themselves, yielding to them in all political matters." This was especially true in Rhode Island, where slave dealers were active as late as the 1820s and where many of the elite owned slaves themselves. Among those who fought to preserve slavery was Nicholas Brown, whose family founded Brown University.

Nothing stopped the rising of the textile cities. Mill fever broke out all over New England after entrepreneurs saw what was happening in Lowell. George Gibb wrote: "American promoters by 1834 had come to place preposterous valuations on every creek and stream which could conceivably turn a water wheel. Whole townships were purchased in Maine, sight unseen, and Boston land speculators filled the hotels in Portland to overflowing."

The Boston Associates extended their empire. They found a site at the Amoskeag Falls on the Merrimack River in New Hampshire where they built the city of Manchester, named for the British textile center. They built the large Amoskeag mill complex in Manchester and large mills in Nashua, south of Manchester on the Merrimack.

The city of Lawrence, Massachusetts, also on the river, arose during a cotton boom that began when Congress raised the protective tariff yet again, virtually guaranteeing that Amos and Abbott Lawrence would reap fortunes in their new venture.

The Lawrence brothers were born in Groton, Massachusetts, the sons of Samuel Lawrence, who had fought the British at Bunker Hill. Their mother had witnessed the Minute Men battling the redcoats at Concord. As young men the brothers went to Boston, where their company, A. and A. Lawrence, became the most successful mercantile firm in the city. Abbott Lawrence's competitive spirit was evident when he played in schoolyard games and remained with him all his life. He secured his reputation as a brilliant businessman when he hurried to England just after the War of 1812 and, well ahead of his competitors, bought up whole cargoes of British goods. He sold them in America and reaped immense profits.

The Lawrences had already been big investors in the textile industry as members of the Boston Associates when they got directly involved in running mills. Ten miles north of Lowell, they bought up land along the Merrimack River in Andover and Methuen for their first mill, the Essex Company. They hired Charles Storrow to design the city, with Abbott setting the tone he hoped would make the community worthy of the Lawrence name: He stated his belief that "it is no less the duty than the privilege of those who possess influence in creating towns and cities to lay the foundations deep and strong." Within a few years there were fourteen churches, fourteen public schools, and fifteen thousand people. Storrow also built the dam and canal system for the other mills that soon formed the city skyline: the Pacific Mills, the Washington Mills, and others. Emulating the paternalism of Lowell's founders, the Lawrences established a boardinghouse system for women workers and cultural activities to occupy them during their free time. Abbott helped the new city library buy books, which he hoped would "tend to create mechanics, good Christians, and patriots."

Despite Abbott Lawrence's hopes for the city and Storrow's urban plan, there was in the ensuing years "a certain mad haste in the construction, the use of shoddy materials," wrote Hannah Josephson. "The development of Lowell under Kirk Boott, and indirectly, Nathan Appleton," she said, "had been dignified, steady, orderly; the development of Lawrence was crude, thoughtless, boom-or-bust." In time, the city of Lawrence would be the scene of tribulation and turmoil. In 1847, a mill dam collapsed, and fifteen Irish laborers lost their lives. In 1860, the Pemberton Mill collapsed and burned, killing eighty-eight persons, most of them Irish women workers. In 1912, a strike by immigrant mill workers in Lawrence led to bloodshed and death.

Amos Lawrence personified the early New England businessman. He was faithful to the principles of hard work and thrift. One of his tenets was, "Business before friends." He did not drink or smoke, and he demanded that his employees abstain, too. When someone asked him about the propriety of being so rich, he reportedly snapped back: "There is one thing you may as well understand. I know how to make money, and *you* cannot prevent it." When his mill workers protested a newly imposed pay cut, he arranged for newspapers to publish a letter to the editor describing awful working conditions in Naples, Italy. The letter was from his son.

When Amos was forty-five his health failed, and he became an invalid. He spent the final two decades of his life tortured by stomach ulcers, existing on a bland diet. He gave away most of his money to educational and charitable organizations while he was still living. He gave advice freely, and after his death his writings on how to succeed were collected in a book that became required reading for ambitious young men in New England. Decades later, John D. Rockefeller also read the book and said the life of the old mill owner "was a great inspiration to me." The founder of Standard Oil was impressed when he read how Lawrence gave away crisp bills. "Crisp bills! I could see and hear them," Rockefeller said in 1917. "I made up my mind that, if I could manage it, some day I would give away crisp bills, too." As an old man, Rockefeller gave away shiny dimes to people who greeted him on the street; his family established a foundation that gave away billions in crisp bills to support worthy causes.

Amos Lawrence disliked the idea of anyone in business serving in public office. When his brother Abbott was a leading candidate for the vice presidential nomination on the Whig ticket with Zachary Taylor in 1848, Amos refused to contribute money to his campaign. "If my vote would make my brother vice president, I would not give it," he said, "as I think it lowering his good name to accept office of any sort, by employing such means as are now needful to get votes." Abbott Lawrence did not pursue the nomination, serving instead as ambassador to Great Britain. He might have been president of the United States; the vice presidential nomination that year went to Millard Fillmore, who became president when Taylor died in office.

Unlike his brother, Abbott did not tire of acquiring wealth. A relative said of him: "He still grasps at money though he has more than a million and is the richest man of his age here. He loves power, too, and office."

Abbott Lawrence and Nathan Appleton both served briefly in Congress and pursued policies beneficial to their industry. They lined up members from other Northern textile centers to work with Southern congressmen in mutual self-interest on proslavery issues. John Greenleaf Whittier looked on all of them with contempt:

> Yet, shame upon them! there they sit,
>   Men of the North, subdued and still;
> Meek, pliant poltroons, only fit
>   To work a master's will.

> Sold, bargained off for Southern votes,
>   A passive herd of Northern mules,
> Just braying through their purchased throats
>   Whate'er their owner rules.

Abbott Lawrence was not dissuaded by criticism that associated him with the evil of slavery. He lived and socialized with abolitionists like Longfellow, Emerson, and Harriet Beecher Stowe. Their words on the subject pricked the conscience but did not change his mind. "I am for the Union as it is," Lawrence said. "I have no sympathy with the abolition party of the North and East. I believe they have done mischief to the cause of freedom in several States of the Union." A Boston newspaper said he had "covered old Massachusetts with shame." Even a rising member of the Lowell clan joined the abolitionist cause. James Russell Lowell, who was beginning his writing career, declared, "There is something better than Expedience, and that is Wisdom, something stronger than Compromise and that is Justice." Abbott Lawrence looked south to the great plantations and to the mills in his own New England, and declared, "We are not only destined to be the greatest cotton growers but the most extensive cotton spinners in the world. We have all the elements among ourselves to do so."

Lawrence and Appleton supported Daniel Webster as he took the most controversial step of his career—voting to enact the Fugitive Slave Law in 1850 that empowered the federal government to pursue escaped slaves and return them to bondage. Henry Clay of Missouri had proposed the law as part of a compromise to keep the United States intact as a union in the face of deep conflict between pro- and antislavery states, between extremists and moderates on both sides of the slavery issue, and between states' righters and supporters of a strong federal role in settling the slavery question. Webster believed the factionalism was tearing the country apart and that the Southern states might secede from the Union. He voted for the compromise despite his longtime opposition to slavery.

Abolitionists were enraged. Ralph Waldo Emerson railed that "the word *liberty* in the mouth of Mr. Webster sounds like the word *love* in the mouth of a courtesan." He called the Fugitive Slave Law a "filthy enactment" and vowed, "I will not obey it, by God!" Harriet Beecher Stowe called Webster the "lost archangel of New England." Even as Webster lived, Whittier wrote his epitaph:

So fallen! So lost! The light withdrawn
  Which once he wore!
The glory from his gray hairs gone
  Forevermore . . .

All else is gone; from those great eyes
  The soul has fled;
When faith is lost, when honor dies,
  The man is dead!

After Webster's political star faded, the mill owners found that it was not just poets and writers they had to contend with on the slavery question. One of the fiercest New England abolitionists also had political power. He was Charles Sumner of Massachusetts, who followed Webster into the Senate. Sumner stood six feet two inches tall and was a renowned orator. He was, Longfellow wrote, "a colossus holding his burning heart in his hand to light up the sea of life." Sumner disagreed profoundly with Webster's toleration of slavery in order to preserve the Union and attacked Massachusetts mill owners for doing business with slaveholders. It was clear he was an abolitionist to be reckoned with. When he was elected, many Bostonians wore black crepe armbands as symbols of their sorrow.

To those who told Sumner that sometimes there was more than one side to an argument, he countered, "There *is* no other side." To those who advised him to be politically practical, he answered, "I am in morals, not politics." Boston society shunned him. Longfellow, despite family ties to Nathan Appleton, remained a friend and often had the senator to his home for dinner. On one occasion, the poet tripped over his invitations. First he asked Sumner to dine with a visiting New York merchant. Then in a forgetful moment he decided to ask his father-in-law to meet the New Yorker, too. He wrote to Appleton:

My dear Sir . . .
   It would give us a great pleasure if you would join him, and favor us with your company at dinner.

64

Sumner had once condemned Appleton as "the living embodiment of the cotton industry," a man whose mills used slave labor for his cotton. The prospect of these opposites in his home was too much for Longfellow. He returned to his writing desk:

Dear Sumner,

 Pray do not come to dinner tomorrow Wednesday, as I expect some one whom you might not care to meet. Come on Thursday, when I shall have another one, whom you will care to meet—namely Hawthorne.

When Sumner first spoke out in the Senate against slavery, some members thought him hypocritical because he came from a state where thousands of textile workers were themselves exploited. But before his election, he had raged against Northern textile industrialists as well as Southern cotton planters for protecting each other's interests at the expense of human freedom. This was, he said, "an unholy alliance or rather conspiracy between the cotton planters and flesh-mongers of Louisiana and Mississippi and the cotton-spinners and traffickers of New England— the lords of the lash and the lords of the loom."

In the Senate, Sumner assailed Senator Stephen Douglas of Illinois as "the squire of slavery . . . ready to do all its humiliating offices." He attacked Senator Andrew Pickens Butler of South Carolina for choosing "a mistress to whom he has made his vows, and who, though ugly to others, is always lovely to him; though polluted in the sight of the world, is chaste in his sight. I mean the harlot Slavery."

A few days after the speech, Senator Butler's nephew, Congressman Preston Brooks, also of South Carolina, walked onto the Senate floor when the day's session was over. He approached Sumner, who was writing at his desk. Brooks beat him nearly to death with a cane. Sumner raised his arms to ward off the blows, but fell to the floor, bleeding and unconscious. Southerners praised Brooks for the attack. Some sent him canes bearing the legend, "Hit him again!" Proslavery members of the House blocked a congressional attempt to punish him for the assault. A court fined him three hundred dollars.

Sumner suffered brain and spinal trauma and was disabled for three and a half years. After he recovered, he resumed his Senate seat and served until 1874. He became one of Lincoln's advisers during the Civil War, especially on the emancipation issue.

Sumner holds a secure place in history as a champion of human rights. Webster's name remains tainted. In his old age, when he was ill and almost destitute, the textile men came to Webster's rescue. They established a trust fund that provided income for him during his lifetime and, after his death, for his widow. His enemies derided him as a chronic dependent of the manufacturers.

Webster did not live to see the Civil War he had so feared. In their own final years, the textile barons refused to believe the country could be so savagely ripped apart. "The Union cannot be touched," Abbott Lawrence had declared as rebellion spread through the Southern states. "Two million swords would leap from their scabbards if it should be seriously assailed by enemies from without or within." But twelve years before the war began, Longfellow sensed that the country would endure a great trial:

> *. . . sail on, O Ship of State!*
> *Sail on, O Union strong and great!*
> *Humanity with all its fears,*
> *With all the hopes of future years,*
> *Is hanging breathless on thy fate!*

By the time war did break out, most of the Lords of the Loom were dead. Patrick Tracy Jackson, who helped build the city of Lowell, died in 1847. Abbott Lawrence died in 1855. A memoir of his life described him as "dying with everything around him to soften the bitterness of death—above all, with the sweet consciousness that he had not lived in vain." He left generous bequests to establish a school of science at Harvard and for other institutions, but his generosity did not silence those who detested the mill system. An Albany, New York, newspaper editorialized, "How many, many thousands of extra hours of wearisome, life-wearing toil did it add to the over-wrought limbs and hands of the operatives, in order that *one man* may be gazetted as a great public benefactor?"

The last to go was Nathan Appleton, in 1861, just after the guns of Southern rebellion were fired at Fort Sumter in Charleston Harbor. Appleton began as a mill owner full of idealism as he welcomed New England's young farm women to join his enterprises. In the end, they refused to work for him any longer. Still, he believed his greatest possession was his reputation as an honest man who did not pursue profits for the sake of wealth alone and who was a generous contributor to New England's public institutions. "Accident and not effort has made me a rich man," he said. When he was eighty years old he fell ill and knew death was approaching. "I am not afraid," he said. "To tell you the truth, I believe I am not afraid of anything." Grief was another matter. On his sickbed, he learned that his daughter, Frances Appleton Longfellow, had been killed in a horrific accident. She had been using hot wax to seal a paper package containing a lock from one of her children's hair; the wax spilled on her hoop-skirted muslin dress and flames consumed her almost instantly. Henry Wadsworth Longfellow was burned on the face and hands while trying to save her. When the news reached Appleton, he said calmly, "She has gone but a little while before me." He died a few days later. Both were buried at Mount Auburn Cemetery in Cambridge, the Brahmins' final resting place.

Hannah Josephson composed a rueful epitaph for all the Boston Associates when she said of Appleton that "it was during his time, and largely through the form he gave to the corporation mills, that the distance between the owners and operatives became so great, and their interests so seemingly disparate. It was of the textile companies that the term 'soulless corporation' was first used in American journalism."

As civil war approached, the new generation of textile families acted to stop the spread of slavery. "We went to bed one night, old-fashioned, conservative, compromise Union Whigs, and waked up stark mad Abolitionists," said Amos A. Lawrence, son of the original Amos Lawrence and the new leader of the clan. The awakening occurred with passage of the Kansas-Nebraska Act of 1854, which provided that people living in the two territories would decide whether slavery would be allowed there. In response, the New England Emigrant Aid Society gave money to hundreds of antislavery New Englanders so they could take up new lives on the Western plains and stop the spread of slavery. The Lawrence family contributed to the society, and Amos A. Lawrence was its treasurer. The family's roles in the Emigration Society and in the establishment of the University of Kansas were commemorated by the naming of Lawrence, Kansas, in its honor.

The Lawrences gave money to John Brown for his campaign against slavery but did not support the violence he resorted to when he took up arms against U.S. troops at the federal arsenal at Harpers Ferry, Virginia. In the raid, to the horror of Amos A. Lawrence, Brown armed his men with rifles that once belonged to the Emigrant Aid Society. Despite his condemnation of Brown's zealotry, Lawrence helped pay for Brown's legal defense. When Brown was executed for treason and murder, Lawrence said: "Old Brown hanged with great ceremony. He died grandly. Nevertheless he must be called a fanatic."

The Civil War brought chaos to the New England textile industry. Union forces blockaded Southern cotton ports, shutting off supplies to the Northern mills and to their overseas competitors. Blockade runners loaded their ships with cotton and eluded Union patrols to get the cargo to European mills. Speculators who had bought cotton before the war at low prices sold high to New England mills that had failed to stock up as the war approached.

A few of the mills did build up cotton supplies before the war and stayed in production, manufacturing clothing and tents for the Union army. For the most part, though, the war idled many mills. Some managers opted for quick profits by shutting down operations and selling their cotton inventories to foreign buyers. According to one history, "nine of the great corporations of Lowell, under a mistaken belief that they could not run their mills to a profit during the war, unanimously, in cold blood, dismissed ten thousand operatives penniless into the streets." Men left the mills in great numbers to serve in the Union army, but the women workers were stranded without jobs.

During the war, the sons of the textile clans honored the tradition of noblesse oblige. Three Lowells were killed in combat. Brigadier General Charles Russell Lowell Jr., twenty-nine years old, died at the Battle of Cedar Creek in 1864. He was, said his uncle, James Russell Lowell, "the pride of the family . . . by far, the best we had." A brother of Charles, James Jackson Lowell, was killed in action in 1862. William Putnam, whose mother was a Lowell, died on the battlefield at Ball's Bluff, Virginia. A son and a Longfellow grandson of Nathan Appleton were wounded in combat. Daniel Webster had feared that America would be drenched in "fraternal blood" if civil war came; his son, Daniel Fletcher Webster, was killed in the Second Battle of Bull Run.

After the war, mill managers, some of them relatives of the original investors, showed little concern for the welfare of their employees. They cut corners. The lighting in some mills was so bad that workers' eyesight failed and they were forced to quit. The mills bought inferior cotton and there was so much thread breakage that production was slowed while the damage was repaired. Profits, and only profits, seemed to interest the owners. "If every dollar earned by a Lowell corporation became a dollar in dividends," wrote Robert F. Dalzell Jr., "it must have been because the stockholders—or more accurately those of them in a position to exercise control—wanted it that way. And evidently they preferred such a policy despite the obvious constraints it placed on future growth. The question is why."

Labor crusader Jennie Collins denounced the new managers with the force of a freight train. Money acquired by their ancestors, not ability, made them aristocrats, she wrote, and in succeeding generations "as each rich man wished his child to marry into a wealthy family, they were obliged to marry cousins. This defiance of nature brought upon the state a race of half-witted, mental cripples, if not idiots, at least possessing unevenly balanced minds." Workers who dared fight for better conditions in the mills had to deal with managers who, wrote labor historian Herbert Harris, "desired dividends more than celestial grace and . . . deplored any fuss and feathers about the well-being of people who made dividends possible."

These were not the mills that Dickens and Davy Crockett and Andrew Jackson had admired. Writing about the city of Lowell, John Coolidge noted that "Americans stopped thinking of the industrial Utopia as one of the seven wonders of the new republic. Distinguished Europeans no longer felt obliged to visit the community and marvel in print at its sudden rise, its physical cleanliness, and its high moral tone."

During the years of industrial decline, the Brahmins still gathered for dinner parties in their elegant Boston mansions. They gorged on creamed oysters, roast mutton, and fine wines. Their wives and daughters learned to ride at new equestrian academies. The families took grand tours of Europe. They came together for evenings of classical music and art exhibitions. They danced by gaslight in Papanti's Hall. They hosted debutante balls for their daughters at the Copley Plaza Hotel and the Country Club in Brookline, and invited visitors from out of town to join them. Oscar Wilde was a guest. He gazed at the debutantes, judged them unattractive, and said he understood why Boston artists limited themselves to painting only millionaires and Niagara Falls.

The unconventional belle of Boston society was Isabella Stewart Gardner, whose husband, Jack Lowell Gardner, was of the textile family. Her friends had a taste for sherry and champagne. "Mrs. Jack," as she was known, drank beer. Most Brahmins were Unitarians or Episcopalians. Mrs. Jack was a Buddhist. Society matrons rode down Tremont Street in horse-drawn carriages. Mrs. Jack walked down the street with a lion on a leash. If she was late for the symphony, the audience had to wait. The symphony would not start without one of its most generous patrons.

For all her eccentricities, Mrs. Jack left to the city one of its finest cultural institutions, the Isabella Stewart Gardner Museum, a Florentine mansion brought from Italy brick by brick and reassembled in Back Bay. The museum is rich with art treasures, including paintings by Italian, Flemish, and Spanish masters.

The Brahmins tried to ensure that Boston would remain the Hub of the Universe and the Athens of America. They were generous supporters of Harvard University where more than sixty male descendants of Cabots and Lowells were educated, along with numerous Appletons and Lawrences. They helped establish the Boston Athenaeum, a library and cultural center on Beacon Hill, where women were banned so they would not "cause embarrassment to modest men." They were principal donors of the Museum of Fine Arts, which was designed by one of their own, the architect Guy Lowell. They supported the Massachusetts Institute of Technology, Massachusetts General Hospital, and numerous religious and educational institutions. The Lowells established the Lowell Institute, which underwrote lectures by distinguished leaders of the arts and sciences. Percival Lowell, a prominent astronomer of his day, was invited to lecture at the institute, but his sister, Amy Lowell, was kept out because she was a woman. The decision was made by her other brother, Abbott Lawrence Lowell, president of Harvard.

As the Lowells of the early textile industry had brought culture to the Yankee women who worked in their mills, so the descendants of those women who remain in greater Boston enjoy cultural benefits brought to them in part by the Lowell fortune. The Lowell Institute's influence has lasted into the electronic age. Public television and radio stations in Boston went on the air with the institute's financial support.

The Brahmins longed for a staid world and preferred that everyone live by their rules, to the annoyance of those with lustier appetites. The aristocracy supported the New England Watch and Ward Society, a quasi governmental group that took upon itself the task of censoring stage plays, books, and all other activities that had the potential for stirring licentious thought. The police closed down offending theaters and bookstores, and broke up gatherings that the Watch and Ward Society branded immoral. "Banned in Boston" became a national phrase of scorn. The Brahmins themselves were mocked, too. At a Holy Cross College alumni dinner in 1910, John Collins Bossidy first recited the impudent verse that they were to endure in perpetuity:

> And this is good old Boston
> The home of the bean and the cod,
> Where the Lowells talk to the Cabots
> And the Cabots talk only to God.

Bossidy's humor reflected an underlying animosity that working classes felt toward the Brahmins. Sometimes the feeling was mutual. In his later years, James Russell Lowell became anti-immigrant, anti-Semitic and anti-Irish. C. David Heymann wrote that the old poet looked back longingly to the quiet days "before our individuality had been trampled out of us by the Irish mob." Amy Lowell abhorred Irish trade unionists, believing they wanted to overthrow democracy. Another poet in the family, Robert Lowell, alluding to the flood of immigrants in Massachusetts and the rising politicians among them, lamented that "strangers hold the golden State House dome."

Louis Brandeis, a Boston lawyer who was the first Jew to serve on the U.S. Supreme Court, said the Brahmins were people "blinded by privilege, who have no evil purpose, and many of them have distinct public spirit, but whose environment—or innate narrowness—has obscured all vision and sympathy with the masses." The political observer Walter Lippmann called Boston "the most homogeneous, self-centered, and self-complacent community in the United States."

No one was allowed to trespass for long into the world of the Boston blue bloods. When John F. Kennedy was a Harvard student, his mother, Rose, daughter of an Irish-American mayor of Boston and wife of an Irish-American millionaire, asked her son's Brahmin friend, "Tell me, when are the nice people of Boston going to accept us?" If not acceptance, there was usually a respectful symbiosis between the Brahmins and the rest of Boston. Kennedy won election to the Senate by defeating a Brahmin, Henry Cabot Lodge Jr. When Kennedy became president, he chose Lodge to be ambassador to South Vietnam. And when Kennedy died, the Boston Symphony Orchestra performed at a memorial Mass in the heart of Irish-Catholic Boston. The man who brought the musicians to the service was a Brahmin, symphony president Henry B. Cabot.

The Cabots and the Lowells and all the other textile families remain an important part of the Boston community. Even as politicians with immigrant names govern the region, the Brahmins are in the Hub of the Universe to stay. In 1946, when Godfrey Lowell Cabot hosted a family Thanksgiving dinner, 161 members of the clan attended. "Godfrey," one of them said, "this doesn't look like race suicide to me."

Generations of Brahmins and their workers lived with the knowledge that textile manufacturing was associated with violence, from the time of the Luddites to bitter strikes in New England. Always, there was resentment among those in the mills toward the blue bloods who, the workers believed as an article of faith, reaped their fortunes on the backs of the exploited.

In private, Amy Lowell viewed the textile workers in the family mills with fear and, said her friend Louis Untermeyer, "the implications of her wealth worried her." Untermeyer, writing an introduction to Lowell's *Collected Poems*, recalled, "We were attending a performance of Gerhard Hauptmann's *The Weavers*, a drama of class conflict which pictured an uprising in the 1840s.... Hauptmann's play reached its climax as the Silesian workers, starving and desperate, destroy not only the machines, which they hold responsible for their distress, but proceed to smash the home of their employer. Amy Lowell could not help thinking of the industrialized town of Lowell which had been named for her forbearers and she, who sometimes referred to herself as 'the last of the Barons,' flinched. 'This is the future,' she whispered as the curtain came down on a scene of pillage. 'That is what is going to happen to me!' "

A member of the Lawrence family witnessed the desperation that could ignite violent revolution in the mill cities. In the 1870s, William Lawrence went to the city of Lawrence as a young Episcopal priest at Grace Church. He recalled "going from tenement to tenement, sitting in the kitchens, talking to the women at the tub and the cook stove, or in the evenings meeting the men." The grandson of old Amos Lawrence walked along the cheerless streets through blocks of slums in the city his family had founded, with the family's grimy mills always in view under smoky skies. A generation later, on these same streets, the mill workers would strike out against the slums, against hunger, against exploitation. William Lawrence said he "learned much and thought more" about the way the textile workers lived. "It has been passing strange to me," he reflected, why those who ran the mills "have been so blind to their best interests and to humanity." As the waves of Irish, French Canadians, and Europeans entered the mills, it seemed passing strange to other New Englanders, too.

4

From Across the Irish Sea

In the spring of 1822, Hugh Cummisky heard talk in Boston about the huge mills planned for the new city of Lowell. Cummisky, a native of County Tyrone in Ireland, anticipated the need for strong arms and brawny backs. He rounded up thirty men in his Charlestown neighborhood on Boston Harbor and led them on a day-long walk to Lowell. They were the first of thousands of Irishmen bound for New England's new mill cities. They built the factories, dug the canals to carry water to the mill wheels, and constructed the boardinghouses for women workers.

The first person Cummisky and his men looked up in Lowell was the boss of all the mills, Kirk Boott. The Irishmen and the former British military officer hit it off at the saloon where they met. Boott bought drinks all around and hired Cummisky's crew immediately. Over the years Cummisky, working on commission, arranged for the arrival from Ireland of hundreds more laborers for the mills. They earned less than their Yankee coworkers, but at least they had their first real jobs in the new land. They were willing to work from sunrise to sunset until, an Irish laborer said, "our sweat mixes with the nightly dew."

Many people left Ireland in the early nineteenth century aboard cargo ships that brought the emigrants to ports in Quebec and New Brunswick.

When the Irish arrivals saw the Union Jack fluttering in the breeze, a symbol to them of eight centuries of English repression, most of them left Canada as soon as they could. They had no money, so they turned south and walked several hundred miles to whatever jobs they could find in New England and beyond. Among them were many Catholics from northern counties in Ireland, including Tyrone, Antrim, Armagh, and Fermanagh.

There was no housing for the Irish laborers in Lowell, and Kirk Boott did not concern himself with the problem as long as the immigrants did not corrupt Yankee neighborhoods with their lusty language and beery brawls. So the Irish settled on a tract of vacant land, and over the next two decades the area was variously known as the Paddy Camps, New Dublin and, finally, The Acre. One observer thought The Acre resembled "an Irish village, with the real Irish cabins and shanties built of board, sod, and mud such as can be seen in Ballyshannon." To most people in Lowell, the place was an eyesore.

Horatio Wood, a Protestant clergyman who ran a ministry to help needy immigrants in Lowell, took his mission to The Acre and saw six to ten people, on average, living in dank cellars. Wood crawled around one cobweb-covered cellar and reported finding two small rooms where "four families, amounting to twenty-two souls, were living!"

John Coolidge wrote that life in The Acre was a prelude to what was to afflict many people who worked in the mills and workers in other parts of the country. These conditions, Coolidge wrote, "were one of the first signs of that social callousness which in a hundred years has allowed rural and urban slums to become the normal habitat of one third of the nation. The tragedy of Lowell lay not so much in the horror of the initial situation, but in the fact that it grew progressively worse. Not only did a constantly increasing proportion of the population live in squalor, but the squalor deepened as the century went on."

The New England textile industry became forever linked to the growth of urban slums, and the Irish were only the first of many ethnic groups that would inhabit them. Community leaders grew to resent the Boston Associates. A Lowell publication, *Vox Populi*, wrote of the mill owners, "These men look only to the means by which they shall most successfully and certainly increase their dividends; and if it costs the sacrifice of every individual enterprise in our midst, they will doubtless persist in their unjust and despicable policy...their love for Lowell is all cotton."

Trouble erupted in The Acre when new laborers arrived from counties in the south of Ireland, including Cork, Wexford, and Waterford. There were vicious fights between men of different regions of the old country despite the efforts of Hugh Cummisky who was trying to maintain good relations with the Yankee community and especially with Kirk Boott. Cummisky presented himself as a friend of all the Irish and tried to stay above regional differences among them, but it was a struggle. "In a fundamental way," Brian Mitchell wrote, "an Irishman had little in common with anyone beyond those who shared his narrow, tribal, parochial outlook. Even in Lowell, a Corkonian considered an emigrant from Tyrone as foreign as the Yankees who lived around both of them." The Yankee natives detested The Acre and its inhabitants. An anti-immigrant newspaper said that "the mass of Irish are just what we have called them, stupid, negligent, and abominably filthy." Another newspaper called them "affable simpletons who needed constant supervision."

Cummisky campaigned for the construction of a church, hoping that the common bond of the Catholic faith would restore peace among the Irish factions. His ally was Bishop Benedict Fenwick of Boston, who often dined at the Boott home when he visited Lowell. Fenwick persuaded the mill agent to donate corporation land for a church and a parochial school. It was not a simple request; some Yankees in town contended that parochial schools were un-American. Boott had no patience with the argument. He believed that workers with at least a good grade-school education would be more productive in his mills, and that the Catholics had a right to establish their own school system.

The Irish built St. Patrick's Church. Yankee laborers, already angered because the mills were hiring so many immigrants, feared the church as a symbol of Irish permanence in Lowell. A mob attacked The Acre in 1831, determined to burn down St. Patrick's. Neighborhood men hurled rocks at the invaders while women stood ready as backups. Irish rage forced the mob to retreat twice, but the women were not through fighting. They loaded rocks in their aprons, pursued the Yankees, and stoned them out of the neighborhood for good. The church was saved. It served all in The Acre, and eventually the county feuds faded away. On St. Patrick's Day, 1835, members of the Lowell Irish Benevolent Society lifted their glasses to toast their Yankee benefactors: "To Kirk Boott, Esquire, and the other liberal and independent gentlemen of Lowell—true and generous friends to industrious Irishmen—remember the gratitude we owe them all."

The Irish middle class in Lowell tried to improve relations with the Yankees. They were proud to be sons of the Gael, descendants of the Celtic people of Ireland, but they made clear that they, too, wanted Lowell to be a model center of American capitalism. They expressed the hope that the city would rise to be "the brightest star in the Union."

Accommodating the Yankees went only so far. The Irish supported Democrat Andrew Jackson and his popular politics, but Kirk Boott, a member of the conservative Whig party, reviled him. Boott threatened to fire employees who worked to put Jackson in the White House. He warned them that with Jackson's election, "grass will grow in your streets, owls will build their nests in the mills, and foxes burrow in your highways." The Irish remained steadfast in their devotion to Jackson and the Democratic party.

Irish farm people had few advantages, but their British rulers had imposed on them the English language, and that made their adjustment in America easier than it would be for succeeding immigrant groups. Because they had a way with words, natural leaders like Cummisky were able to deal with the native-born Establishment on behalf of their Irish communities.

The Irish leader in Dover, New Hampshire, was John Burns, who also worked to have a church built for his people. Burns warned Bishop Fenwick that some of the Irish in Dover would return to Ireland if they could not have a church. Of course, the church was built, and Burns recruited new workers from Ireland for the local cotton factories.

Burns, a skilled weaver in the mills, showed his countrymen how to deal with troublesome Yankees. When the Dover mill agent, the prickly James F. Curtis, was slow to pay him his wages, Burns made a deal. In lieu of wages, he would draw from the plentiful supply of bricks in the mill yards. In time, Curtis traded off enough bricks to build a fine home for the Burns family. Eventually, Burns left mill work to become a successful businessman and a leading citizen of Dover. He and the other Irish who first arrived in the town in the 1820s proudly referred to themselves ever after as the Twenty Pioneers.

As the Irish settled in, native resentment of them smoldered, and the Calvinist minister Lyman Beecher was ready to exploit the antagonism. When Beecher preached in the Park Street Church in Boston in 1830, a reporter wrote that the clergyman "asserted that he never could look upon a Roman Catholic in the light of a fellow citizen" because the pope and priests ruled the conscience of every Catholic. There were fears among some, instilled by Beecher and others, that the pope would lead an invasion of the United States with his "Catholic Irish legions," establish a North American Vatican, and appoint a grand inquisitor.

One of the worst incidents of anti-Catholic violence was the burning of the Ursuline Sisters' convent and school for girls in Charlestown. Prominent Protestant families in Boston sent their daughters to the school because of the excellent education it offered. But during a frenzy of agitation, a mob marched through Charlestown and torched the convent and school. The nuns led their forty-four students away to safety as flames consumed the buildings. Among the students was Maria White, thirteen, the future wife of James Russell Lowell. On the night before the convent was destroyed, Beecher had delivered three anti-Catholic harangues in three Boston churches. The ensuing mob violence shocked Boston, and a contrite Beecher joined those who condemned the Ursuline outrage. Delivering his own sermon after the fire, Bishop Fenwick admonished angry Catholics not to perpetuate religious hatred. He read from the Book of Matthew: "But I say to you, Love your enemies . . . and pray for those who persecute you . . ." Members of the textile families, including Abbott Lawrence, tried without success to convince the state legislature to compensate the nuns for their loss.

There were Catholic church fires in other New England towns, including Burlington, Vermont, and Bath, Maine, as more Irish laborers arrived. Most towns received the hordes of Irish newcomers peacefully, if not with open arms, and considered them just one more social problem. In Fall River, Massachusetts, where two thousand recent arrivals, most of them Irish, were working in mills, a municipal report stated: "There are in the town five blind persons, six insane persons, eight idiots, and 120 persons over twenty years of age who can neither read nor write, eight of who are at the alms house, and a large proportion of the others are Irish Catholic immigrants."

Ralph Waldo Emerson worried about the poverty, racial injustice, and religious discord that were festering in America, "our fortunate home." He lectured on the duty of the privileged young American who encountered suffering: "If a humane measure is propounded in behalf of the slave or of the Irishman or the Catholic or for the succor of the poor, that sentiment, that project, will have the homage of the hero. That is his nobility, his oath of knighthood, to succor the helpless and oppressed; always to throw himself on the side of weakness, of youth, of hope."

Despite Emerson's counsel, native concerns grew with the waves of immigrants after Ireland's Great Famine of the 1840s. Many ethnic groups from all over Europe that settled in New England mill towns would tell of the troubles they left behind, but the greatest calamity was Ireland's famine. A New Englander trying to be humane, trying to understand the Irish newcomers, could not do so without a sense of the anti-English bitterness they held in their hearts, generation after generation, because of the starvation and injustice inflicted on an Ireland under British rule. William Butler Yeats spoke for them:

> Out of Ireland have we come,
> Great hatred, little room,
> Maimed us from the start.
> I carry from my mother's womb
> A fanatic heart.

William O'Connell's parents escaped the famine by leaving County Cavan for America. O'Connell was reared in Lowell among the mill workers and became a Catholic priest, bishop and, in his final years, a cardinal in Boston. He spent a cosmopolitan life among the elite of New

England, counting among his powerful Protestant contemporaries many descendants of the very people who had caused the Irish so much misery. Like other Irish Catholics who knew the history of the British in Ireland, the old priest did not forget and did not forgive. "These memories will never die in the heart or the soul of any man or woman of Irish blood," O'Connell wrote in his autobiography, "and until these crimes are openly confessed by the nation that committed them, until they are openly acknowledged as the bitterest injustice of any one nation against another, until those responsible have made restitution, or at least an attempt at restitution for all their robberies and have begun to show some sense of justice toward the Irish people, they need never expect any fair-minded student of history to consider them other than what they were, the fiercest and most unscrupulous Huns of their time."

The problem with Ireland, theorized political economist Thomas Malthus, was that there were too many people on too little land. Consequently, he wrote in 1817, "to give full effect to the natural resources of the country, a great part of the population should be swept from the soil." And it was.

Under British rule, one million Irish people died of starvation or disease during the famine of 1845-1850. Two million others fled their homeland, most of them to America. The famine struck after a fungus spread through the country, ruining the potato crop, the main food source of rural people.

Ireland had eight million people when the famine began, three million of them tenant farmers who rented small plots of land owned by wealthy Protestant families. Some landlords lived on their Ireland estates, some lived in England. The landholdings were enormous—twenty thousand to forty thousand acres, and landowners reaped fortunes in rent revenues.

The tenants planted potato patches for their own food supply. They worked on the landlords' private holdings, tending grain crops and livestock for export to England. The landlords, greedy for increased revenues, carved out smaller rental plots and packed more tenants on their land. Abbott Lawrence, who had retired from running his Massachusetts textile mills, visited Ireland while he was the American ambassador to Great Britain. He commented on the folly of subdividing the land "a third, fourth or fifth time; the quantity each time reduced until many estates are subdivided in lots of from an eighth or a quarter of an acre." In one case, 294 families were surviving on land that a half century earlier had sustained 42 families.

Lawrence knew the history of Ireland's subjugation, beginning with a twelfth-century English invasion by Henry II, a Catholic monarch. Pope Adrian IV, the only Englishman ever to sit on the papal throne, asked the king to reform wayward Irish Catholics whose strongest allegiance was to their monks and monasteries rather than to bishops and Rome.

After English Catholics broke from Rome and established the Anglican church, they conquered rebellious Irish clan chiefs, seized their land and churches, and granted huge estates to the newly Protestant aristocracy. In 1607, the English defeated the last important holdout, Hugh O'Neill, the Catholic earl of Tyrone. The chief's Ulster plantations were settled with Protestants, and to this day Protestants are in the majority in the six counties of Ulster that comprise Northern Ireland, a part of the United Kingdom.

Through it all the Irish people were true to their Catholic faith but paid a punishing price. In 1649, the English ruler Oliver Cromwell, furious because he thought priests were stirring the people to rebellion, led an army of twenty thousand to Ireland. Cromwell's troops obliterated the towns of Drogheda and Wexford, killing every man, woman, and child they could find. On July 12, 1690, the Dutch-born William of Orange also conquered the rebellious Irish. Fighting for Britain and for Protestant dominance in Ireland, William gathered an army at the River Boyne west of Dublin and led it to victory over Irish nationalist forces. Ever since, Orange societies have celebrated the victory of the "Glorious Twelfth."

As William sat on the throne as king of England, his Protestant followers enforced so-called Penal Laws in Ireland that were calculated to eradicate the Catholic religion and Catholic economic power. The laws dictated that upon the death of a Catholic landowner, the property be equally divided among the sons, an effective means of breaking up large landholdings. There was an exception to the law: Any son who renounced his faith and became an Anglican inherited the full estate. Few of Ireland's sons did so, and in time, Catholics owned virtually no significant agricultural lands.

Catholics were denied the right to education, to enter most professions, to hold public office, to serve on juries, to vote, to speak Gaelic, or to attend their religious services. "The priest was banned and hunted with bloodhounds," Seumas MacManus wrote. "The school master was banned and hunted with bloodhounds." The Penal Laws were often disobeyed, especially by the hunted priests and teachers, who conducted Mass and school lessons in secret emerald clearings shielded from snoops by thick hedges and leafy trees. The great fear was the informer working for the British authorities.

Wherever the Irish gather, in homes, schools, and pubs, at festivals and at St. Patrick's Day concerts, they remember the words of Arthur Colahan's song, "Galway Bay":

> *For the strangers came and tried to teach us their way,*
> *They cursed us just for being what we are.*
> *But they might as well go chasing after moonbeams,*
> *Or light a penny candle from a star.*

The Penal Laws stayed in effect for 150 years. The British banned most industry, forcing Ireland to remain an agricultural country and denying it the economic opportunities offered by the Industrial Revolution. Vengeful authorities even crippled the manufacture of fine linens in the north of Ireland because most of the linen workers were Presbyterians of Scottish heritage, and the Anglican church considered them Nonconformists. Jobless Scots-Irish Protestants left home and played a major role in the growth of the United States.

Jonathan Swift, Anglican dean of St. Patrick's Cathedral in Dublin from 1713 to 1745, ridiculed British legislators for governing Ireland not with the lofty ideals of framers of law but "with the spirit of shopkeepers." And since London insisted on strangling the economy of a nation filled with poor people, Swift offered a solution in his satrical essay *A Modest Proposal:* Let Ireland export its newborn infants as a food product, to be baked as a delicacy for consumption at Europe's elegant dining tables.

When Abbott Lawrence arrived in Ireland in the early 1850s, he still could observe, "Ireland is a conquered country, governed by conquerors." He noted the burdensome presence of Protestant churches in the lives of Catholic farm people: "The difficulties and quarrels growing out of the religious differences in the country have also had important influences on its condition. The Church of England is established and supported by law, while three-fourths of the people profess the Catholic faith; and tithes for the support of the Established Church are levied upon the property of all alike." Anglican pastors collected their tithes from the Catholic tenants in the form of potatoes and the occasional chicken or pig.

The landlords continued to grow grains and livestock, which they exported to England; the tenant farmers rarely partook of these harvests. Still, a tenant family of six could survive because the potato was cooked in several ways and even ground into flour. Potatoes provided as many as 3,800 calories a day, with healthy amounts of vitamins. They could be grown anywhere—along peat bogs, on the sides of hills and mountains, on the smallest patch of marginal land.

The people had survived on one variety of the potato since England introduced the crop in Ireland in the sixteenth century, but that one variety, from the Andes Mountains of Peru, was vulnerable to fungus. Agricultural experts tried to introduce other crops to end dependence on the potato, but British government officials dismissed their efforts. There had been famines in 1817 and 1822 because the potato crops failed. A government report in 1837 estimated that at the end of most summers, just before the potato harvest, more than two million people had run out of food and were in a state of semistarvation. During the shortages, London launched relief programs to get food to the people.

In the Great Hunger of the 1840s, the government chose not to give food aid. British Prime Minister John Russell explained that he did not believe in interfering with the law of supply and demand. In her definitive history of the famine, *The Great Hunger,* Cecil Woodham-Smith wrote, "The influence of *laissez faire* on the treatment of Ireland during the famine is impossible to exaggerate." She added, "Adherence to *laissez faire* was carried to such a length that in the midst of one of the major famines of

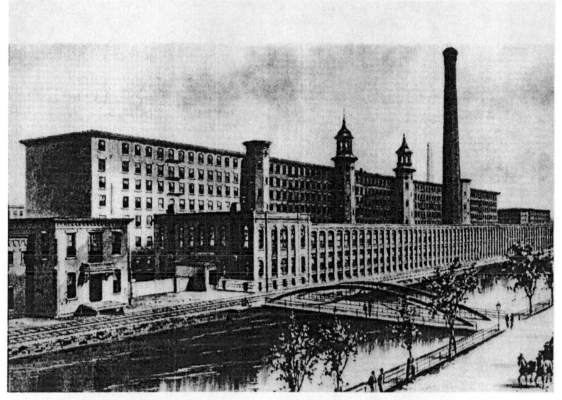

In eighteenth-century New England, huge new mills dominated the skylines of textile cities. This is the Pacific Mill in Lowell, Massachusetts. (COURTESY OF THE AMERICAN TEXTILE HISTORY MUSEUM, LOWELL, MASSACHUSETTS)

Winslow Homer's depiction of mill workers responding to the factory bells that summoned them to labor. (COURTESY OF THE COLLECTION OF THE BOSTON ATHENAEUM)

Eliza Adams of Derry, New Hampshire, worked in several mills in the mid-eighteenth century. Hers was a strong voice for labor solidarity. (COURTESY OF JO ANNE PRESTON)

Lucy Larcom, mill worker, teacher, poet. (COURTESY OF THE LOWELL HISTORICAL SOCIETY)

Harriet Farley, a mill worker and editor of the *Lowell Offering*. (COURTESY OF THE BOSTON PUBLIC LIBRARY)

Harriet Hanson Robinson wrote of early mill days in *Loom and Spindle*. (COURTESY OF THE BOSTON PUBLIC LIBRARY)

Francis Cabot Lowell. This is the only known likeness of the founder of large-scale textile manufacturing in the United States.
(COURTESY OF THE COLLECTION OF THE BOSTON ATHENAEUM)

Nathan Appleton, one of Lowell's original partners.
(COURTESY OF THE UNIVERSITY OF MASSACHUSETTS LOWELL)

Abbott Lawrence, whose family built the mill city of Lawrence, Massachusetts.
(COURTESY OF THE UNIVERSITY OF MASSACHUSETTS LOWELL)

Kirk Boott, who oversaw the creation of the industrial city of Lowell, Massachusetts.
(COURTESY OF THE LOWELL HISTORICAL SOCIETY)

Daniel Webster
(COURTESY OF THE COLLECTION OF
THE BOSTON ATHENAEUM)

Charles Sumner
(COURTESY OF THE
BOSTON PUBLIC
LIBRARY)

Ralph Waldo Emerson
(COURTESY OF THE COLLECTION
OF THE BOSTON ATHENAEUM)

John Greenleaf Whittier
(COURTESY OF THE BOSTON
PUBLIC LIBRARY)

A young worker delivering full bobbins of thread to the looms at a mill in Lawrence, Massachusetts. (COURTESY OF THE AMERICAN TEXTILE HISTORY MUSEUM, LOWELL, MASSACHUSETTS)

history, the government was perpetually nervous of being too good to Ireland and of corrupting the Irish people by kindness, and so stifling the virtues of self reliance and industry."

In August 1845, *The Freeman's Journal* in Ireland predicted an abundant potato yield "of the most luxuriant character." But the summer had been rainy and at its end the potato fungus descended on the land without warning. All over Ireland the stories were the same: In the morning, a tenant farmer saw a healthy field of potatoes; by evening, he smelled the stench of diseased crops. In one day, the potatoes had become a black, gooey, putrefied horror. The rot infected even the winter supply the tenants stored in pits near their cottages. Scientists were unable to develop chemicals to combat the fungus, which they later identified as *Phytopthora infestans*. England's senior official in Ireland, Lord Heytesbury, offered comfort. "There is no cause for alarm," he told the terrified tenant families. "The Government is carefully watching the course of events." Lord Heytesbury did not offer food. "God sent the blight," people said, "but the British brought the famine."

Ireland prayed but was not redeemed. The wind carried the fungus everywhere—across the fields of Cork and Mayo, through the green valleys of Galway and Wicklow, to Kildare and Killarney. As the blight spread, millions of rural Irish had no food. The famine plagued the country for five years as crop after annual crop succumbed to the fungus. When the blight ruined the potato patches, landlords evicted the starving tenants and razed or burned their homes so they would not return. The tenant land was used to raise cattle, a more profitable enterprise. An eyewitness described the eviction of 143 families—men, women and children—from an estate in Tipperary as "the chasing away of 700 human beings like crows out of a cornfield." A history of the famine said those who were driven from the land looked like "evicted skeletons." Lines written by an unknown author recount the times:

> Oh, well do I remember the bleak December day,
> The landlord and the sheriff came to drive us all away;
> They set my roof on fire with their cursed English spleen,
> And that's another reason that I left old Skibbereen.

85

Some tenants and members of secret societies murdered landlords in retaliation for eviction. Queen Victoria asked Parliament to strengthen law enforcement in rural areas, but her government offered no solution to the problems that led to the violence. As the hungry people of Ballin-robe, County Mayo, watched the British Seventh Hussars march by, a villager said, "Would to God the government would send us food instead of soldiers."

Not even people by the sea were spared. After the famine struck, many of them panicked; they sold their fishing boats and nets to buy food. Along the shore some caught fish and shellfish. Then they went after the seabirds; they robbed cliffside nests of eggs, fighting off fierce parent birds. They ended up combing the rocky shore for seaweed, one of the few food sources left to them. People near brooks and streams consumed the abundant fish life. Then they went after the worms. Some people had the means to plant turnips as an alternative to the rotten potatoes. When the turnips were ready for harvest, the growers had to dig human traps in the fields to keep away starving thieves.

Homeless families roaming the countryside were desperate to eat. John Leo wrote, "They ate dogs and rats, often dogs and rats that had already eaten human corpses. When one English traveler spat out some gooseberry skins from a passing carriage, a mother raced to pick up the skins and placed them in the mouth of her starving infant. The roadways were littered with bodies of people with green stains around the mouth, from eating grass as a desperate last meal." Seumas MacManus recalled learning these lines during his childhood in Ireland:

> On highway side, where oft was seen
> The wild dog and the vulture keen
> Tug for the limbs and gnaw the face
> Of some starved child of our Irish race.

An officer of the British Royal Navy told a County Mayo newspaper of the starvation he had witnessed, but could not finish his story. "We must stop," he wrote. "The recital is horrible. Will the Government still refuse to interfere? Alas, we fear so." A British army officer wrote to a government official, "I am a match for anything else I may meet with here, but this I cannot stand."

Those who did not starve died of typhus, dysentery, bloody diarrhea, and scurvy. It was estimated that for every person who starved, ten more died of diseases. Wherever the blight had descended, the afflictions reached out to kill middle-class and wealthy people as well as the hungry poor. Protestant congregations throughout England recited the "Dearth and Scarcity Prayer," but it was not enough; the Irish people seemed destined to suffer every affliction in the Book of Job. Typhus, spread by lice, fleas, and ticks, attacked the small blood vessels, especially of the skin and brain, swelling the face, turning the skin dark. Victims whose bodies were consumed by fever staggered into cooling streams for relief. Hunger edema filled the body with liquid, causing hideous swelling. Cecil Woodham-Smith told of a boy of twelve in Skibbereen "whose body had swollen to three times its normal size and actually burst the garment he wore." The body of a two-year-old child "was swollen to the size of an adult." Children looked like enfeebled old people; hair fell from their heads but grew on their faces. They lost their voices. They lost their eye sight. On stately Georgian squares, wealthy Dubliners kept to their social schedules, with sumptuous dinner parties and grand balls.

Travelers riding in carriages in the mist and dark of night were jolted as teams of horses lurched over yet another dead body. In daylight, passengers saw children on roadsides pushing wheelbarrows containing the bodies of their dead parents. A priest told of visiting the home of a mother and her infant child, both dead: "Two others lay beside her just expiring, and, horrible to relate, a famished cat got upon the bed, and was just about to gnaw the corpse of the deceased infant, until I prevented it." The churches enlarged their cemeteries, but many of the victims ended up in shallow graves along the roads where they perished. The smell of death was everywhere. Like Job, people cursed the day they were born.

A contemporary writer saw people lose their humanity as starvation approached. At first, he wrote, those who are hungry clamor aggressively for relief. In the second stage, those who are starving display a "patient, passive stupidity . . . they will stand at a window for hours, without asking charity, giving a vacant stare, and not until peremptorily driven away will they move." In the last stage, the victims fall into idiocy. The head "bends forward, and they walk with long strides, and pass you unheedingly."

John Mitchel, the Irish patriot, went to a village to check up on a family he had known. He remembered "the strong man and the fair dark-eyed woman and the little ones, with their liquid Gaelic accents that melted into music two years ago." When Mitchel revisited the family, now starving, "they shrank and withered together until their voices dwindled to a rueful gibbering, and they hardly knew one another's faces; but their horrid eyes scowled at each other with a cannibal glare."

In the valleys of death, the Protestant landlords prospered. They loaded their rich harvests on wagons. Horses and mules hauled the food to port towns where it was taken aboard ships bound for English markets. The wagons, escorted by armed guards, passed along roads and through villages teeming with wandering, half-crazed people. The people watched the wagons pass by and heard the wheels creak under the weight of butter and eggs, barley and oats, hams and beef—a cornucopia brimming with the promise of survival but always rolling away from the famine victims. The gunmen kept the people at a distance.

In the absence of a government relief program, others tried to rescue the Irish people. Protestant and Catholic clergymen, nurses, and doctors worked side by side, risking their lives to bring comfort to victims of disease. One of the doctors asked in disbelief: *"Are we living in a portion of the United Kingdom?"* Quakers opened food stations. The sultan of Turkey sent aid. "Ladies Work Associations" in England sent food and clothing. The elite of English society formed the British Association for Irish Aid. Although Queen Victoria's government was doing nothing, she contributed two thousand pounds.

The Choctaw Indians of Oklahoma sent money for food relief. Boston businessmen financed a ship and crew that carried food to the stricken. American groups from all religions formed relief committees to send food and money to Ireland. It was one of the first times in U.S. history that, as private citizens, Protestants, Catholics, and Jews worked in national unison for a common cause. Ships loaded with donated food from America sailed *into* Irish harbors; as they headed for the docks, they passed British ships carrying food *away* from Ireland to English markets. The preposterous situation led one observer to comment, "The moment the very name of Ireland is mentioned, the English seem to bid adieu to common feeling, common prudence and common sense, and to act with the barbarity of tyrants and the fatuity of idiots."

When the donated food arrived among the starving, there often was chaos. In 1847, the worst year of the famine and forever after called Black 47, a contemporary novel described scenes of food distribution: "Here were wild crowds, ragged, sickly, and wasted away to skin and bone, struggling for the dole of charity like so many hungry vultures about the remains of some carcass which they were tearing amid noises, and screams, and strife, into very shreds."

Finally, the British government launched a massive food program of its own. Three million gaunt men, women, and children lined up every day for soup tickets. After the famine, coroner's juries in Ireland, with no power to effect the prosecution of the British prime minister, nevertheless returned verdicts of "willful murder against John Russell."

George Bernard Shaw, born in Dublin a few years after the Great Hunger ended, remembered Britain's role in the suffering when he wrote his play *Man and Superman:*

MALONE: My father died of starvation in Ireland in the Black 47.

VIOLET: The famine?

MALONE: No, the starvation. When a country is full of food and exporting it, there can be no famine.

When Abbott Lawrence made his ambassadorial visit to Ireland, the crisis was over, but he saw no laughing girls, no nimble young men chasing them. He saw no dancing, heard no songs or poetry, and sensed only spiritlessness in a people who had been among the most spirited on earth. "The most striking modern objects which meet the eye of a stranger in Ireland are the alms houses," he said. "They are on a large scale...

and in every locality where man is to be found." He told of all the people who wanted to leave the country, foresaw a huge emigration, and added, "They entertain the idea that the United States is a land of promise, where they may be prosperous and happy." The Irish poet Ethna Carbery wrote of the exodus:

> *They are going, going, going from the valleys and the hills,*
> *They are leaving far behind them heathery moor and mountain rills,*
>
> *They are going, shy-eyed cailins, and lads so straight and tall,*
> *From the purple peaks of Kerry, from the crags of wild Imaal,*
> *From the greening plains of Mayo, and the glens of Donegal.*

Victoria visited Ireland in 1849, and some people sneered at her as the Famine Queen. But huge crowds cheered her, shedding for a moment their black despair. Three million of the queen's Irish subjects were dead or had fled the country. The ravages brought on by the famine and England's repressive governance of the past are still reflected in Ireland's population figures. Today the population numbers only four million people. A century and a half after the famine, Mary Robinson, the president of Ireland, lamented that Britain had yet to apologize for its role. "Even now," she told a London audience, "it is not too late to say sorry. That would mean so much." In her subsequent post at the United Nations, Robinson saw new famines inflicted on people in the undeveloped world. Always, she was compelled to talk of the same catastrophe that had struck in her own country.

In 1997, two years after Robinson's comments, British Prime Minister Tony Blair expressed words in Belfast that were the closest thing to an apology ever offered. "Those who governed in London at the time failed their people through standing by while a crop failure turned into a massive human tragedy," Blair said. "That one million people should have died in what was then part of the richest and most powerful nation in the world is something that still causes pain as we reflect on it today." One wonders whether embittered people of Irish heritage accepted Blair's words as adequate. One wonders whether Cardinal O'Connell of Boston would have withdrawn his condemnation of the English as "the fiercest and most unscrupulous Huns of their time."

One million or more survivors of the famine made their way to Dublin, Cork, Galway, and other ports. On the docks they held "American wakes" with those who were staying behind. The ritual acknowledged without spoken words that relatives might never see each other again.

The emigrants sailed on ferries across the Irish Sea to England, most of them to Liverpool, for steerage passage to the land of promise. They were full of trouble but they sailed with hope. One of their priests told them, "Your sons in Ireland would be oppressed laborers, your sons in America may sit in the highest places in the land."

Nathaniel Hawthorne, who was the American consul in Liverpool at the time, wrote that the Irish arrivals in the city "were as numerous as maggots in cheese." American relatives sent them steerage money and the British government also helped finance the exodus. British shipping firms, which had profited from carrying slaves to America decades earlier, transported the emigrants and profited again from human misery. This time the vessels were called "coffin ships" because death claimed so many passengers during the sailings.

The ships' crews put their human cargo in filthy holds belowdecks that were freezing in winter, stifling in summer. Sailings took four to eight weeks, depending on the weather. Gales, fog and, worst of all, icebergs, terrified crews and passengers alike. All endured the constant pitching and rolling of the fragile vessels on stormy seas. Passengers shared meager meals of biscuits and oatmeal in crowded quarters amid rats, lice, disease, and the stink of their own bodies. Some passengers, with eyes of stone and jaws gone slack, slipped out of suffering into insanity. The main escape route was death. By the light of the stars, crewmen collected the dead and dumped them into the Atlantic. One in six of the passengers was never to see America. It is believed that seventeen thousand of them perished during the six years of sailings. The Atlantic was, the Irish people said, their "bowl of tears."

Their fate in Black 47 is told by maritime records of some of the coffin ships:

The Lartch, 440 passengers, 108 deaths.
The Queen, 493 passengers, 137 deaths.
The Avon, 552 passengers, 236 deaths.
The Virginius, 476 passengers, 267 deaths.

Henry David Thoreau came upon the wreckage of a coffin ship on the shores of Massachusetts. Almost 150 Irish emigrants and crew of the brig *St. John* had died. Some bodies were still trapped inside. "I saw many marble feet and matted heads," Thoreau wrote. He told of a girl's mangled body lying on the rocks "so that the bone and muscle were exposed, but quite bloodless—merely red and white—with wide open and staring eyes, yet lustreless, dead-lights."

Seaworthy ships sailed to Boston or New York, but most coffin ships were too decrepit to pass inspection in American ports and so carried their passengers to Canadian points in Quebec and New Brunswick. As they approached land, crewmen fished the Grand Banks, and all aboard had their first fresh food in weeks. The last leg of the sailings took the debilitated emigrants up the St. Lawrence River where they saw neat white houses, rolling farmland, pine forests and, commanding the horizon, the majestic peaks of the Laurentians. For many, it was the last beautiful sight of their time on earth.

The busiest immigrant processing center was on Grosse Isle in the St. Lawrence, thirty miles east of Quebec City. The island, three miles long and a mile wide, was uninhabited before Ireland's Great Hunger, but the Canadian government opened an immigration station there to deal with the arrival of thousands of passengers. Public health workers and immigration officials quarantined the emigrants in drafty wooden structures called fever sheds. An estimated twenty thousand men, women, and children died at Canadian quarantine centers, half of them on Grosse Isle. Some were so alone that their names were recorded only by the doctors, nurses, and priests at their deathbeds. Even as women were dying in the sheds, they gave birth. Canadian families adopted many of the infants.

The fever sheds on Grosse Isle have long since turned to dust, but visitors stop by the "Irish cemetery," a green expanse of mass graves covered by symbolic white crosses. A memorial there bears so many names of the dead that most visitors of Irish heritage see a family name.

In 1909, the Ancient Order of Hibernians erected a granite Celtic cross on the island. It stands on a promontory overlooking the St. Lawrence and beckons all who sail by to stop and ponder the fate of the honored dead. Those attending the dedication ceremony almost a century ago read an inscription in English at the base of the cross: "Sacred to the memory of thousands of Irish emigrants who to preserve the faith suffered hunger and exile in 1847-48, and stricken with fever ended here their sorrowful pilgrimage." Another inscription is in Gaelic, a language that the strangers to Ireland did not know. It remembers the victims with harsher words: "Thousands of the children of the Gael were lost on this island while fleeing from foreign tyrannical laws and an artificial famine in the years 1847-8. God bless them. God save Ireland!" Surely kinspeople in Ireland and America who were at the dedication recalled a proverb they shared in bad times with bittersweet laughter but on that day with tears: For a person to be happy in this world *and* in the next, one should live as a Protestant and die as a Catholic.

By the turn of the twentieth century, scientists had developed a crop spray that virtually wiped out the potato fungus in Ireland. The threat of famine was over. By that time, millions more Irish made it to American soil and began new lives. Their skill at growing potatoes was not needed. There were few carpenters or butchers or tailors among them, and they had never seen a factory, but in the mill cities they found jobs. The Massachusetts statesman Edward Everett was pleased that they filled the labor vacuum created by the exodus of so many New England people to the Western frontier. "Their inferiority as a race," Everett said of the Irish, "compels them to go to the bottom of the occupational scale and the consequence is that we are all the higher lifted because they are here." To mill managers the situation was ideal: They had a source of labor that was powerless, poor, and desperate for work.

The arrival of huge numbers of Irish gave rise to anti-Catholic, anti-immigrant organizations that called the Catholic church "the whore of Babylon." New England audiences attended lectures on "the dangerous influences of Romanism" and the "cruel practices of Roman Catholicism." The virulent views of Samuel F. B. Morse, inventor of the telegraph, had earlier contributed to the mania. "Popery," Morse wrote, was opposed to democracy as well as "to civil and religious liberty, and consequently to our form of government."

The most powerful force of bigotry was the "Native American" political party, whose members were called Know-Nothings because they professed to outsiders an ignorance about the party's activities or philosophy. In the 1850s, Know-Nothing candidates were elected to the Massachusetts governorship and to a huge majority of seats in the state legislature. They enacted laws prohibiting naturalized citizens from voting until they had been in the United States for twenty-one years; even immigrants who became citizens were barred from elective office.

The Know-Nothings appointed legislative committees to search for evidence of subversion in Catholic institutions, including Holy Cross College in Worcester. The inspection teams rummaged through convents and schools in Roxbury and Lowell as the Sisters of Notre Dame watched with puzzlement. Know-Nothing mobs swept through Irish neighborhoods in Lawrence, Clinton, and Southbridge, Massachusetts; Manchester, New Hampshire; and Lewiston, Maine, vandalizing Catholic churches. In Ellsworth, Maine, a mob attacked Father John Bapst, a Jesuit missionary, stripped him, tarred and feathered him, dragged him out of town, and left him to die. Then the mob burned down a Catholic chapel. Bapst survived and later became president of Boston College.

During the Know-Nothing rampages, and several years before he became president, Abraham Lincoln wrote to a friend: "Our progress in degeneracy appears to me to be pretty rapid. As a nation we began by declaring that 'all men are created equal.' We now practically read it 'all men are created equal, except Negroes.' When the Know-Nothings get control, it will read 'all men are created equal, except Negroes and foreigners and Catholics.' When it comes to this, I shall prefer emigrating to some country where they make no pretense of loving liberty." The Irish also noticed the Know-Nothings' affinity for rewriting the Declaration of Independence and joked that the bigots would bestow upon themselves the right to "Life, Liberty and the Pursuit of Irishmen."

By the time the Irish arrived, the textile industry had become a colossal presence in New England. Mill buildings that once were 150 feet long were replaced by structures three times longer to make room for hundreds more looms. The big factories filled the last open spaces along the rivers, locking the workers in sunless industrial gloom. The Irish found that Sarah Bagley's *Voice of Industry* described life in the mills all too accurately: "The Factory operatives must work by rule, eat by rule, and sleep by rule. What weary hours, from sunrise to sunset, then eat and go to sleep, then sleep, rise, work, eat, work, sleep."

When the Irish entered the mills, they collided with their unhappy history. Waiting to give them their orders were Protestant overseers from the north of Ireland and from the English textile centers. After their years in the mills, workers had different memories of their bosses. Some women found that they were fair, especially the English overseers. Some remembered them as brutes. Cardinal O'Connell formed a low opinion of them when he was growing up in Lowell. "Their chief work and task," he wrote, "was to act as slavedrivers of the immigrant Irish population, for which they were handsomely recompensed." The workers, O'Connell said, "were treated precisely as if they were part of the machinery which ground out the millions being produced for the rich managers and mill owners, who spent the money, not in Lowell, but in New York, Boston, Paris, and London."

At first, the Irish workers were willing to work for lower pay and to tend more machines, causing friction with the Yankee women still in the mills who were protesting work speedups. Hannah Josephson wrote that the Irish women millworkers had "no standards the textile manufacturers might feel obliged to respect." Harriet Farley, in her closing days as editor of the *Lowell Offering*, wrote of a "downward tendency" in the new workforce, less moral supervision of employees by the mills, and growing immorality in the city. Mary Halpin, a young Irish immigrant who worked in a Nashua, New Hampshire, mill, felt the animosity and wrote in the Nashua newspaper on behalf of the Irish workers. "Deal gently with them," she pleaded with the Yankee population. "For behold they come from many a distant land and a loving home. Deal gently, e'en as God has dealt with thee."

The mills changed Irish family life. In the old country, the father was the boss of the tenant farm and of the household. The mother had a distinctly subservient role in family matters. Daughters were considered inferior. Thousands of the daughters, weary of old attitudes, left home on their own and went to America.

In Ireland, the parish church bell rang morning, noon, and evening, beckoning the tenant farmers to pause for the prayers of the Angelus. In the American textile centers, the father answered the bell in the mill tower that dictated when he started working and when he could go home. He took orders like everyone else and because of his meager wages became financially dependent on his children who also worked in the mill. While they contributed their share to the family, both sons and daughters achieved more independence than they had in Ireland, creating hostility between the once-dominant fathers and their children. The children married earlier than they had in the old country.

As it was back in Ireland, the wife's role, if she did not work in the mill, was to run the house. But increasingly she no longer accepted the husband as boss. She bellowed at him if he drank away the food money while carousing with friends at the neighborhood tavern. As the men shared a pint, they moaned of feeling beleaguered and whined about the burdens of domestic life. They found fleeting comfort in the "creature" alcohol and muttered that the three things most difficult to teach were a mule, a pig, and a woman. The women waiting at home had their own adage: The three things that leave the shortest traces are a bird on a branch, a ship on the sea, and a man on a woman.

Parish priests exhorted their congregations to avoid the evils of alcohol and tongue-lashed men who neglected their families. The Irish journalist John F. Maguire wrote, "Were I asked to say what I believed to be the most serious obstacle to the advancement of the Irish in America, I would unhesitatingly answer—*Drink.*" In Lowell, arrest records for one year indicated that 70 percent of the men and 84 percent of the women charged with drunkenness were Irish. The Yankee elite of the city feared that the problem was out of control and asked for the help of a Capuchin friar

from Ireland. Father Theobald Mathew had launched a temperance movement that encouraged people in Ireland and in the United States to pledge
that they would drink no more. Mathew went to Lowell, and in three
days of mass meetings with the immigrant mill workers persuaded four
thousand of them to take the pledge. It is not known how many stayed
reformed after Mathew went away. Equally difficult to confirm is the
number of Irish who drank in moderation, or who never took a drink at
all.

The church was a powerful influence as it guided Irish immigrants in
their new industrial surroundings. "In the process," Brian Mitchell wrote,
nineteenth-century American Catholicism "became anti-intellectual, traditional, and blue-collar—a religion of the working class which posed no
threat to Lowell's mill owners. Catholicism preached obedience, good
citizenship, and tradition, urging its followers to turn inward to find
comfort and fulfillment."

Hasia R. Diner's study of Irish immigrant women detailed how the
church took on social problems. The Sisters of Mercy harbored battered
women in Mercy Houses. The wives, obeying their church's disapproval
of divorce, stuck with their harrowing marriages. The nuns ran employment agencies for the women, taught them clerical and nursing skills, and
opened day nurseries for the children of working mothers. The mission
of mercy was daunting. In 1881, Massachusetts prisons reported that they
housed 336 Irish-born women, the largest female ethnic group behind
bars. French Canadians, who were in second place, accounted for 71 inmates. Most of the women ended up in jail because of problems related
to poverty, alcohol, domestic violence, and desertion. There were few
social agencies to deal adequately with these problems. But there were
the nuns.

Single women, including deserted wives and widows, went into the
mills, now commonly described by newspapers as tombs for the living,
living hells, and prison factories. They stayed at their jobs not only to
support themselves but also to save enough money to bring their brothers
and sisters from across the ocean. The bosses, when short of labor, paid
bonuses to employees for recruiting family members to work in the mills.

Working women were earning a few dollars a week when *Godey's*

Lady's Book was circulating in the New England mill cities. To mill hands, the magazine must have seemed to be of another world. It offered advice to young brides on managing the household allowances provided by their affluent husbands: "The amount once in the possession of the young housewife, whether it be ten dollars, fifteen dollars, or twenty-five dollars weekly . . . let her take every care of it and devote it *only* to the purpose for which it is given; let no inducement cause her to appropriate it to any other use."

Irish women in the mills could only dream of having a hundred dollars a month in spending money, but they could at least try to escape to another life. Many became domestic servants. At the turn of the century, their average weekly wage was nine dollars plus food and shelter. The textile workers earned seven dollars, and saleswomen, six dollars.

Protestant women who competed with the Irish for jobs knew that their religion was an advantage, as reflected in newspaper classified advertisements. These "Situations Wanted" ads appeared in the *New York Times:*

AS CHAMBERMAID AND WAITRESS,—A situation wanted by a Protestant young woman, as chambermaid and waitress . . .
AS COOK,—Wanted, a situation by a Scotch Protestant girl as cook; understands cooking in all its branches . . .
AS COOK,—A Protestant young woman wants a situation in a private family, as first-class cook . . .

The Irish immigrant who wanted to move beyond the job of domestic or factory hand was told in plain words: No Irish Need Apply. The phrase was used in help wanted ads in newspapers, it was posted at businesses, and hung in store windows. Some Irish Catholics refused to accept limits on their lives in America because of who they were. They left the church and changed their names. Murphys became Murfies, O'Briens became Bryants, Delaneys became Delanos. "Contemptible toadies," Cardinal O'Connell called them, who "went over body and soul to the enemy and sold their glorious inheritance for a mess of pottage. No sooner had they taken their places among the Protestants than they were given places which as Catholics they never would have obtained." It was not just the Irish who capitulated; other ethnic groups who fol lowed them to America also included people who camouflaged their her itage for a better chance of success.

The Catholic Irish changed the face of New England. By 1860, just fifteen years after the Great Famine began, 60 percent of the people in Lowell, Lawrence, Fall River, and Boston were foreign born, and most of them were Irish. Native New Englanders heard plenty of their blarney. The Irish told them of their heroes—of Brian Boru, the first Christian king of Ireland, and of the freedom fighters Wolfe Tone, Daniel O'Connell, and Robert Emmet. The Yankees were informed that it was Ireland's St. Brendan the Navigator who discovered America. They learned about Ireland's saints and scholars and wee folk and leprechauns and banshees wailing of oncoming death. At Irish parties, people were weepy-eyed as they sang of the River Shannon and the green hills of Donegal. They crooned lachrymose melodies like "Sing an Irish Song To night (For Your Daddy)" and "When They Play the Rosary on the Uku lele." They mourned their dead at wakes with keening and lamentations, feasting and drinking, and in long processions walked behind the hearse to the cemetery. They tapped their feet with dancers from Kilkenny. They marched in St. Patrick's Day parades, with shamrocks on display, shil lelaghs in hand, and fiddles filling the chilly air with the music of Mayo and Killarney.

As their numbers rose in New England cities, the Irish assumed a greater voice in American life. They established their own newspapers, notably *The Pilot*, edited by John Boyle O'Reilly, an Irish poet and patriot who had joined them in Boston. The papers supported immigrants when they were under attack from bigots, and were quick with editorials at the slightest appearance of perceived denigration of the Irish. Ralph Waldo Emerson wrote himself into trouble by making the sympathetic but seemingly cavalier observation that slaves and downtrodden immi grants, including the Irish, "have a great deal of guano in their destiny. They are ferried over the Atlantic, and carted over America, to ditch and to drudge, . . . and then to lie down prematurely to make a spot of green grass on the prairie." *The Pilot* condemned Emerson's "heathenish, soul less, immoral remarks." But Emerson's words proved all too accurate for Irish mill workers in Lawrence, Massachusetts. They *were* ferried across the sea and they *did* lie down prematurely, not on the prairie but in the rubble and flames of the Pemberton Mill.

On Monday, January 9, 1860, rain fell in Lawrence. On the fourth story of the Pemberton, Rosanna Kenney, twenty-one years old, felt a rocking sensation. She had heard that stones in the mill foundation had slipped out of place sometime before, and she attributed the rocking to a thaw. She turned back to her work. One floor down, Maria Yeaton approached overseer Elbert Moses who supervised her and the other operators of one hundred looms. She asked him if he expected the rain to develop into a downpour. "Why do you ask?" Moses said. "Because," Yeaton responded, "we are always afraid of the big mill when the water is high."

The next afternoon, Mary Desney, who had immigrated to Lawrence from Anderson, Scotland, went to the Pemberton Mill looking for a job. The overseer she was supposed to see was not immediately available. As she waited for her job interview, Mary Desney said later, she sensed impending danger and hastened out of the building. Those who glanced at her saw only a fleeing figure. They could not know that her flight was an omen.

The Pemberton was the newest, most modern mill in Lawrence. It was 284 feet long and 84 feet wide, twice the width of most other mills. Because of the greater width, larger windows than usual were installed, giving the employees more natural light in which to work. The five stories each had oak floors six inches thick, and each floor was supported by cast-iron pillars. From the fireproof tin roof down to the foundation, the building was designed for sturdiness and safety. Two members of the Lowell textile clan, John A. Lowell and his brother-in-law, J. Pickering Putnam, built the mill in 1853 with their chief engineer, Charles H. Bigelow. They spent a fortune, $850,000, on construction, and for their money had what was considered the finest mill possible. They installed their looms and spinning machines, and hired hundreds of workers. The

Pemberton seemed good for the city of Lawrence. It was making money for the owners and it offered jobs to young immigrants from Ireland like Bridget Ryan, Ellen Dineen, and Mary Burke. But Lowell and Putnam, squeezed by a financial depression, sold the building in 1858 to George Howe and David Nevins for only $325,000. The new owners installed more machinery to increase output. The added weight strained the load limit of the upper stories.

Ten minutes after Mary Desney ran out of the mill, twilight fell. It was just before five in the afternoon on January 10. All the looms were operating, and hundreds of men, women, and children were busy on all five floors. Suddenly the building trembled. Then it tottered. The big windows rattled. The thick floors creaked. The heavy metal looms rocked. Steam pipes burst and scalded workers including Rosanna Kenney on the fourth floor. Then there was a terrifying roar heard miles away as the huge building collapsed. Within seconds the Pemberton was in ruins, with clouds of dust hovering above. The only sounds were the groans and screams of the dying, the injured, and the trapped.

Sixty-five women and 23 men, most of them Irish, lost their lives. Another 275 workers were injured, many of them seriously; 375 escaped harm.

News stories about the disaster were collected in a book titled *An Authentic History of the Lawrence Calamity*. Olive Bridges from Calais, Maine, was on the fifth floor when she felt the building tremble. She immediately sensed what was happening. She ran to the elevator shaft, grabbed the hoisting chain, and descended to safety. Then her floor and all its workers and machinery fell down to the fourth floor; more humanity and looms and bricks fell to the third, and so the fall continued down to the foundation.

On the third floor, overseer Moses thought that the factory boilers had exploded. The gaslights went out, and the women working for him ran screaming to the windows. Moses looked out and saw that an adjacent building had not collapsed. He broke a large window and guided his workers to safety. As the young women stepped through the glass shards, they saw the extent of the collapse and realized that friends were probably dead. Several of them fainted, but Moses got them out. Among the survivors in the Moses group was Maria Yeaton, who had told the overseer that she worried about the building's safety.

Lizzie Flint and Darius Nash were together on another section of the third floor when Nash saw the southern end of the building collapse. He shouted at her, "For God's sake, let's go to the lower end!" As they ran, falling debris from the fourth floor hit Nash and he fell on Flint, breaking her leg. They were trapped.

Bystanders stared at the aftermath: shattered bricks and mortar, mangled iron shafts, huge machines twisted into grotesque shapes, and torn, bloody bodies. Only the two tall mill chimneys remained standing, like grim sentinels on a battlefield of the dead and dying. Dust spiraled upward like gunsmoke.

A five-story wing at the north end of the main structure did not collapse. It was filled with workers assigned to the counting room, the cloth room, and the mill offices. Several other detached buildings that were part of the Pemberton complex also remained standing. In each of these buildings the employees could hear the death cries of their coworkers close by. In the office, John E. Chase, the Pemberton agent, and S. G. Howe, the treasurer, heard the crash and rushed toward the main building's ruins. Howe fell and was trampled by terrified workers racing to escape, but he survived.

Spectators, many of them surviving workers, huddled on the edge of the ruins. They built bonfires to help the rescue parties see better in the black piles of wreckage. Relatives arrived to learn who had lived and who had died. Firemen assembled squads of volunteers to retrieve the bodies of the living and the dead. Darkness fell, and the rescue workers used fire lamps to search for victims. They could hear the shrieks and moans of men and women and teenage girls in the wreckage. They could smell seared flesh, singed hair, and scorched clothing. They heard firemen urge each other on by reciting psalms and singing gospel songs. Hour after hour, the rescuers stumbled out of the rubble with more bodies. "Headless, armless, crushed, torn and [severed] bodies, soaking in blood," labor agitator Jennie Collins wrote, "were drawn out to get at the living, whose cries could be heard far, far down beneath the rubbish. Fainting ones, slashed and mangled ones, living and dying ones, came swiftly on the shoulders of the stout men, while the wild and frenzied assembly of relatives shouldered, crowded and fought for a glimpse of each bleeding mass, to know if it were the body of their beloved."

At about ten P.M., a spark or a dropped lantern ignited flooring that was soaked in oil and blanketed with cotton waste. Flames spread rapidly, and now the terror of fire threatened those waiting to be saved. Mary Bannon, pinned in the wreckage, handed her pay envelope to the friend comforting her and asked that it get to her father. "Bid him good-bye for me," she said. "You will be saved; I will not." Mary Bannon died. Survivors remembered another young woman who was on the second floor when it collapsed. The looms around her had plunged downward and so had she. Her hand was caught in the machinery and she struggled to free herself. Then the flames neared. She pulled her hand away with all her force, ripping off two fingers. She crawled to an opening, stripped the burning clothes from her body, and raced past the flames to safety.

News of the disaster spread quickly. The Associated Press reported to newspapers throughout the country: "Within the past ten minutes the whole mass of ruins has become one sheet of flame! The screams and moans of the poor buried, burning and suffocating creatures can be distinctly heard, but no power on earth can save them." Doctors and other volunteers in several New England cities boarded special trains that sped them to Lawrence. At the Pemberton, they were sickened by what they found. Ellen Mahoney's legs were crushed. So was Celia Stevens's head. Both of them died. A reporter wrote that Samuel Martin's eye was "crushed out so that it hung down on his nose; the bone of the socket was broken." Mary Crosby's ear was nearly severed. Both survived, but Mary's sister Bridget perished. Rescuers found Kate Cooney, whose head and shoulders were severely burned. Her arms were burned off at the elbows, but she lived. Doctors prepared to amputate Mary Callahan's shattered leg, but her mother refused to consent, raving that Mary's "condition in heaven" would not be happy if she were maimed. Mary Callahan died. There was no help for Owen Brennan or Margaret Corcoran or

Bridget Gallan or Martin Hughes or Mary Murphy. All died. So, too, did Bridget Ryan and Ellen Dineen and Mary Burke who had left Ireland for better lives in America.

The rescue workers found three girls who died in an embrace. They found the coupled bodies of Lizzie Flint and Darius Nash, with his weight crushing her. "They'll have to get you out first," she told him. The workers lifted him away as fire approached, then for a fleeting moment were distracted by piercing screams from other victims. In that instant Lizzie Flint was incinerated.

Elizabeth Stuart Phelps, who was to become the first American novelist to deal with the effects of factory life on women, was a fifteen-year-old girl living in nearby Andover when the Pemberton disaster occurred. Decades later she recalled the awful night: "With blanching cheeks we listened to the whispers that told us how the mill-girls, caught in the ruins beyond hope or escape, began to sing...their young souls took courage from the familiar sound of one another's voices. They sang the hymns and songs which they had learned in the schools and churches.... Voice after voice dropped. The fire raced on."

Rescue workers were sometimes helpless. One of them found two young women, gave them coffee, and assured them they would soon be freed from the wreckage. But the women could see fire and they screamed for help. "Men redoubled their exertions, but in vain," a news report said, and "the flames enveloped the poor creatures, who perished before the eyes of their would-be deliverers." Overseer Morris Palmer, also trapped, gave up hope of rescue and slit his throat. There were reports of others also cutting their throats, and of doomed victims begging rescue workers to shoot them. A rescue crew, unable to penetrate the flames, stood by in anguish as two workers, trapped together and awaiting death by fire, sang a hymn:

> My Father's house is built on high,
> Far, far above the starry sky...
> I'm going home, I'm going home,
> I'm going home, to die no more...

As the night passed, the rescue workers experienced an eerie awareness: The more the flames spread, the fewer screams they heard. Finally, no one else was left alive in the embers and wreckage of the Pemberton.

Mayor Daniel Saunders Jr. ordered that City Hall be made into a hospital and morgue. Doctors, nurses, and volunteers treated the sick and comforted the grieving relatives of the dead. Among the volunteers was Olive Bridges, the quick-witted Maine woman who had saved her own life when the Pemberton began collapsing. She worked through the night, nursing her coworkers. Among those who did not survive was overseer Palmer, who died of his self-inflicted knife wound.

Unclaimed bodies were buried in a mass grave in a Lawrence cemetery. Other victims were not identified for days as relatives waited for definitive word from the doctors. The body of Mary Burke, seventeen years old, was finally identified by her mother, who cried out, "Oh, God forgive me for ever coming to America."

The Pemberton disaster stirred national outrage. A *Vanity Fair* poem railed at the textile barons:

> *A curse on ye, ye millionaires,*
> *Who sit at home in your easy chairs,*
> *And crack your nuts and sip your wine,*
> *While I wail over this son of mine!*

Financial aid poured into Lawrence from all over the country. Donations came from New England mill workers, the Masons, the New York Stock Exchange, the Philadelphia Corn Exchange, the Pittsburgh Club, churches and synagogues, the "Italians of Boston," a War of 1812 pensioner, the Odd Fellows, the Knights Templar, and hundreds of other individuals and organizations. Amos A. Lawrence, heir to his family's textile fortune, assembled twenty wealthy business leaders in Boston and formed a relief committee that raised thousands of dollars for the stricken workers and their families.

Three days after the disaster, a physically and emotionally exhausted Mayor Saunders wrote to Amos Lawrence of an orphan girl about fifteen who worked in the Pemberton to support her younger brothers and sisters. She was burned and trapped in the ruins but still alive. "We had nearly extricated her; ten minutes more and she would have been safe but the flames came," the mayor wrote. "You must imagine the rest. I can't write. Oh, how fervently our prayers joined with hers to God. There are many very sad cases. I can't write—it unmans me."

The press and the public attacked the original Pemberton builders, John A. Lowell, J. Pickering Putnam, and Charles Bigelow. An inquest found that the building had collapsed because the cast-iron pillars were defective, too weak to support the structure. A coroner's jury censured Bigelow, the supervising construction engineer, but found "no evidence of criminal intent." The jury's findings led to stricter standards and safety requirements for the construction of factory buildings. Within two years of the disaster, a new Pemberton mill was built on the site of the old one and stayed in operation for almost sixty years.

The mills remained a principal source of jobs for the Irish of New England, but the personal cost of working in a factory continued to be high. Fifteen years after the fall of the Pemberton, fourteen Irishwomen died in flames that destroyed a mill in Fall River.

The new immigrants in the mills had no experience with unions, but they found leaders among their own people who stepped forward to fight on their behalf for better working conditions. Many of the leaders had worked as union activists in the British cotton industry.

Robert Howard, born in England of Irish parents, began working in a Lancashire mill at the age of eight. He became a skilled cotton spinner, but the British mills blackballed him because of his union activity. Like many other militant union leaders in the British mills, he immigrated to Fall River, and the city became known as the strongest center of unionism in New England.

Mill workers chose Howard to be their representative in dealings with management. He taught his followers that they had to think together and act together when it was time to present their demands to management.

Labor's adversaries in Fall River were not the Boston Brahmins who controlled the huge mills of Lowell, Lawrence, and other northern New England cities, but a group of local families who owned most of the mills in the city. Howard was more than a match for them. William F. Hartford wrote that part of Howard's wage-negotiating strategy was to know conditions in world cotton markets as well as the owners did. He sensed when to press for pay increases and when not to push too hard if the mills were in financial trouble. Howard negotiated with the owners on a friendly but firm basis, and whenever the moment seemed right, insisted on expanded workers' rights.

Howard was spurred by social conditions in Fall River that were as Dickensian as those he had witnessed in Lancashire. William Beard Hale, a Protestant churchman and reformer who worked among the mill people of Fall River, went into their slums to minister to their needs and came away devastated by the alcoholism, prostitution, and hopelessness he witnessed. "The heart sickens at the sight of the crowds who sit on the stoops and hang out windows and gaze at their misery," Reverend Hale wrote. "Among them all, hatred of the rich, and rage against life [are] inevitable. In such a place, what can men do but sit on the steps and curse their employers; what can women do but nurse their crippled babies and wish them dead."

Robert Howard saw the misery, too. He saw men and women in the summer heat almost stripped to the skin as they toiled at the looms. He saw them slip into the liquor stores and taverns after work to buy bottled solace, and he proposed a solution: "If our manufacturers would give over preaching so much about temperance and ... try to bring about a reform in the conditions of their operatives, it would be better than all the many thousand temperance lectures and temperance tales." After his years in union leadership, Howard was elected to the Massachusetts legislature and continued to champion the labor cause.

Another Fall River textile worker, Cassie O'Neill, symbolized women's solidarity during textile strikes in many cities. She persuaded women in Fall River to form their own unions so they could more effectively demand equal pay. She also was loyal to the men when their jobs were threatened. When the mills in Lowell tried to eliminate the jobs of skilled men workers known as mule spinners and replace them with unskilled women who tended spinning machines, O'Neill urged women workers to support the mule spinners' union. "Let it not be said that the women are a dead weight to the mule spinners of Lowell," she declared. Eventually, however, the mills had their way and the mule spinners disappeared.

By this time Irishwomen had staged several strikes and were much more aggressive than the Yankee women in demanding better working conditions. They refused to accept management policy that dictated that men get more pay because they were the family breadwinners. The women argued that the widows and deserted mothers among them had the same family responsibilities but were paid much less.

The first important national union in America, the Knights of Labor, formed in the late nineteenth century, produced a champion for the cause of women in industry. She was Leonora Barry, a union investigator of conditions in mills and factories. Barry was born in County Cork and with her family had emigrated from Ireland to upstate New York. She has been described as "tall, with a commanding presence, contagious smile, and flashing blue eyes under a broad brow, gifted with characteristically Irish humor, pathos and spontaneity."

Barry became a schoolteacher at the age of sixteen. Then, widowed at a young age and with two children to support, she worked in a hosiery mill in Amsterdam, New York. Her first week's pay was sixty-five cents. The exploitation she experienced prompted her to become a labor organizer, working for the enactment of laws mandating improved factory conditions. Although she readily took on factory owners who forced workers to endure dangerous or unsanitary conditions, she abided by the mores of the times and declined to lobby politicians on behalf of workers' rights because, she explained, such activity was not "ladylike."

Barry also saw women in the mills who were beaten down by apathy. She wrote that through long years of repression, such women "have acquired, as a sort of second nature, the habit of submission and acceptance without question of any terms offered them, with the pessimistic view of life in which they see no hope."

As long as the Irish stayed in the mills, leaders like Robert Howard, Cassie O'Neill, and Leonora Barry fought to make things better for them.

Over the years, the number of Irish workers dwindled, but the mill managers had little trouble replacing them with the next wave of immigrants, the French Canadians of Quebec. By the beginning of the twentieth century, little more than 10 percent of married Irishwomen were mill workers, while 30 percent of married French-Canadian women were toiling at the looms. The French Canadians soon became the largest ethnic group in many mill cities.

The Irish in large numbers vowed, as Robert Howard had done in Fall River years before, that no child of theirs would follow them into the mills. The nuns of the parochial schools prepared high school girls for teachers' colleges, and thousands upon thousands of young Irish-American women taught in the public schools. By the turn of the century, just five decades after the famine, they held a quarter of the teaching jobs in Fall River and Providence. In Lowell it was almost a third; in Worcester, half. Other young women became nurses as the Catholic hospital system expanded. The advent of the typewriter and adding machine created thousands of office jobs for them, and so did the growth of the telephone system. The sons of Irish-American mill workers, beneficiaries of a patronage system run by Irish politicians, became policemen, firemen, and public works employees. The church drew many men and women who became priests and nuns. The college-educated among them went on to achieve success in the professions that had been so long dominated by their Yankee neighbors. Out of Ireland their people had come full of trouble but clinging to hope. And now, in America, their sons and daughters sit in the highest places in the land.

5

***

Voyagers South

Voltaire dismissed Quebec as "a few acres of snow." The Algonquins called their land *kabek*, a word variously interpreted to mean a shut in place or a spot where the river narrows. It is indeed a land of snow much of the year and it is immense, covering six hundred thousand square miles. It is bigger than Alaska, bigger by far than the combined vastness of California, Texas, and Montana; and ten times bigger than New England. It stretches from Hudson Bay and Labrador in the north to border villages in the south that touch New York, Vermont, New Hampshire, and Maine. Seven million people live in the French-speaking Canadian province, half of them in the metropolitan areas of Montreal and Quebec City. The people of rural Quebec have plenty of space to share, a profusion of mountains, rivers, lakes, and ocean shore in what has been called "America's attic, an empty room."

The French Canadians who migrated to New England came mostly from rural Quebec. They answered the call of the textile mills that needed new workers, first in the mid-nineteenth century and through the decades until the massive mill closings in the 1950s. A century and a half after their arrival they remain a large presence in all six New England states even though many of them have married into other ethnic groups, and long after the looms fell idle. Because of the emigrants from Quebec, people of French heritage are the fifth biggest ethnic group in the United States after the English, Germans, Irish, and African Americans.

The French arrived in the New World almost a century before the Pilgrims, when Jacques Cartier raised the fleur-de-lis on the remote, rocky shore of the Gaspé Peninsula and claimed Quebec in the name of France. But in 1763, the British, victorious in the French and Indian Wars, took control of the province. The *habitants* continued their lives as farmers, fishermen, and trappers. In the long, frigid winters, men trudged through snowdrifts deep into the forests and harvested timber. In the short, sweltering summers, families carried tin pails into the woods and fields to pick wild berries. On the farm they were almost totally self-sustaining. They made their own furniture and clothing, they were efficient managers of agricultural production, they bartered in the town market for what they needed and rarely dealt in cash.

The people had powerful emotional ties to the land, their language, and their Roman Catholic faith. Their churches and cathedrals dominated the skylines of their villages, towns, and cities. The Quebecois venerated St. John the Baptist as the patron saint of their province. They prayed to St. Anne de Beaupré, revering her as a guardian of the French people. They named sons in honor of St. Joseph, patron saint of all Canada. On April 25, feast day of St. Mark, they asked God to provide bountiful crops. They were determined to hold on to their religion and culture even though their English rulers treated them as second-class citizens. Life was hard, but they persevered. "I suffered and I cried but I never despaired," sang their balladeers.

"Country folk do not die for love, nor spend the rest of their days nursing a wound," wrote Louis Hemon in his novel of Quebec, *Maria Chapdelaine.* "They are too near to nature, and know too well the stern laws that govern their lives. Thus it is, perhaps, that they are sparing of high-sounding words, choosing to say 'liking' rather than 'loving,' 'ennui' rather than 'grief,' so the joys and sorrows of the heart may bear a fit proportion to those more anxious concerns of life which have to do with their daily toil, the yield of their lands, provision for the future."

The British were more tolerant of the Catholic church in Quebec than they had been in Ireland. London allowed the church to maintain its authority, and the parish priests continued in their role as community leaders. Besides ministering to matters of the spirit, the priests counseled the people in affairs of the family, finances, even the law. They dealt with the English authorities on behalf of their people. But other than freedom of religion, French-speaking people in Quebec had few rights under British rule. They could not hold public office or vote, and the government largely ignored them. So the French began their long struggle for *la survivance*, the preservation of their heritage. The struggle is still vigorous in Quebec but weak in the American cities and towns where Franco-Americans live.

The pent-up emotions of French-speaking Canada burst like a blister in July 1967, when French President Charles de Gaulle visited Quebec. Addressing a throng from the balcony of the City Hall in Montreal, the imposing symbol of modern France declared, *"Vive le Québec Libre!"* The cheers of the crowd told the world that the Quebecois wanted full liberty, equality, and fraternity in the land of their birth, rights they had before the English arrived two centuries earlier. *Je me souviens*, their auto license plates read: I remember. American journalist Lansing Lamont, who spent years covering events in Canada, interpreted the phrase his way: *Born French but screwed by the English ever since.*

For the generations of people who left Quebec, economic opportunity in the New England mills seemed a better choice than staying on the farms. The land was worn out from too much planting, and crops were lean. The government did little to help farmers, and many sank into debt at the hands of moneylenders who gouged them with high interest rates.

Those who had already migrated to New England beckoned relatives to give up the struggle in Quebec and join them in the mills. A labor museum in Woonsocket, Rhode Island, displays a letter that typifies countless messages sent across the U.S.-Canadian border:

Dear Basile,

We are settled now in Woonsocket, staying with Uncle Francois until we can find our own place. The pay is good, Basile. We work from sunrise to sunset, sometimes longer, but on Sunday the mills are closed and it is like a church holy day. The work is not hard though it can be tedious.... Let me know what you decide, and if you want to come I will speak to the foreman.

Your loving brother,
Emile.

In America, everyone in the French-Canadian family, including children, worked for a better life, and there were many children— a dozen or more in a family was not unusual. The birthrate in Quebec had been high for practical, religious, and political reasons: Farmers needed the labor of the children, the church prohibited birth control, and the French were determined not to vanish despite English political dominance in the province. In just fifty years, from 1800 to 1850, the number of French Canadians increased from one hundred thousand to one million. *"La revanche du berceau,"* they explained: Revenge of the cradle.

The Quebecois in New England eventually began referring to themselves as Franco-Americans as they started their new lives. Families still recall how their parents or grandparents left their Quebec farmland in the care of a relative and sold their household goods to finance the voyage south to the United States. For almost all the emigrants the uprooting was painful. Many planned to spend just a few years in the mills and then return home. The veneration of home was reflected in an oral-history interview conducted in the 1930s with an elderly woman who lived out her life in Manchester, New Hampshire, site of the Amoskeag Mills. She remembered how a merchant in her Quebec village pleaded with her father not to take his family away to a mill city. "Nothing hurts me more," the merchant told him, "nothing makes me sadder or more utterly discouraged for our future, than to see a Canadian—a man whose ancestors have opened this soil, have tilled it, have lived on it and now sleep under it—admit that he is willing to see his children spend their lives for the profit of these capitalists who draw hard gold from sweat and blood.... A man is not poor who has all the substantial food he can eat, and all the wood he can burn. That is not poverty ... when you open the door of your little house every morning, you put your foot onto your own land."

Despite the merchant's plea, the farmer did leave, taking his family to Manchester. The priests and the government condemned those who left, accusing them of "desertion of the Fatherland." They warned that the United States was a Protestant nation tainted with heresy, impiety, and materialism. A French political leader in Quebec gave up in frustration as the *dépopulation en masse* continued. "Let them go," he shrugged. "It's the rabble that's leaving."

The songs of the emigrants reflected the conflicts they struggled with as they pondered whether to leave Quebec:

> *Where are you going?—To the States—*
> *You are headed for poverty*
> *Turn around, don't go there!*
>
> *Don't do like those folks*
> *Who go to the States,*
> *And are plunged in poverty*
> *As well as trouble*

But they went, leaving behind the fields that could not give them sustenance. People in the Richelieu Valley migrated to the mills of Woonsocket, and it became the most Franco-American city in America. The villagers of the Coaticook area went to Berlin, New Hampshire. Farm families from the Yamaska River Valley set out for Fall River. For people of the Beauce region the destination was the mills of Augusta and Waterville in Maine. Between 1860 and 1900, about six hundred thousand people, one-quarter of Quebec's population, migrated to New England and accounted for 10 percent of the population in the six states. So many left the village of St. Hilaire that the local baker closed his shop, followed his neighbors to Lowell, and opened a new bakery.

"My grandmother and grandfather came from Canada with eighteen children," Lucy Blouin recalled of her three-week journey south. "And my grandfather built the wagon that he brought the family down with." As an old woman, she remembered that "every three days my grandfather would stop at a farm and work for a day to get flour, eggs, milk, and butter if they had it." The family made it to Lewiston, Maine, and Lucy Blouin spent all her working life in a mill there.

The Quebecois came by horse-drawn wagons at first, then in huge numbers by rail. Native New Englanders passing through the train stations witnessed daily scenes of the new arrivals with their large families. Fathers carried suitcases and burlap bags bulging with family possessions, and mothers carried crying babies.

Often, amid tears of reunion and embraces and merry babble, not a word of English was spoken. In Biddeford, Maine, wrote Dane Yorke, "the Sunday evening train from Boston seems to have been a favorite with incoming immigrants and it became the custom for relatives and friends to meet that train each week for what was known as a 'greenhorn greeting' to the new arrivals. Sometimes the long wooden platform of the Biddeford depot would be crowded with nearly 500 'greeters,' and impromptu dances would start while the train was awaited."

The French-speaking arrivals had little in common with the staid Yankees, but they had come to take jobs no one else wanted. Some went into shoe factories, some went into the paper mills of northern New England, but most of them went into the textile mills. Proud to have jobs, the men wore jackets and ties as they walked to the mills, then changed into work clothes. The tradition soon ended; respect for one's occupation seemed out of place when conditions forced everyone in the family to work just to survive. The mills almost totally consumed family life. Nine out of ten Franco-American women and children were textile workers because, labor leader George E. McNeill charged in the 1870s, the mills were paying "pauper wages." McNeill told the Massachusetts legislature that many mothers and children were thus taken "from the sanctity of the home and had become the prey of this devouring monster." There were weakly enforced state laws to limit child labor, but the parents themselves violated minimum-age restrictions by misrepresenting the ages of their children to hiring bosses.

In her novel *Canuck*, the Franco-American novelist Camille Lessard-Bissonnette wrote of fathers sending children into the mills at an early age. A character in the book, a young woman embittered because her brother was forced into child labor, says to her father, "Don't forget that you committed a crime when you forced Maurice to work in the mills when you should have sent him to school. You passed him off as a fifteen-year-old in order to exploit his health and the sweat of this child for your own profit."

Frances H. Early wrote that children's earnings "represented thirty-nine percent of the income of these families, twenty-two percent of which was contributed by children under the age of sixteen. Clearly, working children were crucial to the French-Canadian working family." A 1908 Maine labor report concluded, "It is said that American parents work for their children, but the foreigner makes his children work for him."

Despite the mills' dependence on the women, and the families' dependence on their wages, government and religious authorities opposed the hiring of mothers. Carroll D. Wright, the first commissioner of the U.S. Bureau of Labor, believed that the employment of a mother in the mills "is a crime to her offspring and, logically, a crime to the state; and the sooner law and sentiment make it impossible for her to stand at the loom, the sooner the character of mill operatives will be elevated." The Catholic bishop of Fall River told working mothers that they had entered into contracts to be wives and mothers. "Violation of this law would ruin domestic life and ultimately undermine the foundations of society," he said.

Some Franco-Americans also disapproved of mothers working in the mills. Editor Alfred Bonneau of *La Justice* in Biddeford lamented, "We have seen their tired faces—pale, drawn, haggard, tearful—and worn-out bodies always susceptible to consumption. They return home half-deaf because of the noise of the looms. These mothers have a contract with their husbands to manage the house—they should not break it because working mothers are detrimental to the whole family." Mill owners, state legislatures, and the women themselves paid no attention to these expressions of concern. Neither did the succeeding waves of immigrant women who entered the mills. They had bread to earn. "If a woman's place is in the home," said union activist Carrie Allen in 1912, "why not pay her husband enough to keep her there?"

When the Franco-Americans joined the Irish workers already in place, the permanent workforce of men, women, and children that Francis Cabot Lowell saw as an evil in England became a reality in the American mill system he created. Normand R. Beaupré, a Franco-American scholar in Biddeford, wrote that factory lives had changed little over the century that began when Yankee farm women first entered the mills. Describing twentieth-century conditions—heat, constant noise, lung diseases, and monotony among them—Beaupré said the Franco-American mill workers "endured them stoically since, in their estimation, it was dignified work, work that brought them an honest wage."

Mill work for Rose Duplessis meant helping relatives left behind in Quebec. "When we came we didn't know a word of English," said Duplessis, who arrived in Waterville, Maine, with her sister in 1922. "We stayed with one of my uncles in Waterville. We arrived one day and the next we started work in a cotton mill at thirteen dollars a week. We spent our first paycheck of thirteen dollars on clothes. After we had worked another five weeks, we were able to send another twenty-two dollars to my mother, who was sick."

Juliette Durette Quinn, who arrived in Biddeford by train in 1912, worked for decades in a mill there. Asked if the job was hard, she said, "Oh, God, yes it was, but we didn't have any other choice." Normand Beaupré interviewed her and other southern Maine mill workers and wrote that they held to a "belief in fatality as well as duty, meaning things happen the way they happen because God ordains it that way, that they had no choice, they had to go to work in the mills and they had to work hard.... So many of these women lived [in] their dreams but never saw them to fruition and most of their lives were spent working in the mills... following in a religious way the dictates of fatality, one's lot."

There was loneliness, too, wrote Eva Shorey, a mill inspector for the Maine Labor Bureau. "Transplanted to the unattractive life on the blocks," she said, "with no opportunity for the enjoyment of the out-of-doors in their immediate vicinity, with a strange language and strange customs, is it any wonder that many sigh for their native land and spend homesick hours in the noisy rooms of the great mills, which are so different from the life they have left?"

The Franco-American scholar Gerard J. Brault wrote that "the process of acculturation was stressful and often left psychological scars. Many of the newcomers, for example, would never get over being ridiculed for their accent or for cultural *faux pas*." From the start the Franco-Americans endured bigotry. Maurice Violette remembered when the train brought him and his family to Augusta, Maine, in 1921 and how everyone, wearing stocking caps, scarves, and coats sewn from homespun blankets, piled into a hay wagon for the ride to their new home. "In the middle of February," he recalled, "we paraded down Water Street, up to what they called Sand Hill, getting pelted with snowballs. And the whole way we were called all sorts of vile names by the people because we were from Canada." Such malice created within the Franco-American communities a disconnection from New England society that would last for generations. *La Justice* in Biddeford expressed a typical attitude when it urged its readers not to shop in stores run by Yankees because "they laugh at us behind our backs even as they take our money."

The Franco-Americans found no sanctuary in the churches. The Irish-American bishops and priests who dominated the Catholic church in New England preached that immigrants must become part of society by speaking English and by studying American history. The newcomers also were told they must obey their new clergy in all matters of the church. As the church tried to impose its views, the Franco-Americans resisted what they saw as a threat to *la survivance*. Incidents of petty priestly behavior increased tensions. Some pastors refused to baptize Franco-American infants or to preside at Franco-American funerals and burials.

In Maine, the bishop allowed the Knights of Columbus, at that time a predominantly Irish-Catholic organization, to wear their fraternal uniforms at church ceremonies but withheld such permission from Franco-American societies. Some Franco-Americans, despite their centuries-old adherence to the Catholic faith, became so embittered that they stopped attending services in churches with Irish-American pastors.

Le Progrès, a French-language newspaper in Lawrence, editorialized often about these tensions and noted that while Franco-Americans represented three-fifths of the Catholics in New Hampshire and two-thirds of the Catholics in Maine, there were no Franco-American bishops, a situation that lasted until 1907.

There were other differences with the Irish-American church leaders, particularly over the issue of parish control. In Quebec the pastor and the congregation, not the bishop, controlled a church's destiny, including its finances. In the United States the bishop exerted authority over all aspects of church operations in his diocese, including the power to appoint or remove pastors. There were constant battles between the bishops and French-speaking parishes over the appointment of Irish-American pastors. The Franco-Americans insisted on having their own priests. It was a battle they won only after being in America for many years.

In Rhode Island, there was trouble when Bishop William Hickey launched a fund-raising drive in 1922 to build a bilingual high school in Woonsocket. Franco-Americans protested because they feared the dilution of their native language; they boycotted the drive. The bishop imposed the most severe punishment possible for a devout Catholic: He excommunicated sixty-two leaders of the uprising. He also suspended Franco-American priests who supported the boycott. The standoff ended only when the protestors gave in to the bishop and formally repented.

As the bishop in Maine, William O'Connell confronted issues arising from the huge numbers of French-speaking Catholics in his diocese. A haughty man with a sometimes forbidding demeanor, O'Connell dealt with these problems by fiercely asserting his authority in church matters. The Franco-Americans in Biddeford called their parish St. Andre's, but O'Connell insisted on calling it St. Andrew's. He demanded that the French-speaking Sisters of the Good Shepherd learn English. He backed off only when the nuns threatened to stop teaching at two parochial schools. O'Connell later moved on to the cardinal's mansion in Boston. The people in Biddeford continued to call their church St. Andre's.

The more trouble the Franco-Americans encountered, the more they united. Members of the educated middle class from Quebec came to the United States to lead their communities as doctors, lawyers, newspaper editors, and priests. The immigrants formed cultural organizations with names like *Societé de Jean Baptiste, Institut Jacques Cartier,* and *Survivance*

Française. Club meetings were times for conviviality, for raising a glass or two.

Madeline Giguere recalled the earlier tradition of eighteen or twenty children in a family and said of the club activity: "The men's French societies in the American cities were viewed as a kind of birth-control device. Wives didn't mind them going off to them at night and staying late—they'd be gone for the night at least." Allegiance to Revenge of the Cradle faded away, but before it did many Franco-American wives bore children year after year with the usual announcement to family and friends: "One in the crib and one in the oven." Cora Pellerin, a mill worker in Manchester, remembered, "You were a wreck for a man. That's what you were, a wreck for a man!"

Franco-Americans were not free of such problems as alcoholism and domestic violence, but most of them clung to the traditions that emphasized family life. They became among the most culturally stable ethnic groups in the country, staying in New England despite their rocky road to acceptance.

The more conservative families brought with them the strict customs of rural Quebec. At dinner, the father was always served first. After the meal, the family recited the rosary, with images on the walls of the Sacred Heart, the Virgin Mary, and the crucifix. On Sundays it was off to church twice—Mass in the morning, Benediction in the afternoon. On holy days of obligation they attended Mass at five A.M. and then rushed to work before the mill gates closed out latecomers at six. Girls were forbidden by parents to wear lipstick, and one woman recalled that she had to observe the ban even on her wedding day. Some Franco-Americans cannot recall their parents ever going out for an evening's enjoyment at a restaurant or at the movies.

Fathers taught their children that it was their duty to obey the mill bosses. Yves Roby wrote: "The fathers, invoking the authority of the Church, would remind them that in the world there are those who command and those who obey; the roles and duties of individuals were clearly defined. A good employer risked his capital to provide work for employees, a fair wage, and decent working conditions. In return for that risk, the employer had the right to expect of his employees that they would work long and well, that they would be on time, sober, skillful, honest, and keep their nose to the grindstone."

Until the day the children left home for good, the father ruled in all matters, especially money matters, and that included control of the mill earnings of every working member of the family. Rose-Anna Bellemare, who became engaged while still working in the Manchester mills, recalled, "My last pay day, I threw it [her wages] on the table just before I got married." Her father took all the dollars. "There was ten cents in the envelope that Papa said we could keep," she said.

Within the first two decades of the arrival of the Franco-Americans in New England, the streets were crowded with people speaking many languages. For the first time in their lives, the Quebecois saw Greeks, Armenians, Poles, Russians, Italians, and Jews. They feared Jews most of all because they had been taught from childhood that Jews had crucified Christ. They worried about losing their jobs as all these strangers came to work in the mills. They didn't want the new immigrants around them and sometimes told their bosses so. But people from Quebec were themselves among the targets of bigots who rejected all immigrants.

The relentless tide of European immigration to big American cities contributed to the rebirth of the Ku Klux Klan in 1915. The new Klan's primary campaign was against the black population in the South with lynchings and floggings that revived memories of the original KKK that terrorized freed slaves after the Civil War. The reborn Klan reached a nationwide membership of perhaps five million in the early 1920s as it targeted Catholics, Jews, and immigrants. It was active throughout New England, where the Know-Nothings had waged war against Irish immigrants in the 1850s.

Klan members were lawyers, doctors, ministers, government officials, and others in the middle class. The women's auxiliary, the "Klaxima," sponsored church suppers and Christmas socials. Cities and towns provided facilities for their parties in municipal halls. The Klan's summer-time barbecues attracted hundreds of people who socialized on meadows in the shadows of New England's mountains. Governor Percival Baxter of Maine called the Klan "an insult and an affront to all Maine and

American citizens." In 1924, he was succeeded in office by Ralph Owen Brewster who won with strong Klan support.

Klan couples posed in photography studios in their white robes, their hoods pulled back to show smiling faces. They proudly displayed the pictures on the living room mantel for their children and grandchildren to see. They drew the hoods over their heads as they paraded through their cities and towns past monuments to American patriots who had believed that all people were created equal. But the KKK message in the 1920s was that Franco-Americans, Polish-Americans, Irish-Americans, and Italian-Americans did not belong in this country. "The future America is not going to put up with hyphenates," vowed the king kleagle of Maine.

Cross burnings in the New England night underlined the message. There were few violent confrontations between the Klan and their Northern targets, but only because the KKK was outnumbered. By the mid-1920s, the Klan fizzled away in all but the Southern states, and the "hyphenates" continued to arrive in America.

Senator Henry Cabot Lodge of Massachusetts led a congressional effort to limit eastern European immigration but did not oppose immigration from Quebec. The Franco-Americans had, Lodge noted, "become a strong and valuable element of our population. But the French of Canada scarcely come within the subject we are considering, because they are hardly to be classed as immigrants in the acceptable sense. They represent one of the oldest settlements on this continent. They have been, in a broad sense, Americans for generations, and their coming to the United States is merely a movement of Americans across an imaginary line, from one part of America to another."

The Franco-Americans lived in their own enclaves, known as "Little Canadas." It was in these tenements that the role of the immigrant woman in an industrial society was defined. She began her day by rising before the sun in a cold-water flat. Exhausted, she dressed three or four small children, fed them breakfast, and delivered them to relatives or a neighbor who cared for them. If her husband was out of work, the children stayed home with him. She trekked to the mill in the early morning with her older sons and daughters. She spent only fleeting minutes in sunshine, and her day had few moments of charm and grace. In spring and summer, the song of birds and the scent of flowers were rare joys that renewed her hope that one day she would move her family away from the city to a suburb with fields and forests of Quebec memories.

Home from work, she walked up the two or three flights of stairs to her tenement rooms and longed for rest after her mill labors, but it was time to begin a new round of tasks. She boiled water to heat dinner, mostly soups and stews prepared the previous night. When she opened the cupboards, cockroaches scattered. At mealtime she waited on the boarder she had taken in for extra income at the price of her family's privacy. When dinner was done, she put the younger children to bed. Then she boiled water again to do the laundry with the help of older daughters, silently hoping they would not marry too soon and leave more housework to her. She scrubbed the clothes by hand on a washboard, rinsed them by hand, and guided them through a hand-turned wringer. She hung the wash outside, and the splash of colors on the clothesline brightened her drab neighborhood. If clothes were tattered, she mended them. If new clothes were needed, she made them. She prepared the dinner that she would serve her family the next evening.

Unrelentingly, men came by for money. The landlord came by for the rent money. The men who delivered milk, ice, and coal wanted their money. The life-insurance agent collected money on policies that cost five to ten cents a week.

There was little money for amusements or recreation for her children. If she were blessed, her husband was not an alcoholic, drinking away the household money and beating her when she protested. If times were hard, she cut back on food, especially meat. When she was desperate for money, she sold spare furniture. She lugged family heirlooms to the pawnshop. She went into debt at the grocery store. She borrowed money from friends. She cashed in the insurance policies. As a last resort, she went to the neighborhood loan shark.

When her evening labors were done at last, she went to her bed, knowing that on this day, as on so many others, she had been true to the old Quebec creed: *Pas de croix, pas de couronne*—No crown without the cross.

The greatest enemy of those in the tenements was filth. Leaking privies in the yard contaminated the drinking water. Measles, whooping cough, diphtheria, and typhoid constantly threatened the lives of children. Mortality rates in the tenements were as high as forty-seven deaths per thousand people. Half the victims were children under the age of five. In these neighborhoods, *la mort subite*, sudden death, was a common cross to bear. When illness struck, few families could afford the costs of a hospital, so those who were doomed to die accepted their fate with "Christian resignation." When death came, some families could not afford the services of a funeral parlor. The mortician came to the home and the embalming took place in the kitchen. On the other side of the closed door, children huddled in the sleeping rooms, whispering about death, the "intervention from heaven."

In happy times, the kitchen also was the place for parties. For six days a week the family worked long and hard, but Saturday night was for good times, for the music of fiddles and harmonicas and concertinas, for manifesting through song and dance their resolve to survive in America while clinging to their culture, too.

Their love of a good time startled their neighbors. In the horse-and-buggy days in Brunswick, Maine, Franco-American weddings were followed by speedy carriage rides through the streets of the town. A. G. Tenney, editor of the *Brunswick Telegraph*, editorialized: "Has a crisis arrived with racing on the streets? On Monday morning, as frequently happens, there was a French wedding, a part of the fun always being a ride after the ceremony is over. Three sleighs driven abreast as rapidly as livery horses can travel were going down Federal Street in high glee when William Mountford was knocked down." Tenney facetiously suggested that a wedding chapel be built next to the town racetrack. On the whole, though, Tenney liked the Quebecois. "They are quiet, orderly and industrious," he told his Yankee readers.

The painter Marsden Hartley grew up amid the textile mills of Lewiston, Maine, and remembered the spirit exuded by the Franco-Americans: "The Canadians came to the city—giving it new life, new fervors, new charms, new vivacities, lighter touches, pleasant shades of cultivation, bringing no harm to the city, bringing what it now has—a freshening of city style, a richer sense of plain living."

In the Little Canadas, the mill bells pealed all day, summoning or dismissing the workers. Children were given time off from school to deliver lunch to their families in the mills; they lugged three-tiered pails that contained a hot liquid in the bottom, meat and vegetables in the middle, and dessert on top. If children took the long way, they could walk for two miles through a mill's aisles, hallways, and workrooms. They shouted above the factory racket to greet dozens of relatives and neighbors, most of them covered with cotton lint. They saw children from their neighborhood standing on platforms or boxes so they could reach the machines they were assigned to tend.

Eva Shorey, the Maine factory inspector, saw urban misery in the Little Canadas of Lewiston and Biddeford, but on summer days she saw children playing games like *la cachette* (hide-and-seek), and *sauter a la corde* (jump rope). In one of her annual reports she wrote: "A passerby can appreciate some of the joys in tenement house life when observing the verandas of a five-story tenement, filled to overflowing with crowds of excited children, in various stages of apparel and non-apparel, their shrill voices raised in shouts or other exclamations, while the older people are at the windows, conversing with their neighbors across the street."

After coal-fed boilers were installed in the mills, everyone was exposed to the carbon monoxide pouring out of the smokestacks. Inside, workers waged a futile war against filth. The buildings were infested with rats that squirmed into lunch food; at the end of the shift, workers shook out their clothes to get rid of vermin. In Lewiston in the 1880s, sanitary conditions were so bad that the city established a board of health, but the board could accomplish little, citing inadequate funding, public apathy, or outright opposition.

One of the worst disasters resulting from such neglect occurred in Brunswick, Maine, on the Androscoggin River. In the late nineteenth century it was a popular summer resort. It was the home of Bowdoin College and the Cabot textile mill, which employed seven hundred workers, most of them Franco-Americans and some of them children only seven years old. The Boston Brahmins who owned the mill maintained about one hundred housing units for the workers in four tenement blocks along the river. The Cabot Mill's dividends were averaging 8 percent, but despite the steady profits, the managers were constantly pressuring the town to lower taxes on company property.

The *Brunswick Telegraph* was usually filled with news about town government and the social activities of the Yankee population. There were items about farm crops and commericial fishing, and sports and academic events at Bowdoin. There were advertisements for Dr. Flower's Lung Cordial, "without question the most wonderful lung remedy ever discovered," and for Ayer's Sarsaparilla, "the best blood purifier." Castoria for Infants and Children claimed a cure for "colic, constipation, sour stomach, diarrhea." At Town Hall, the "Dublin Dan Comedy Company in their latest laughable success" was appearing in the summer of 1886.

Editor Tenney, riding his horse and carriage, was making his usual rounds that same summer, picking up news here and there, when he heard about widespread illness in the mill neighborhood. There also seemed to have been more funerals than usual in recent weeks at the Franco-American parish.

For several years Tenney had been nagging the mill managers to clean up the filth in the "disgracefully neglected Cabot houses," but the managers ignored him. Some of the old *habitants* in the houses kept pigs and cows, and the yards were covered with manure. A town history said that "a man from the Middle Ages would have felt at home amidst the dirt and the smells of Brunswick." This scene was within walking distance of the town's finest homes and the green expanses of the Bowdoin campus where Tenney had studied five decades earlier.

Tenney learned that many children were afflicted with high fever and a tough membranelike obstruction in the air passages of the lungs that made breathing difficult. The sick were being treated by a young Franco-American physician, Dr. Onsime Pare, a graduate of the University of Michigan. Pare told Tenney that Brunswick had a diphtheria epidemic. There had been 126 cases in just thirteen weeks. Tenney rarely published news about the factory workers, but now he began chronicling the deaths on the front page of every edition of his weekly paper. The September 10, 1886, edition carried a long list of the latest victims, including:

Marie Forten	Diphtheria	2 years
Joseph Carou	Diphtheria	15 months
Marie L. Dubie	Diarrhea	1 year
Rosanna LeBlanc	Diphtheria	9 years
Michael Quintal	Diphtheria	4 years

By the end of the summer, the *Telegraph* had listed the deaths of more than seventy people, mostly children, and still the mill did not clean up the neighborhood. Tenney suggested that because some members of the Brunswick health board were friendly with Cabot management, they did not insist on a cleanup. "This is a record which should consign to eternal infamy the management of this corporation," Tenney told his readers. He declared that the Boston owners had "no tender mercy for the poor slaves bound to it by the necessities of existence, they dying by slow poison . . ."

The neighboring *Bath Times* carped that "Tenney will frighten everybody into keeping away from this really beautiful and thriving village." Tenney resisted pressure to stop reporting on the public health disaster, writing that "could we believe ourself capable of *concealing* facts as monstrously heartless as the record of the Cabot company shows, we should think ourself a fit subject for a madhouse."

The state board of health finally stepped in, telling town officials: "Here are seventy-one deaths in all occurring in eight months, and almost all from diseases which need never largely prevail and from conditions which it is scandalous to let exist. Typhoid fever, diphtheria, diarrheal diseases, cerebro-spinal-meningitis (spotted fever)—all these belong to that group of maladies which have been characterized as 'filth diseases.' The death rate . . . in your town probably cannot be equalled elsewhere in New England."

Under orders from the state, the Cabot Company eventually cleaned up the tenement district. Dr. Pare, who had worked day and night through the summer to treat his fellow countrymen, died of pneumonia six months after the epidemic. He was thirty-two years old. The mill managers who had ignored his pleas for cleaner tenements closed down operations on the day of his funeral. His family took the body to Quebec for burial. The Cabot Company started up the looms again and stayed in business for another fifty-six years, then sold out to new owners and left town.

Many Franco-Americans who lived in conditions as perilous as those in Brunswick tolerated their plight. They regarded themselves as temporary residents of the United States who would eventually return to Quebec. To the natives of New England they became known as birds of passage. By 1887, there were 306,000 Quebec immigrants in America, and only 28,000 of them were citizens. They did not become citizens for several reasons, principally because of the language barrier. Those who kept their farms in Quebec were paying taxes in the province and did not want to be taxed again in the United States. As World War I approached, some men dreaded the draft because the loss of their wages would push their families deeper into poverty. They may have been influenced, too, by events back in Canada. Young Canadians of English heritage displayed valor on the European battlefields, but the French-speaking people of Quebec opposed conscription. This resistance, wrote Lansing Lamont, underscored the "French-Canadians' unwillingness to participate in the wars of an Empire whose anglophone constituents denied them equal rights at home." Many Franco-Americans did serve in the U.S. armed services; the inscriptions on New England war memorials are replete with names rooted in Quebec.

In the past, few history books mentioned the great Quebecois migration to the United States. Few newspapers bothered to report on the social activities of Franco-Americans, or even their births and deaths, except for disasters like the Brunswick diphtheria epidemic. When they were written about at all in English-language newspapers, their names were often misspelled. Sometimes they were deliberately ignored. In Lewiston, Maine, the Franco-Americans built the Sisters of Charity Hospital, which Yankee doctors in town dismissed as the "French hospital," an institution not up to their medical standards. Even government officials attacked them because they chose to live apart from the rest of society. During the late nineteenth century, when railroads depended on Chinese immigrant labor to build their Western routes, the Bureau of Labor Statistics in Massachusetts issued a report that criticized the Quebec immigrants while managing also to insult the Chinese. "With some exceptions the Canadian French are the Chinese of the Eastern States," the report said. "They care nothing for our institutions, civil, political or educational. They do not come to make a home among us; but their purpose is merely to sojourn a few years as aliens, touching us only at a single point, that of work . . . they are a horde of industrial invaders, not a stream of stable settlers."

The Franco-Americans also dealt with pressures from community leaders who preached *fierté*, ethnic pride. Much of the pressure came from the four hundred French-language newspapers published in New England during the peak years of the textile industry. The editors relentlessly admonished their readers to cling to their ethnic identity, their faith, their language, and their culture. "He who loses his language loses his faith," wrote Alfred Bonneau of *La Justice* in Biddeford. In Lewiston, *Le Messager* preached: "Learn the history of the United States well, for it is the country where you live, but do not neglect that of Canada. . . . In becoming acquainted with the beauty and grandeur of the lives of your ancestors, you will understand what you owe them and the direction you must, yourself, go in. Especially, speak French in your family so that your parents will not be forced to impose this duty of primary importance to you." The editorial urged readers to learn English, too: "English penetrates you from the air you breathe because every hour of the day it is made to ring in your ears."

Because the church was the strongest tie to their heritage, Franco-Americans scraped together nickels and dimes and dropped them in the Sunday Mass collection baskets so they could build their own churches. In old mill cities and towns across New England, these majestic granite structures still add architectural beauty to the skylines. The churches were the people's spiritual and cultural *citadelles*. The parishioners loved their *choeurs de chant*. They joined the *Cercle Catholique, Les Dames de Ste. Anne*, and *Les Dames de Charité*. Revered parish priests were the sturdiest guides leading the Franco-Americans through the pitfalls of American life. Outside the old church of St. John de Baptiste in Lowell is a statue of a long-ago pastor, the Reverend A. M. Garin. Its inscription reads: "He went about doing good." Father Garin was one of hundreds of priests from France and Quebec who became important leaders of their Franco-American communities. They were spiritual advisers, they were symbols of stability in times of great social adjustment, and they were builders. They built schools, hospitals, colleges and universities, homes for unwed mothers, and orphanages at a time when young parents often died of lung diseases associated with mill work.

The priests taught the people that hard work was their destiny, that they were born to suffer in this life, but that they should not blame society for their condition. It was a difficult credo but not very different from the Puritanical teachings accepted by their Yankee bosses and neighbors. The people for the most part obeyed the stern curés. The priests put the fear of God into any young parishioner who flirted with the idea of marriage to someone not Franco-American. They refused to consider marriage between a parishioner and a non-Catholic. If an unmarried woman became pregnant, the priest often dictated that the couple be married in the basement hall of the church, not in the sanctuary, humiliating the couple and their families as well. A Franco-American woman who required a cesarean delivery had to receive permission from the priest. Children were discouraged from participating in recreational and educational activities sponsored by non-Catholic organizations like the YMCA and YWCA. To send Franco-American children to public schools would be to send them into a world without God. The children belonged with the nuns who led them in the Pledge of Allegiance to the American flag but also in the Pledge to the Sacred Heart.

Like other Catholic ethnic groups, the Franco-Americans idolized some of their priests as saintly authority figures. Parents prayed that a son would be called to the priesthood or that a daughter would enter the convent. When it happened, it was considered such a blessing that the family pooled hard-earned wages to pay the education bills. Sometimes it meant that a younger boy or girl who showed promise in school had to drop out and go to work in the mills to help the older sibling realize a religious vocation. Laurette LaCasse Bouchard of Manchester left the classroom for the mill to help two older brothers become priests. "I felt bad when I couldn't go to school," she said. "I cried. Boy, did I cry!"

Franco-American children who left school for similar reasons included candidates for academic honors and scholarships. They remembered when teachers scolded inattentive students with the frightening question: Do you want to spend the rest of your life in the mill like your parents? Now, pressured by those same parents, honor students went to the principal, stammered through the announcement that they had to drop out and, like Laurette LaCasse Bouchard, surrendered their dreams with tears in their eyes. Their situation was similar to Lucy Larcom's a century before, when she, too, put aside her books and poems and went into the Lowell mills. "I had looked through an open door that I was not willing to see shut upon me," Larcom recalled. "I began to reflect on life rather seriously for a girl of twelve or thirteen. What was I here for? What could I make of myself? Must I submit to be carried along with the current and do just what everybody else did?" Larcom did escape from the mills and realized her ambition, but few Franco-American children did. In some areas of New England, in the years before school attendance laws became effective, 70 percent of them were working.

The mill managers welcomed the child workers. "There is such a thing as too much education for working people sometimes," said Thomas Livermore, agent at the Amoskeag Mills. "I have seen cases where young people were spoiled for labor by being educated to a little too much refinement." The Fall River school board agreed. "An exclusively bookish education," the board said, "has created in the minds of many of the [mill children] a radically wrong attitude toward life which would make the child look upon working at cotton manufacturing" as something to avoid.

Franco-Americans spent their whole working lives in the mills, in contrast to the Yankee women and Irish immigrants who passed through them in a few years. Like their predecessors, the Franco-Americans worked in conditions that were dangerous and unhealthy. Alice Blais recalled the deafening noise of the Lewiston cotton mill where she worked fifty-four hours a week: "If someone wasn't used to it, he was nearly deaf when he left. When there were fifty to sixty machines in the same room, they all made the same noise. What a racket that made! . . . it was a drone, a boring noise. It was necessary to talk real loud because there were so many machines. There were five to ten machines to each operator, and they weren't that far apart." The women learned to tolerate the bedlam just as earlier workers had done. "It came to a point where there was a rhythm to it," Cecile Doyon said. "And we'd start to sing to that rhythm when the work was going fine, but when the work was going badly, there was no singing." Long after the mills went out of business, a common badge of service for retirees was the hearing aid.

Damaged eyesight was another price they paid. Marie Proulx spent thirteen years in a Manchester mill, working in a poorly lighted room where she checked for imperfections in a hundred variations of colored thread. In her retirement she recalled, "I lost my eyes in Number Four mill."

The work was repetitious to the extreme. Robert Fournier recalled its effect on his mother, Germaine LeBlanc Fournier, who worked most of her life in the weave room of a New Hampshire mill. "When she was home her hand would involuntarily bob up and down, simulating her hand movements in the mill," LeBlanc said of his mother. "It wasn't a physical condition. It was just that so many hours were spent with her hands moving over the fabric that even in her relaxed moments her hands would be moving."

Corrupt floor supervisors victimized the workers. Melanie Cote remembered that on payday, bosses sometimes kept part of the wages that were due her and her coworkers. The boss would "steal our money—about five to ten dollars," she said, explaining that it was futile to appeal to higher-ups because "that's what the bosses did in those days." Henry Paradis, a loom fixer in the Newmarket silk mill in Lowell, recalled how a supervisor could misuse his authority to have sex with the women. "Let's say this girl comes and gets a job," Paradis said. "Well, hey, he likes her, you know? 'I'll get you a raise. It won't be much but I'll get you a raise.' But he's not saying when. A week goes by. 'Oh, I'll get you your raise. But you know what would be nice? To go out.' So, they would go out. First thing you know, she can't work any more, if you know what I mean. But she never got that raise because she got into trouble. Oh yes.

That happened many times in my father's time, in my time . . . because the supervisors, the Romeos, they think they can do anything they want to do or have anything they want."

Other workers curried favor with the bosses by bringing them fresh vegetables from their gardens. Men who dreaded being laid off during economic slowdowns were victims, too. When ordered to do so, the most desperate of them went to the boss's home and performed such chores as mowing his lawn or painting his fence, anything so they would not end up on the layoff list.

Conditions in the mills spurred campaigns to unionize the workforce. This created pressures for Franco-Americans who traditionally did not like unions, especially unions led by radical agitators from Europe. When union leaders called for work stoppages, coworkers demanded that the Franco-Americans join in the protests, but their priests and community leaders told them that strikes were wrong. During a series of strikes in the late nineteenth century, a convention of Franco-Americans condemned the walkouts as detrimental to the public interest and "against the moral and religious duties of Catholic citizens." In Fall River, Father Pierre J. B. Bedard commanded his parishioners not to strike during labor troubles. Other ethnic groups in the city accused him of importing strikebreakers from Quebec on behalf of the mills. This was in the era when many leaders of the American Catholic church were sympathetic to the labor cause. Franco-American priests clung to their own views.

When strikes broke out in Biddeford in 1926, the pastor of St. Joseph's Church told a reporter that his Franco-American parishioners did not take part. "I was proud of them—of their restraint during the recent labor disturbances at the Pepperell Mills," the priest said. "Deeply as they felt in the matter it was certainly a striking illustration of the kind of men and women they are that they kept their heads and resorted to no violence." And, he added, "the French people have no superiors as textile workers. Moreover they are industrious, thrifty and law-abiding."

Franco-Americans have told interviewers over the years that their own French-language newspapers took management's side during strikes just as strongly as the establishment press did. During a major 1922 strike at the Amoskeag Mills in Manchester, *L'Avenir* tried to shake the workers' solidarity by attacking a Franco-American leader of the United Textile Workers Union. Manchester mill worker Cora Pellerin said that Franco American editors considered the workers their inferiors.

In Woonsocket, Rhode Island, there was a notable exception to the generalization that Franco-Americans were passive in their dealings with management. During the Great Depression of the 1930s, French-speaking weavers from Belgium founded the Independent Textile Workers, which affiliated with the national Congress of Industrial Organizations, the CIO. The goal was to enlist all the mill workers in the city, unskilled laborers as well as accomplished craftsmen, into one big union. The concept had rarely been accepted in the textile industry. Well-paid skilled workers could not often be persuaded that they had common cause with those who earned the lowest wages. But Woonsocket became a symbol of labor unity. Even workers not associated with the mills joined the union, in cluding barbers, electricians, retail clerks, and public employees. Mem bership grew to eighteen thousand in the small city.

By 1943, the Independent Textile Workers became the Industrial Trades Union. It survived charges by priests, business leaders, and poli ticians that it was a Communist organization. It pioneered in offering its members day care centers, public housing, adult education, and medical coverage. It sponsored social and cultural programs. "For many French Canadian workers," wrote Carl Gerstle, "membership in the ITU meant accepting America as their home; and the cumulative discontent of their years of harsh labor became anger towards those who had denied them the right to enjoy the life promised by America. The ITU provided a focus for discontent but also a vehicle for transforming it into effective struggle." The union's influence faded away as the mills started moving south, but it had compiled an admirable chapter in New England's labor history.

Regardless of whether their experiences in America were fulfilling or demeaning, first-generation Franco Americans felt the emotional pull of their homeland. In his novel *Maria Chapdelaine*, Louis Hemon depicts a young man in Quebec who wants Maria, the woman he loves, to join him in the New England mill town where he has found a job. She agonizes about whether to move to an English-speaking place or stay in Quebec.

Hemon describes her dilemma: "Then it was that a third voice, mightier than the others, lifted itself up in the silence: the voice of Quebec—now the song of a woman, now the exhortation of a priest. It came to her with the sound of a church bell, with the majesty of an organ's tones, like a plaintive love song, like the long high call of woodsmen in the forest. For verily there was in it all that makes the soul of the Province: the loved solemnities of the ancestral faith; the lilt of that old speech guarded with jealous care, the grandeur and the barbaric strength of this new land where an ancient race has again found its youth." Maria stays in her homeland.

The Franco-Americans went back to Quebec as often as they could, especially during strikes and temporary mill shutdowns. Many older people went back twice a year to check the condition of the family farm. "I want to see if it is still where I left it," was their common explanation, said Philip Lemay, who emigrated from Quebec to Lowell with his family. "At heart, *Monsieur*," he told an interviewer, "they were still farmers like their ancestors had been," and the farms they owned had been in the family for generations. They sang:

> *Oh, how deep my joy would be*
> *To go back to die in Canada,*
> *To the cradle of my birth*
> *Where I must go to end my days.*

The Canadian government tried to lure its people back home with repatriation programs that offered them land for as little as fifteen dollars an acre in Quebec Province and in the richer farm country of the Canadian western plains. The government hired American-based agents to recruit people to return; the agents included priests, editors, and other professionals in the French-speaking communities of New England. Editor Bonneau of *La Justice* in Biddeford, a repatriation agent for the Colonization Society of Montreal, ran an advertisement in 1922 that declared: "Canada made me rich. That's what thousands from the United States are saying after taking a homestead in Western Canada."

Bonneau quoted a visiting Quebec priest: "I have seen the French in Biddeford, especially working-class *Quebecois*, who love their homeland

and want to come home to die in peace. They are facing competition from Armenians and Poles who are bringing wages down.... We must show the Franco how happy and prosperous he would be if he returned to Canada."

Albert Berubé, a priest and repatriation agent, played on the misery of his countrymen in his messages from Quebec. "You are tired of life in the mills," he wrote. "You have told me so... and I have seen it with my own eyes. Your financial status is not what it should be. For a long time you have served masters without hearts; for too long you have built fortunes for rich Americans. It is time to think about yourself and your children. Your fifteen to twenty years' experience in the United States shows you that there is nothing but a life of a mercenary there. Do you want to be truly free? Do you want your independence? Do you want to be your own boss for one more time? Come here and we will provide you and your sons over seventeen with very good and spacious lots of land." In 1910, Berubé led a group of 118 Franco-Americans away from the mills and tenements of Biddeford into western Canada where he settled them on prairie farms.

Always, those who stayed struggled with their loneliness and reached out for emotional lifelines to loved ones in Quebec. The unnamed old woman interviewed for an oral history in Manchester during the Depression remembered: "My father never said he was sorry that he had left Canada. He had a few thousand dollars when he died. He probably would have had as much, not in money but in property, if he had worked as constantly and as hard on his farm in Canada. And the feeling of loneliness, of being a stranger, of being nothing but an obscure cog in a gigantic machine, must have put a bitter taste in his mouth.... I think my mother was awfully lonely here. She never complained, but she lived her life watching for the postman."

The repatriation movement faded away in the 1930s as the second and third generations of Franco-Americans got their own jobs in the mills and elsewhere. They absorbed the English language, and their ties to American communities grew stronger as they cast aside the dictates of the old pastors and married into other ethnic groups. "Now Francos began to regard their ethnic background as detrimental to their prosperity," Robert Perrault wrote. "They felt that by shedding their 'foreign traits' and attempting to appear as American as possible, they would find greater acceptance in society. Consciously, Franco-Americans slowly abandoned certain customs which they had observed for many years." President Franklin D. Roosevelt approved, writing to Canadian Prime Minister Mackenzie King in 1942 that the United States and Canada should encourage assimilation of their French-speaking people "into the whole of our respective bodies politic."

Like everyone else, the Franco-Americans experienced the great upheaval in their lives brought on by World War II and contributed heroes to the cause. In Manchester's city park, a memorial honors a native son who played a role in a memorable moment of the war. René Gagnon of Manchester was in the group of Marines who raised the American flag on Mount Suribachi as his comrades defeated the Japanese in the Battle of Iwo Jima. In Lawrence, the park that had been donated by the first mill owners is now Campagnone Common in honor of three Franco-American brothers from the city who died on the battlefields of Germany—Albert, Carmen, and Bernard Campagnone.

The educational opportunities offered by the GI Bill, the growth of the defense and electronics industries in New England, and the collapse of the textile industry all helped weaken Franco-Americans' cultural isolation. In the course of these events their language began fading away. "Especially, speak French in your family," they had once been admonished. But Michael Guignard, a Franco-American scholar raised among the Biddeford mills, wrote, "I haven't taught my children French because raising kids is hard enough without having to be constantly searching for words. Francos of my generation have forgotten much of their French. Few of our children speak French. We have forgotten much of our heritage, culture and history. In short, our commitment to *la survivance* is, at best, weak. Yet, most young Francos have become productive members of society, whose parents, teachers and priests are, I think, proud of them."

Memories of days past are revived at Franco-American festivals in many old mill towns. The *Petit Canadas* are mostly gone, demolished in the name of urban renewal or repopulated with new ethnic groups. In

Lowell, the church of St. John de Baptiste on Merrimack Street is now Nuestra Senora del Carmen, serving Hispanic Catholics. The statue of the old French pastor, Father Garin, still stands by the door to welcome them.

The mill cities are filled with new faces from Asia, Central America, and Africa, but Franco-Americans remain in great numbers. Poets like Paul Marion write so that they may remember their heritage:

> ... *the stars like a connect-the-dot game*
> *transmitting my root tongue,*
> *language of those who carried my name down*
> *and down through Quebec backwoods, villages,*
> *down through New England hills,*
> *down through pine cone valleys*
> *to this mill town whose brick factories*
> *make a great red wall along the river ...*

In 1961, the city of Lewiston, Maine, observed its centennial with a celebration that filled the downtown streets with Franco-Americans who had worked in the mills there. The setting was rich with historic landmarks. Along the Androscoggin River, there were the great red walls of the once-mighty Bates Manufacturing Company where bedspreads had been "Loomed to be Heirloomed." There was Bates College, named for the mill's founder who contributed to the building of the school. There was the beautiful Catholic church, Sts. Peter and Paul, its twin spires visible for miles. There was the hospital built by the Sisters of Charity, the "French" hospital once scorned by the Yankee doctors but still serving people in central Maine.

The political and community leaders who spoke had names carried from the snowy farms and villages of Quebec generations ago: Jacques, Couture, Levertu, Landry, Boisvert, Gagne, Poliquin. Dean Emeritus Harry W. Rowe of Bates College also spoke. "As we pay tribute to those who helped make our city prosperous, strong and good," he said, "we salute the Franco-American contribution. Much of this history is found in the record books of our parishes. Out of the church came schools, homes for children, a house for the elderly, credit unions, charitable societies, a magnificent hospital and a youth center." These were the people who came to America and its mill cities with only a few possessions, endured social ostracism, worked hard all of their lives, and made lasting contributions to the culture of New England.

Some surviving workers remember the mill days with nostalgia. Madeline Giguere recalled her great-aunts saying they enjoyed those days. "When the looms were running, there would be time to talk, watch the children, visit in a social way," Giguere said. "You could never do that on a farm. And there were lasting friendships made in the mills. My maternal grandmother worked in the mills when she was young. For years after she left, she met at least once a year with the girls she had known in her section of the mills. And they would talk about those old days."

Juliette Durette Quinn worked long years in the Biddeford mills. She kept working while experts made their studies of the declining textile industry. She kept working at the side of those who never could shake off despair, who never could find an escape route from the mills. And she worked with those who, like her, thanked God they had jobs in the mills. She expressed her own conviction: "When I think about it we loved it. We had nothing else."

6

Wretched Refuse

When Abraham Lincoln was reelected president in 1864 during the Civil War, Karl Marx sent congratulations from London and included a comment about America. "While the workingmen, the true political power of the North, allowed slavery to defile their own republic," the father of communism lectured the president, "they boasted it the highest prerogative of the white-skinned laborer to sell himself and choose his own master." A State Department aide sent a polite, noncommittal reply of thanks.

There was irony in Marx's message. He had spent years thrashing out his ideas with the financial support of his associate, Frederich Engels. In turn, Engels lived on the profits of his family's textile factory holdings in Germany and England. As the two political philosophers cursed capitalism and proclaimed that their ideas would be the salvation of the world, the Engels mill workers toiled to fund the birth of communism.

Marx's daughter, Eleanor Aveling, carried on the Marx-Engels mission. She toured New England mill cities in the 1880s, speaking on the "Wage Slavery System and Its Remedy." From the time immigrants first worked in the mills in huge numbers, the principles embodied in communism, socialism, and sometimes anarchy were part of labor's arsenal in its struggles with employers. The ideas were alien to most Americans, but many in the working class clung to them until leaders in labor and politics worked to end the worst abuses in the long, tortured, history of labor-management relations.

In the years after the Civil War, reformers and political agitators in the United States who agreed with Marx on many social issues attacked the growing wealth—and the growing poverty—that was the fruit of the factory system. In his novel *Looking Backward*, Edward Bellamy portrayed a Utopian society in America with everyone sharing equally in the country's riches, and with no one stuck at the bottom of the economic ladder. Wendell Phillips, a blue-blood Boston social reformer, agreed. "We affirm as a fundamental principle," Phillips asserted in 1871, "that labor, the creator of wealth, is entitled to all it creates." To achieve that goal, Phillips was willing to accept "the overthrow of the whole profit-making system, the extinction of all monopolies, the abolition of the privileged classes . . . and best and grandest of all, the final obliteration of that foul stigma upon our so-called Christian civilization—the poverty of the masses." Phillips ran for governor of Massachusetts on a platform of such radical ideas but was defeated.

The economist Henry George argued in *Progress and Poverty* that despite the enormous output of the factory system and the accumulation of capitalist wealth almost beyond imagination, men, women, and children still worked long hours for little pay while imprisoned in poverty. "Men die of starvation and puny infants suckle dry breasts," George wrote, "while everywhere the greed of gain, the worship of wealth, shows the force of the fear of want. The promised land flies before us like the mirage."

While Marx, Phillips, and George were excoriating capitalism, Jennie Collins worked as an advocate for women mill workers in New England, following in the tradition of Sarah Bagley and other early labor reformers. Her years of activism spanned the departure from the mills of a native-born workforce to the arrival of workers from Ireland, Quebec, and Europe. Collins summed up the relationship between factory owner and employee in her own style: "There is not equity or justice in giving to one man a [million dollars] a year, while fifty thousand of his partners in the work receive only six or seven hundred."

Collins was born near the Manchester mills in New Hampshire built by the Boston Associates. As a young woman, she worked in the mills of Lawrence and Lowell. After her self-education, she taught history at a Boston evening school for women. All of that was a prelude to her work for labor reform and women's rights, which began during the growth of women's colleges, including Smith, Vassar, Wellesley, and Radcliffe. It was the dawn of women's pursuit of full equality in American life. A century before the issue of equal opportunity arose in the workplace, Collins wrote, "If there were found in the ranks of women some who were able and willing to shoulder a musket or accept the position of a sea captain or police officer, as absurd as it seems at first thought, I would not deny them that privilege."

Collins wanted most to protect working women "against the cruel encroachment of capital." For years she was a popular speaker at meetings of women mill workers and saw the poverty into which many of them and their families had sunk. "How can it be," she asked, that capitalists have the power to burden "disinherited ones with a life of bondage, in which they earn much and get little, see plenty and have nothing?"

In 1868, Collins led the fight to reduce the working day in the mills to ten hours and accomplished victory on a local level during a strike in Fall River. She convinced the mill owners there that instituting a ten-hour day resulted in more efficient production than driving the workers to exhaustion through twelve or thirteen hours at the looms and spinning machines. She told the owners that British textile workers who had won the ten-hour day did as much work in a year as they had when the work day was twelve hours long. Amos A. Lawrence, the second-generation leader of the textile family, did not often agree with Collins and other reformers, but he did on this issue. He told a Massachusetts labor commission, "The physical, intellectual, moral, and religious interests of our people require a reduction" in work hours. He acknowledged that "the present system of labor is debasing the native New England stock and forcing them to emigrate to the West." As for the immigrants in the mills, his Brahmin view was that "the population which displaces ours is inferior in every respect." Despite Collins's efforts and Lawrence's testimony, Massachusetts did not enact the ten-hour law for another decade, and then applied it only to women and children. Collins and the other women who struggled to improve working conditions in the mills were accustomed to delayed victories.

On a cold December day in 1869, Collins stepped off a train into the deep snowdrifts of Dover, New Hampshire, to lead eight hundred women in another strike against the cotton mills of the Cocheco Manufacturing Company. The mill managers had usually prevailed over the women strikers in earlier decades. This time they announced a pay cut of 12 percent and an increase in the corporate boardinghouse charge. The workers struck, arguing that their high production made the company prosperous enough to pay dividends of 16 percent, and that it was their efficiency in the mills that made possible these high profits. Many of the strikers had lost husbands, sons, brothers, and fathers in the Civil War, which had ended four years earlier, and were on their own, depending on the mill for economic survival. Collins later wrote that people in Dover supported the strikers and that no one thought the corporation "could hold out against such a strong current of public opinion." For her, "it did not seem possible that the wishes of such an intelligent and considerate class should be ignored when they asked for bread." She also was realistic, noting that while politicians addressed the Cocheco workers' rallies and promised them support, it was easy for the mill owners "to buy the votes of servile men and defeat the advocates of justice."

Collins contacted women mill workers throughout New England to win their support for the Dover strikers and organized a boycott of Cocheco's famous calico fabrics. She rallied the workers day after day in Dover's Exchange Hall. Despite her warrior status in New England's labor battles, what she saw in Dover shocked her. At one rally, as she waited to speak, she noticed a row of little girls sitting by themselves in the hall near the speakers' platform. She wondered why no adult was looking after children so young. One of the girls explained to her that they, too, were strikers.

While the Cocheco mills were cutting the workers' pay they required the women and children to work harder. Previously a woman had worked two looms; at the time of the strike she was tending six or seven. Collins met a widow who had worked for twenty-six years and was earning less than when she started while being required to double her production at the looms. "Time after time the company had cut down the pay," Collins wrote, "always reducing when the market was dull and never raising when the goods were in active demand."

As the Cocheco mill managers dispatched recruiters throughout New England and Quebec to enlist scab workers, Collins urged the strikers to stay the course during the difficult, dreary winter. A strike, she said, requires "courage to face starvation for the sake of justice, perseverance to hold out until the loss of money, often the only avenue to a capitalist's heart . . . [brings justice, and] fidelity to each other in order that the traitorous behavior of a few shall not defeat the purpose of the many."

Despite her leadership and her organizing talents, Jennie Collins could not win the strike for the Dover women. They finally gave up and returned to work, failing to win better pay or reduced hours. "So the Dover strike closed," Collins wrote, "and as noble an assembly of human beings as ever congregated under one roof were defeated, captured, and bound by their avaricious taskmasters, for no other reason than that the captives had none of the arms which political power supplies, and were consequently bare-handed, defenseless and impotent." She concluded that women would never win justice in the workplace until they won the right to vote. That victory was delayed for another fifty years.

During the Dover women's futile struggles, native-born workers in other mills pursued goals that promised better lives as they confronted a society that threatened to deny them their dreams. Mary Wheelwright, working in the Bates mill of Lewiston, Maine, supported her family but managed to save enough to pay her way through college. She spent her childhood in Dover-Foxcroft, Maine, working on the family farm. Relatives remembered her determination to get an education. Wheelwright's goal was to study at the new Bates College in Lewiston, across town from the mill where she worked in the 1860s. Bates began as an all-male institution and was proud of it. The school president had admitted several women, but the students and faculty made life so miserable for them that they all dropped out. Mary Wheelwright was not any more welcome, as reflected in these lines that passed for campus humor:

How many college students have they down at Bates Seminary?
Five, and a nigger and a woman.

"In spite of the uncongenial atmosphere in which she found herself," a college history noted, "in spite of occasional slights and constant ill-concealed dissatisfaction with her presence, she persisted in claiming and maintaining her right to the opportunities which broad-minded men had gained for her." Wheelwright was twenty-three years old when she completed her studies with the class of 1869. She was the first woman graduate in the school's history. She married and reared a family, and as Mary Wheelwright Mitchell, opened a private school in Boston. She became a friend of literary figures, including Ralph Waldo Emerson and Louisa May Alcott. She had escaped from the mill.

The departure of native-born workers from the mills and their replacement by immigrants heightened public disgust with the Boston mill owners. The animosity was a dark cloud over Lowell as the city celebrated its fiftieth anniversary on March 1, 1876. A children's choir of five hundred voices sang in Huntington Hall; the Germania Orchestra came from Boston to perform, and the audience stood for Handel's "Hallelujah Chorus." The banners and parades reflected Lowell's pride in its historic role in the nation's textile industry, but the speeches that day had a bittersweet tone.

Speakers recalled the city's promising beginnings when the Boston Associates purchased swampy farmland and turned it into an ideal place in which people could live and work. They also spoke of Lowell's decline. The model city had become an aggregation of dusty mills and drab slums.

One of the speakers was the Reverend Warren Cudsworth, a native of Lowell, who refashioned a morality fable of greed. He told of three men who had been paid a total of four dollars for their labor. One of them held the wages; he gave one dollar to each of the others and kept two dollars for himself. "Well, that is the arithmetic of a great many people in this world," Cudsworth said. Alluding to the mill bosses in the audience, he continued, "They may amass wealth, they may gain fame, they may for a while seem to be the lions of their day but public opinion sooner or later finds out the man who makes it two dollars for himself when he is taking in money and only one or less when he is paying away any, and very soon the lion is dismissed with a kick."

Dr. John O. Green, who had watched over the health of the boardinghouse women when the mills first opened, spoke of the industry's founders. They had, the old doctor said, "established a wise system of business, and by various means in their power fostered good order, temperance, purity, schools and churches, intending to make the city an honor in Massachusetts." Now, in 1875, the city of forty thousand was dealing constantly with problems of crime, alcoholism, prostitution, illiteracy, and disease. Just four years earlier, Green had struggled to save lives during a smallpox epidemic in Lowell's tenement neighborhoods that killed more than 170 people. Green spoke directly to the industry bosses: "Let those upon whom the destinies of the city now devolve see to it that the power of moral prestige which once made the young town so attractive in the esteem of our neighbors be not forfeited and lost."

The next speaker never minced words, whether in war or in Massachusetts politics. General Benjamin Butler was a commanding presence on the stage, a fierce-looking man with crossed eyes and a walrus mustache. During the Civil War, he was merciless to the vanquished Confederates, and Southerners called him "the Beast." As military governor of the conquered New Orleans, he ordered his troops to treat Southern women like whores if they were disrespectful to Union authority. At home in Lowell, the mill owners despised him but the workers considered him a friend. He grew up in a Lowell boardinghouse run by his mother and witnessed the struggles of the textile workers. After the Civil War, Butler won election to the Massachusetts legislature as an advocate of the ten-hour day. The mill owners tried to defeat him by intimidating the workers not to support his candidacy. Butler ran for governor but lost on the ten-hour issue. (He subsequently did win the governorship.)

During the Huntington Hall ceremony, Butler recounted the exodus of fifteen hundred Lowell men, "the best, most energetic and most enterprising," who saw better opportunity in joining the 1849 gold rush in California. He recalled the shutdown of the Lowell mills during the Civil War as the owners waited for peace while other New England mills had planned well for the war, stocking enough cotton supplies to last them for several years and keeping their workers employed. Butler loathed the circumstances in which absentee owners in Boston determined the destiny of his hometown. He declared they should turn over the mills to business leaders who were born in Lowell "with all their memories of home nativity and pride of birthplace."

When John A. Lowell came to the podium to pay tribute to his ancestor, Francis Cabot Lowell, he committed the faux pas of the day. As he spoke of the earliest days of the Lowell mills he told the audience, "At that time we were not overrun by Irish." The remark passed without serious incident; the Irish and other ethnic groups in the audience were accustomed to Yankee boorishness.

Lucy Larcom, who left Lowell to become a writer and teacher at Wheaton College, was the only person listed on the program who had labored in the mills. She also alluded to the immigrants who had replaced Yankee women like her at the looms. She sent a message to the semicentennial celebration organizers recalling those early years: "There was ample breathing room, and no stifling population about us then. The glory of heaven and earth seemed to enfold us as we toiled for our daily bread."

The immigration that seemed so stifling to Larcom continued to grow because of wars and political turmoil sweeping through Russia, Poland, Italy, Greece, and the Austro-Hungarian Empire. From 1840 to 1880, ten million immigrants arrived in the United States. In the next three decades, there were seventeen million more arrivals. Legends of the mill cities recount that in countless European villages, posters on the streets urged the people to emigrate. Agents for the mills showed village people drawings of mill hands in New England leaving work for the day carrying baskets of gold. The American Woolen Company of Lawrence proclaimed in its posters: "No one goes hungry in Lawrence. Here all can work, all can eat." Priests and ministers in the mill towns helped recruit immigrant workers, too, in return for the mills' contributions to parish funds. For the European villagers, many of whose homes displayed portraits of prosperous-looking relatives in America, the message was irresistible. They were for the most part hardworking and energetic but illiterate peasants who were living a pastoral existence when the mills pursued them, promising them jobs in America.

Workers, probably in the Amoskeag Mills, Manchester, about 1915. (Courtesy of the American Textile History Museum, Lowell, Massachusetts)

Eva Shorey, a state factory inspector in Maine, who sought to better the lives of mill workers. (COURTESY OF STEVE SHOREY)

The Desrochers twins, Eva (left) and Alvana, were among hundreds of thousands of French Canadians who left Quebec to work in the New England mills. (COURTESY OF THE LOWELL HISTORICAL SOCIETY, LOWELL MUSEUM COLLECTION)

The Lawrence strike, 1912. (COURTESY OF GEORGE H. KERR PUBLISHING CO., CHICAGO)

Arturo Giovannitti and Joseph Ettor, strike organizers for the "Wobblies," the Industrial Workers of the World.
(COURTESY OF THE IMMIGRANT CITY ARCHIVES, LAWRENCE, MASSACHUSETTS)

William Wood, president of the American Woolen Co.
(COURTESY OF THE AMERICAN TEXTILE HISTORY MUSEUM)

Father James T. O'Reilly, implacable foe of the IWW during the Lawrence strike.
(COURTESY OF THE IMMIGRANT CITY ARCHIVES, LAWRENCE, MASSACHUSETTS)

State militia troops confront Lawrence strikers.
(COURTESY OF THE IMMIGRANT CITY ARCHIVES, LAWRENCE, MASSACHUSETTS)

The militia protects mill entrances from strikers.
(COURTESY OF THE IMMIGRANT CITY ARCHIVES, LAWRENCE, MASSACHUSETTS)

Josephine Lis
(COURTESY OF GEORGE H. KERR
PUBLISHING CO., CHICAGO)

Both were in their early twen-
ties when they assumed major
leadership roles as representatives of 25,000 workers during the Lawrence strike.

Annie Welzenbach
(COURTESY OF GEORGE H. KERR
PUBLISHING CO., CHICAGO)

Women lead a street demonstration during the Lawrence strike.
(Courtesy of the Immigrant City Archives, Lawrence, Massachusetts)

Elizabeth Gurley Flynn, a star organizer for the IWW in the early twentieth century.
(COURTESY OF THE LABADIE COLLECTION, UNIVERSITY OF MICHIGAN)

And they came. Greeks came from Mikonos and Messenia and Thessaly. Germans came from the dying mill towns of Saxony and Bavaria. Russian Jews fled the oppression of czars and their marauding Cossack troops. Poles fled from Russian rule in their homeland.

European men had nightmares about the prospect of army service. "The peasants dreaded the bloody disasters which no pen could describe, no mind embrace," wrote historian Oscar Handlin. "Men were so fearful at the very thought of it that they wept; they knew that all would perish when it came. It was not glory the trumpets blew for them, but doom, in ravaged fields and flaming homes and men on horseback trampling over the supplicating bodies."

Emily Greene Balch wrote of a fourteen-year-old Croatian village girl who explained to neighbors why she had cast aside her peasant petticoats for "citified" clothes. "Tomorrow," she told them proudly, "I am going to America." A teacher in the village described the departure of fifteen girls and young women: "They were all blessed by the priest after Mass. The prayer for their happiness away from home was very moving. All who knelt before the altar were pale, struggling against the tears in eyes which may never see this church again. On this consecrated spot they took leave of the fatherland, our dear Croatia, who cannot feed her children . . . and the old people die in peace because they have hope the little ones shall fare better than ever they have done."

In the late nineteenth and early twentieth centuries, emigrants sailed from Rotterdam, Antwerp, Hamburg, Le Havre, Naples, Genoa, and other ports. When their passenger liners entered New York Harbor, destined for Ellis Island, the newcomers stood on the decks and stared in wonder at the Statue of Liberty towering above them. They saw the inscription at the base of the statue but did not know for whom the words of Emma Lazarus were written until someone translated. They they knew:

> *Give me your tired, your poor,*
> *Your huddled masses yearning to breathe free,*
> *The wretched refuse of your teeming shore,*
> *Send these, the homeless, tempest-tossed, to me:*
> *I lift my lamp beside the golden door.*

The immigrants submitted to a process that consumed hours of waiting in lines for every step required to qualify them for entering American life: They were showered with disinfectants while their baggage and clothing were sterilized in steam chambers. Doctors looking for symptoms of contagious diseases poked and probed their bodies. They were questioned about their personal histories, and about where they intended to live and work. If the clerks found their names too difficult to spell, the immigrants were given simpler, American-sounding names. And always, overworked officials barked out orders. The immigrants stood and waited, they sat and waited, they huddled and waited, until uniformed strangers allowed them to leave Ellis Island, set foot on the streets of New York City, and begin their journey to new homes.

Their destination was wherever they could find relatives, whether on the farms of the Great Plains, in the mining towns of Pennsylvania, in the meatpacking plants of Chicago, or in the sweatshops of New York. Among the New England textile cities, the Greeks headed for Lowell in large numbers and saw the familiar sights of countrymen, *patrioti*, chatting in Greek coffeehouses. They met men with familiar names like Ulysses, Socrates, and Euclid while bargaining at fruit stores and bakeries. One Greek man, arriving in Lowell, told a prayer meeting of his compatriots: "I thank God I have reached the Holy City." By 1910, Lowell had one of the largest Greek colonies in the country.

Poles went into the Holyoke, Massachusetts, mills and eventually to other textile cities. In just fifty years, nine million of them immigrated to the United States. The *Poznaniak* had bitter memories of the constant invasions of their homeland by Russia, Austria, and Prussia but fond memories of their windswept plains. Some who arrived in New England managed to work their way out of mill life and established farms in the Connecticut Valley of western Massachusetts. Armenians, Lebanese, and other ethnic groups also saved part of their mill earnings so they could buy small farms in the Merrimack Valley.

In Scotland, village ministers paid by the New England mills persuaded young women gifted in the weaving of ginghams and tartans to pull up roots and go to America. Portuguese from the Azores and the Madeira Islands, whose fathers had sailed on New Bedford whaling ships, worked in new mills built by enterprising merchants and farmers in New Bedford and Fall River. Rhode Island mills also lured the Portuguese, along with Finns, Germans, Armenians, and Swedes. The city of Lawrence, Massachusetts, attracted so many ethnic groups that some fifty languages and dialects were spoken there. The mills posted signs on the work floors ordering that the employees "speak English only," but obeying the rule was an uphill struggle for everyone. Immigrants learned English in night schools, they listened to their children speak the new language, they learned popular American songs on the new Victrola "talking machines," they flocked to neighborhood nickelodeons and learned to read the captions of silent movies that starred Charlie Chaplin and Greta Garbo.

Most immigrants depended on patrons or, as the Italians called them, *padrones*, to help them find jobs just as the Irish had found work through labor contractors like Hugh Cummisky, and the French-Canadian farm families in Quebec had been helped by recruiters working for the mills. The *padrones* contracted with the mills to help the new arrivals find housing, took care of other immediate needs, and delivered them to their new bosses. Some *padrones* were honest, others cheated their clients out of their full pay. Corrupt mill overseers cheated the immigrants by withholding the first paycheck during the "learning period."

Oscar Handlin wrote that many of the ethnic groups were criticized for living apart in enclaves and were judged incapable of assimilating into American society. He told of a settlement house worker who complained with exasperation, "This family is not yet Americanized; they are still eating Italian food." Eventually, Handlin wrote, new immigration policy "drew a sharp distinction between the immigrants of northern and western Europe and those from southern and eastern Europe." Laborers were welcomed if they hailed from Great Britain, Ireland, Germany, and Scandinavia, but barely tolerated when they came from Greece, Italy, and the Slavic nations because, a U.S. government report said, "all are different in temperament and civilization from ourselves." These conclusions were arrived at, Handlin said, with no evidence to support them. "In forty-two volumes, under the guise of science, the government had published the record of their shortcomings," Handlin wrote. "Learned men had told them they were hardly human at all; their head shapes were different, their bodily structure faulty, the weight of their brains deficient. If they were Italians, they were not really like the Italians who had a claim to the mantle of Rome; if they were Greeks, they were not genuine Greeks descended from the Hellenes." The result was immigration laws based on the premise "that the national origin of an immigrant was a reliable indication of his capacity for Americanization."

Emily Greene Balch, who drew a largely sympathetic portrait of her subjects in *Our Slavic Fellow Citizens*, included her own generalizations: "This type, as it has shaped itself in my mind, is short, thick-set and stocky . . . not graceful nor light in motion. The face is broad, with wide-set eyes and marked cheek-bones; the nose broad and snub . . . the forehead rather lowering, the expression ranging from sullen to serene but seldom animated or genial."

Europeans with radical political ideas were exiled to the United States during this period, among them Socialists and anarchists, and newspapers worried about the invasion of communism. The Hallowell, Maine, *Register* warned its readers: "Communism means, in plain English, that the industrious and economical classes shall divide the fruits of their toil among the idle and the vicious." But there also was concern about mill owners who profited from laborers who did not have the power to demand fair wages. "Even enlightened employers could not resist the more exploitative system, since it was a far more effective mechanism for keeping labor costs low," wrote Jacques Downs. "Here was the kind of situation that Marx would soon find typical of capitalism. . . . For the first time in its history, America had a powerless, landless proletariat ready to work at any wage it could get."

The immigrants were glad to have jobs in their new country. In a history of Greeks in Lowell, Nicholas V. Karas told of an old woman who heard a mill bell and made the sign of the cross. Her young companion asked why. "It's God's work that puts bread on our table," the old woman said. "We must thank Him." Greek men, like the early French Canadians, wore suit coats to their jobs, signifying their *estima* or sense of self-worth. Like everyone else who ever stood in a textile mill for the first time, they were terrified of the howling machinery but felt more at ease when they saw people from their village working in the mill and surviving.

New England natives mocked the immigrants for their ways, their accents, and their religion. But the immigrants kept coming, building their own churches, clinging to their languages and customs, and believing that in their new country, life could be better. "What a magic word—America" said James Palavras, who was a shepherd in Greece before he came to the United States at the age of nineteen. "The name drew you like the voices of the sirens that lured Odysseus, but we couldn't block our ears; we didn't want to."

Neighborhood streets and social halls resonated with the music and dance of Italy, Poland, Portugal, Greece, Lithuania, and dozens of other countries. Portuguese staged their Holy Ghost festivals in their *comunidades*. The Sons of Italy celebrated the feast days of their saints. Muslims from the land now called Lebanon observed Ramadan; Lebanese Christians observed the rites of the Roman Catholic Maronite church. Parading Germans carried banners with words that were strange to New Englanders: *Einigkeit Machete Start*—In Unity is Strength. Ethnic groups took care of their people through mutual-benefit societies organized by the Irish Benevolent Society ("We visit our sick, and bury our dead"), the Polish National Alliance, the American Slovak League, the Croatian National Society, and the Jewish Workman's Circle. Their clubs and coffeehouses and saloons were towers of Babel; the kitchens in their enclaves emitted the pungent aromas of a hundred ethnic dishes.

The immigrants realized they were at the lowest level of society. Eva Shorey of the Maine Labor Bureau quoted an unidentified writer's assessment: "French and kindred nationalities represent already a laboring aristocracy, and the truly lower classes are formed by Armenians, Portuguese, Greeks, Poles, Russians, and other such Slavs as herd together like animals."

Newspaper coverage of them was outrageous. The *Lawrence Tribune* reported a crime story in 1911 with the headline: "Murderous Dago Shot to Kill." The *Manchester Union* told its readers: "A foreigner's knife is an insidious thing. It lurks in the shadow until the man's passion calls it forth from its sheath and buries itself in the back." Some immigrants were even turned away from corporate housing. Luigi Nardella remembered that in Natick, Rhode Island, the mill wouldn't allow the Italians into the tenements on Main Street, "even if the tenement was vacant and the Italians needed it. And Italians were fifty percent of the workers in the mill."

The novelist Elizabeth Stuart Phelps wrote of her new immigrant neighbors in Lawrence that "we did not think about the mill people. They seemed as far from us as the coal miners of a vague West . . . whose names we did not think it worthwhile to remember." Historian Walter Lord suggested, why should anyone bother to remember? "The one belief above all others that obsessed many minds as the twentieth century began," he wrote, "was the conviction that the British and American people were bolder, braver, truer, nobler, brighter, and certainly better than anyone else in the world."

Emily Greene Balch thought that had a New Englander bothered to ask a Slavic woman to talk about herself, she would have told how she enjoyed working in the fields of her homeland at the side of her husband. She would have talked of missing her garden of sunflowers and poppies, and of socializing in the village where "everyone knows everyone else, and there are no uncomfortable Yankees to abash one, and where the children do not grow up to be alien and contemptuous." Polish girls from Galicia would have spoken of their love for dancing on village greens, and of their desire to flee the tenements of the American mill towns for homes of their own. Lithuanians would have shared their memories of singing festivals on the shores of the Baltic Sea. Hungarian textile workers could have told their mill bosses how their people at home were among the most skilled on earth in lace making and embroidery.

All the ethnic groups yearned to stay in touch with families in their native countries, and enterprising business owners helped them do so. An advertisement in Lawrence offered to ship holiday gifts to the old country:

> Make the hearts of the old folks at home rejoice. Picture your old mother or father opening a parcel from you in this country, and ex-

claiming with tears of joy in their eyes: "God bless them. I knew they would never forget me."

Duncan Wood, Forwarder of Foreign Parcels
499 Essex Street, Lawrence

They communicated as best they could with those they had left behind. When an immigrant died in America, the family photographed the body and sent the picture back home. When the immigrants became citizens, they sent photos of themselves proudly posing with the American flag.

Jews also came to the mill gates looking for jobs. The United Hebrew Charities of New York sent letters to Lowell mill agents asking them to hire Russian Jews who had fled from persecution in their homeland. "There are many skilled mechanics among their number," the letters said, and many unskilled people who could work as operatives tending the machines. The New York appeal in the summer of 1891 was ill timed; the mills were laying off workers because of a business slowdown. A Lowell newspaper editorialized that "the shipping of these Hebrew paupers here would mean that some hundreds of people already settled here and paying taxes would be out of employment." Labor unions in Fall River opposed the hiring of Jews in the mills. There were unsubstantiated reports that Jews from Russia were bringing typhus to the American cities where they settled.

Jewish immigrants did find mill jobs, and agent Joseph Ludlam at the Merrimack Mill in Lowell sought to calm the public. He took a reporter on a tour of the mill to see newly hired Jews at work. The reporter wrote that they were industrious, thrifty, and self-respecting. Apparently bedazzled, the reporter also told his readers that "these women are dark with lovely eyes." Jewish neighborhoods with kosher food stores, synagogues, and schools added new sights and sounds to old New England.

Edith Abbott, who worked for many women's causes in the early twentieth century, was not sympathetic toward the immigrant workers in her book *Women in Industry*. She did not find in them the traits she admired in the Yankee women of the mills. "The immigrant woman has no interest in operatives' magazines, improvement circles, or lending libraries," Abbott wrote. "She has no theories about making labor or laborers alike self-respecting and respected. . . . The fact that there are more of the old and the very young in the mills, more married women and more children, is in itself symptomatic of the existence of an inferior factory population."

Jennie Collins saw a loss of self-respect among many workers and believed that management negligence was a cause. She toured a textile mill filled with immigrants and wrote: "Dirty faces, torn dresses, uncombed hair, dull eyes, and expressionless mouths were to be seen everywhere. If threads broke in the warping-machine, the gearing was stopped because the operative lacked the intelligent skill to tie it while the machinery was in motion; if the shafting squeaked for oil, the attendant did not seem to care, or if she did care, could not stop to oil it, owing to the constant attention which the management of so many looms required of her." Collins said of the men who owned such factories: "They do not consider the good will of the operatives of any consequence, and can see no more value in the man who cares carefully for their interests than they do in another who does just what he is told and nothing more."

The flood of immigrants also raised concerns over whether the men among them should have the vote. Elizabeth Cady Stanton and Susan B. Anthony, historic partners in the fight for women's rights, disagreed on the voting issue. Kathleen Barry wrote that feminists who opposed voting rights for immigrants argued that the men "brought with them the patriarchal religious values of Catholic Europe, which could be wielded as political power over women." Stanton said, "the danger is not in their landing and living in this country, but in their speedy appearance at the ballot box and their becoming an impoverished and ignorant balance of power in the hands of wily politicians . . . we should welcome all hardy, common-sense laborers, as we have plenty of room and work for them." But, Stanton added, they should not have the vote. Anthony opposed the notion of granting the vote only to the educated. "The greatest wrongs in our government," she said, "are perpetrated by rich men, the wire-pulling agents of corporations and monopolies, in which the poor and ignorant have no part."

Stanton and Anthony worked against the exploitation of labor. As Kathleen Barry noted, Anthony was the daughter of a mill owner who "had not forgotten the problems and hardships of the working women she saw in her youth." Like the women who led the first labor battles in New England mill cities, Anthony believed that women had to look out for themselves. She told a San Francisco audience in 1871: "I declare to you that woman must not depend on the protection of man, but must be taught to protect herself, and there I take my stand." She organized groups of working women for mutual support. She taught them the tactics of political power, how to stand up for their rights, and how to present labor grievances to their bosses. The influence of Stanton and Anthony was surely strong among the women labor leaders who took on the mill barons during the rise of New England industrialism in the late nineteenth century.

The effort to organize the textile workers was daunting because they came from so many ethnic backgrounds and traditions, and spoke so many different languages. Sometimes the newer ethnic groups did not even like each other because of ancient antagonisms that had originated with past European wars. Emily Greene Balch noted that inviting a group of Slavs to a labor function was like inviting an Irish Catholic and an Ulster Orangeman to work together in unity simply because both were from Ireland.

Mill overseers pitted group against group, and men against women, keeping them disunited and in fear of losing their jobs. In 1904, management at a Fall River mill dealt with twenty-six thousand striking workers by hiring thirteen thousand immigrants to replace them. When workers from eastern and southern Europe organized strikes, the Irish and Franco-Americans usually did not support them. On the production floors, where interdependency was crucial, feuding ethnic groups sabotaged each other's work. "A loom fixer could paralyze an entire section of a weave room by stalling or by refusing to come to a weaver's assistance," wrote Tamara K. Hareven. "A room girl could leave a weaver stranded by refusing to disentangle the warp; and a cloth inspector could make a [mender's] life miserable by steering more of the defective or dark cloth, which is hard on the eyes, in her direction."

Leonora Barry, inspecting factory conditions for the Knights of Labor, wrote a report on bosses who turned men against women in Rhode Island textile mills. "The following is a fair example of the contemptible, mean trickery resorted to by some of the kings of the cotton industry," Barry wrote. "A law in this state prohibits the compulsory labor of women over ten hours per day. Upon one such occasion women weavers were asked to work overtime. They refused. The foreman went to the men weavers, asked them to work overtime, saying it would be money in their pockets, a favor to their employer, and would make the women jealous of their larger month's wages." The men agreed to work overtime, Barry reported. She added, "This is only one instance of how the wage-workers are made the instruments of injury to one another."

Barry expressed her dispirited feelings on factory life at a time when her Knights of Labor union was fading away, to be replaced by the American Federation of Labor. The AFL under the leadership of Samuel Gompers did not believe in one union for all workers and focused membership drives on skilled workers. The federation organized craft unions in industries across the country. By the late 1880s, the AFL had 6,000 locals and 675,000 members. It became a powerful voice for workingmen, but its door was shut to unskilled immigrant workers in New England who were in need of union support. It was they, more than anyone in the mills, who represented the exploitation cited by Karl Marx in the 1860s. "By increasing the intensity of labour," Marx wrote, "a man may be made to expend as much vital force in one hour as he formally did in two."

Those trapped in the mills were producing four times the goods produced by the workers a half century before, but their wages increased by only 80 percent in the same period and even the wages they earned could be taken away. Mill managers were quick to fine weavers and cloth inspectors for flaws that often were virtually invisible, and sometimes the total fines for the week amounted to half of the weekly wage. At a legislative hearing in Rhode Island that considered a bill to end such abuses, a witness testified: "There are four sins for which there is no forgiveness. One is willful murder; the next is oppression of the poor; the third, sodomy and the fourth, defrauding the laborer of his wages." The bill, brought up for a vote in 1886, did not pass.

A prominent religious figure defended industry in its dealings with labor. The Reverend Henry Ward Beecher, brother of the novelist Harriet Beecher Stowe and son of the inflammatory, anti-Catholic clergyman Lyman Beecher, earned generous fees glorifying big business in speeches and magazine articles. Speaking of the labor turmoil in the 1870s, and worker demands for equitable wages, Beecher argued that a dollar a day was adequate to support a worker, his wife, and five or six children, assuming the father did not squander his money on beer and tobacco. "But is not a dollar a day enough to buy bread with?" Beecher argued. "Water costs nothing and a man who cannot live on bread and water is not fit to live." Beecher's weekly income was almost eight hundred dollars at the time he preached that six dollars a week was an adequate wage for others.

William Graham Sumner also opposed the rising demands of the working class. Sumner, a Yale professor of social and political science, was the author of *What Social Classes Owe To Each Other*. Writing of "the poor, the weak, the laborers" in 1883, he argued: "In their view, they have a right, not only to *pursue* happiness but to *get* it; and if they fail to get it, they think they have a claim to the aid of other men— that is, to the labor and self-denial of other men—to get it for them. They find orators and poets who tell them that they have grievances, so long as they have unsatisfied desires." One of the poets was Walt Whitman, who told the American people that "the depravity of the business classes of our country is not less than had been supposed, but infinitely greater."

Even as labor protests spread, there was little change for the men and women in the New England textile mills. The mill agents still ruled their lives. The agent could make or break them, and workers who got in trouble on the job had to beg for his mercy. Mary Langevin of Chicopee, Massachusetts, pleaded with agent J. M. Cumnock of the Dwight Mill on behalf of her daughter:

May 6 79

Sir

 My daughter is said to have gone out of the mill without leave and I believe it is so I am very sorry she disobeyed so much will you be so kind as to see the overseer and ask him to take her back...for we are poor and need her help I hope he will forgive her this time for my sake

yours Mary Langevin

In a later incident, Cumnock fired two workers and received a note from another mill agent:

Holyoke, Mass. June 21st 1882

J. M. Cumnock, Agent.
Dear Sir,
We note the names of Victoria Lenroy and Justine Nadeau and will "blacklist" them.

Yours truly,
Theop. Parsons, Agent

It is not known whether Mary Langevin's plea on behalf of her daughter was successful, but the effectiveness of the blacklist system used by the mills suggests that Victoria Lenroy and Justine Nadeau, unless they resorted to aliases, never found mill work again.

Jennie Collins's visits to the mills convinced her that most workers, men as well as women, were terrified at the prospect of losing their jobs, dangerous and demanding as they were. "What shall I say of the men," she wrote. "Go to the mills and see how the mendicant workman kisses the rod that wounds him, praises the overseer that swindles him, bears curses and even kicks without a murmur, and then tell me if you can that his condition is a desirable one."

Collins thought that many workers lost their humanity in the mills. Lowell mill agent George Oliver didn't view them as human at all. "I regard my work people just as I regard my machinery," Oliver said. "So long as they can do my work for what I choose to pay them, I keep them, getting out of them all I can.... When my machines get old and useless, I reject them and get new, and these people are part of my machinery."

The best of the skilled workers were not immune from discharge. The kings of the mill were the men known as mule spinners because their labor resembled that of a farmer driving his stubborn mule to plow a field. The mule spinners wrestled with fifty-foot-long carriages weighing up to fourteen hundred pounds that were used to spin cotton into thread. The cumbersome machines then wound the thread onto spindles. The mule spinners guided their carriages to the assembly line and delivered the full spindles to the looms. The men walked up to twenty-five miles a day as they pushed the mules from section to section in the mill. They seemed essential, but they were not, especially when they demanded better pay or improved working conditions. "The mule spinners are a tough crowd to deal with," one of their bosses told a reporter in 1902. "A few years ago they were giving me trouble at this mill, so one Saturday afternoon, after they had gone home, we started right in and smashed up a roomful of mules with sledge hammers. When the men came back on Monday morning, they were astonished to find there was no work for them. That room is now full of ring frames run by girls." The women were paid considerably less than the mule spinners to tend simpler thread-spinning machines.

As workers approached middle age, they worried about the future. There was no Social Security, no unemployment benefits, no medical insurance. Only town welfare agencies and church-sponsored charities provided the barest essentials of food, clothing, and shelter to the destitute. And there was the poorhouse. As workers got older, the machines ran faster, and there was a constant struggle to keep up with the accelerated pace or to be fired. Workers shared a rhyme that gave a mocking voice to the relentless machines:

> *Clickity-click, clickity clack,*
> *You've got to stick till I break your back.*
> *Clickity-click, clickity clack,*
> *The longer you stick, the worse your back.*

"They are always on the jump," said ex-mill worker Harriet Robinson after meeting with two hundred Lowell women workers in 1881. "They have no time to improve themselves, nor to spend in helping others. The souls of these mill girls seemed starved, and looked from their hungry eyes, as if searching for mental food."

In Washington, the Senate held hearings on the relations between labor and capital and heard testimony from Dr. Timothy D. Stow whose patients in Fall River were mostly immigrant mill workers. He described them as physically deformed. "They are dwarfed, in my estimation," Stow testified, "as the majority of men and women who are brought up in factories must be dwarfed under the present industrial system; because by their long hours of indoor labor and their hard work they are cut off from the benefit of breathing fresh air and from the sights that surround a workman outside the mill." Stow told the senators that the workers were ill-nourished, and "being shut up all day long in the noise and in the high temperature of these mills they become physically weak."

Reporter Ray Stannard Baker made a similar observation in Lawrence in 1912: "I asked the ages of many young people I met, and they looked (and they were) stunted, not fully developed." A Lithuanian priest worried about the decline in immigrants' health as newer generations of them were brought up in the mill cities. He told an interviewer that while the first immigrants from Europe were sturdy and capable of hard work, their children were not as strong. "And their children's children are even worse, puny little things," the priest said. "I'm afraid this condition is due to uncertain working conditions, to bad living. And I don't believe America can afford to allow each generation of immigrants to get poorer and poorer."

William Lawrence was dismayed by the way mill owners treated workers in the city named for his family. Recalling his days as a priest in Lawrence in the 1870s, he wrote: "Thousands of men and some women wasted a large fraction of their wages in drink, and hundreds if not thousands were 'beery' a good deal of the time. The waste of child life, the privation of wives, and the personal degradation were unspeakable."

Father Lawrence saw hundreds of children working in the mills, growing up in ignorance and living in filthy tenements. He used his family connections in an effort to improve conditions but got nowhere. "My uncle was treasurer of the Pacific Mills, a man of large experience," Lawrence recalled. "I was inexperienced and only twenty-seven years old when I had the temerity to write him that, if he continued to handle the help of the mill as he did then, there would be a bad strike within a few months, that I knew the help and their temper. Nothing was done; the strike came, engendering bad blood, sending many of the best workmen and women out of the city and laying the foundation for a mutual distrust which hampered work for many years."

All through the decline in working conditions, the only major invest ments mill owners were willing to make was in automation of the ma chinery so that the number of skilled workers could be reduced or eliminated. "Indeed, there could scarcely be said to have been a labor policy," George Gibb wrote, "for labor was considered along with tools and metal as a factor of production, to be purchased for as low a price as possible in as small amounts as possible when required to fill orders on the books."

Philip Hubert, an admirer of the industry, summed up management's philosophy: "From an economic, or rather an industrial point of view . . . manufacturing has to be carried on at present with the greatest subdi vision of labor possible. Fierce competition and a small margin of profit demand it." Hubert believed that pursuing profits justified the subdivid ing of labor to the point of making the worker "only a part of the machine and needing to be little more intelligent than one of its wheels." There was little incentive for a worker to take pride in his or her contribution to the manufacturing process.

At the turn of the century, Frederick Taylor offered factory owners what he promised would be the key to an industrial paradise. "Taylor ism," the time-motion studies of factory workers, became the rage among production supervisors. The goal was to determine the most efficient ways workers could perform manufacturing tasks in the least time. Taylor preached that time-motion studies make "each workman's interests the same as that of his employer, pays a premium for high efficiency, and soon convinces each man that it is for his permanent advantage to turn out each day the best quality and maximum quantity of work." Suddenly women who were earning ten cents an hour had time-motion men at their sides, calculating how management could squeeze more work out of them in less time, watching their every move and driving them to distraction as they turned out textiles at obsolete machines in decrepit surroundings. Steve Dunwell wrote that the workers "despised the time study men, with their clipboards, stopwatches, and lab coats, for Taylorism only made their difficult situation worse, adding further dehumanization to their exhaustion." Dunwell also argued that Taylor "laid the groundwork for speedups and stretchouts" to get more and more production out of the workers. "His analysis of industrial work assumed an ignorant, irresponsible laborer," Dunwell wrote. "Increased output had to be sought by means of rigid compartmentalization of jobs and strict behavioral control."

For both men and women, the kind of workplace where they spent their lives was simply fortuitous. In some mills they answered to bullies; other mills had enlightened managers. Workers at the Saco-Lowell textile-machine shops in Maine were fated to work for James McMullan, a Republican who, like Kirk Boott in the early days of Lowell, was intolerant of anyone with differing political views. "So profound was this feeling," George Gibb wrote of McMullan's reign, "that few men in the shop dared admit themselves to be Democrats, and those who were known to have Democratic leanings found little favor if already employed—little chance for employment if a Republican could be found instead."

When agent Franklin Nourse of the York Mill in Saco was transferred to another city, the Maine workers were sorry to see him go, according to historian Roy P. Fairfield. "His leaving marked the end of an era of essentially friendly relationships between employer and employees," Fairfield wrote. "York workers held him in high regard . . . he was an arduous community worker, and he did nothing to lessen the hope that each year would be better than the last."

Unfortunately for the York workers, the mill directors in Boston replaced Nourse with Elmer Page, who ruled by intimidation when profits were down. Page introduced labor-saving machinery that displaced some workers. He cut everyone else's pay. When workers struck, merchants in town, who in previous years sided with the company during labor troubles, supported the strikers. The businessmen extended credit to them and contributed to their relief fund. Apparently fearful of labor violence, Page strung barbed wire on top of the mill fence, which the workers called the "state prison fence." He prohibited lunch breaks in the mills and fired employees who agitated for better conditions. Workers hissed invectives at Page as he walked the aisles of the mill, and people taunted him on the streets.

The Biddeford-Saco community boiled with prejudice and anger when Page imported fifty lower-paid Armenian and Syrian workers. The *Biddeford Record* attacked the new arrivals. "They work for any wage, live like animals, and are a setback to civilization," the newspaper said. "Their advent not only means the displacement of other operatives to a large extent but it also means a distinct loss to the business community." In one of the few concessions he made as the mill agent, Page submitted to community pressure and got rid of the immigrant workers.

In Manchester, three generations of the Straw family were popular agents for the Amoskeag Mills, and workers shared legends and stories about all of them. During the 1860 presidential campaign, Ezikiel Straw gave Abraham Lincoln a tour of the mill and introduced the candidate to the workers. One of them hesitated to shake hands, explaining that he was grubby from his labors. "Young man," Lincoln said, "the hand of honest toil is never too grimy for Abe Lincoln to grasp."

Ezikiel Straw went on to be the governor of New Hampshire. His son, Herman, became the Amoskeag agent and also was respected by the workers. Tamara K. Hareven tells of a former Amoskeag worker who came back to the mill office with a twenty-year-old pay slip and asked for the wages that were due her. Astonished clerks brought the matter to Straw. The woman explained to him that she had been in Nashua all those years and never had a chance to return to Manchester to pick up her money. Herman Straw told the clerks to give her the back pay with twenty years' interest.

William Parker Straw succeeded his father as the agent. William Straw was a demanding boss but was fair to the workers. During a strike at Amoskeag, his young daughter died; the workers suspended picketing for a day and sent the family a funeral wreath. Straw supported his workers, too. When the Boston office ordered him to fire all supervisors over age sixty, he refused, and then resigned. When the Amoskeag Mills closed years later, he used his role as a Manchester bank president to lead community efforts to bring new industries into the empty mills.

Roy Fairfield wrote that when women workers liked their department overseers, they often presented them with canes or watches when they retired. At Christmas, workers in many mills chipped in to buy their boss a present. Agents sometimes closed the mill for the day when the circus came to town; others gave workers the day off so they could attend out-of-town union meetings. Eventually, some mills offered profit-sharing and health-care plans to the workers.

For more than a century Thomas Goodall and succeeding generations of his family provided mill jobs to people in Sanford, Maine. Goodall, a native of England, arrived in the little farm town in 1867 and at the age of forty-four started manufacturing wool blankets there. It is said that in the cold winter months he drove his horse-drawn sleigh through the area and delivered blankets to the needy.

Five thousand people worked for the Goodall Mills, many of them for forty and fifty years, and many of their children worked there, too. There were few labor problems. The company built houses and sold them to the workers at cost. Members of the Goodall family helped build the Sanford town library, the town hall, the hospital, the ballpark, the airport, and a golf club. The company financed college scholarships for public and parochial high school students. Goodall executives organized company parties and opened the doors of their homes and summer cottages to their employees. Like many of the mills, Goodall sponsored such employee activities as sports teams, bands, and social clubs. In many New England communities, statues in the town square commemorate heroes of the American Revolution and the Civil War. In Sanford, Thomas Goodall's statue in Central Square looks out at the town he built. The slovenly, uncaring workers Jennie Collins saw were the exception in mills run by intelligent leaders like Goodall, Franklin Nourse, and the Straw family.

Eva Shorey was among those who looked out for the interests of less-fortunate women workers in the mills. Shorey was born to a newspaper family in Bridgton, Maine. She was a Republican and an activist in the woman suffrage movement. For seven years she was secretary for the governor of Maine, but in 1907 she began touring the textile mills for the State Labor Bureau. She regularly reported to the bureau and to the state legislature on what she saw in the mills.

The legislators, mostly farmers and small businessmen, gained much of their knowledge of big industry and the fate of industrial workers through Shorey's insights. She did not resort to overstatement in her reports; her descriptive powers were enough to make her argument, and very gradually her words brought about laws to improve factory conditions. She wrote of her visit to a mill where women dye workers were spinning red yarn for damask tablecloths: "Some wear caps, as the particles of red lint are constantly in the air. The operatives here stand all day. Some cannot do this work because the dye poisons them. It stains the hands, and on account of the heat and consequent perspiration, one unconsciously rubs the face with the hands." She met one woman who had been doing this work for twenty years, since the age of thirteen. The woman, with grim humor, told Shorey, "It makes us red-headed."

Shorey wrote about a woman who had worked in another mill for forty-three years. At the age of sixty-one, and slightly deaf, she was still working in the weave room. She tended four looms instead of the two that had been assigned to her in previous years, but she had received virtually no increase in pay. Shorey visited the home of the woman's friend who was unable to work any longer. "Her health broke down," Shorey reported, "and after varied experiences she is now living in two scantily furnished rooms, her hands so twisted out of shape by rheumatism that she is able to care for herself but partially and depends largely on the assistance of her neighbors." These two women, Shorey wrote, "represent the varied phases of light and shadow one finds among so large a number of women mill employees."

The condition of textile workers seemed insignificant at a time when inventive and industrial giants dominated the American stage. They gave the people the telephone, electric light, recorded sound, moving pictures, radios, cameras, cars, and flight. Rockefeller refined oil, Carnegie forged steel, and railroad barons connected the country. The titans of American industry created new jobs for millions and, for themselves, untold wealth. Mark Twain called these years the Gilded Age.

It was also the age of strikes by workers who, as Jennie Collins had observed, "saw plenty and had nothing." Labor violence escalated beyond anything the American public had seen, and there was fear of anarchy.

The terrorist Molly Maguires waged war against management on behalf of anthracite coal miners in eastern Pennsylvania until twenty-four of them were indicted for murder. During an 1886 McCormick Harvester strike in Chicago, a dynamite explosion in Haymarket Square killed seven policemen. In the ensuing gunfire, police killed ten workers. Six years later, Carnegie Steel shut down a mill in Homestead, Pennsylvania, in a union-busting drive. There was violence again; a gun battle killed ten Pinkerton Detective Agency men and nine strikers. Two years after Homestead, American Railway Union members struck the Pullman Railroad Car Company to protest wage cuts and organized a national rail strike in support of their cause. Militia troops opened fire on crowds that tried to stop the trains from running, and twenty people were killed.

Out of all the blood and turbulence, the militant Industrial Workers of the World appeared on the labor front and struck fear in the hearts of industrialists and many other Americans. The IWW declared that "there can be no peace as long as hunger and want are found among millions of working people and the few, who make up the employing class, have all the good things in life."

The National Association of Manufacturers, two thousand members strong, met in New Orleans to consider the growing militancy of unions. NAM President David Parry told the delegates, "Organized labor knows but one law and that is the law of physical force—the law of the Huns and Vandals, the law of the savage." He charged that union attempts to shorten work hours and to achieve uniform pay scales in various industries were "cardinal sins of socialism."

While the NAM considered the IWW and Socialists in general an ominous presence, Big Business opposed government action that would provide some measure of protection for exploited workers. In 1891, Pope Leo XIII issued an encyclical in which he urged capitalists to pay just wages. He also defended the role of trade unions. In his 1906 book *A Living Wage*, John A. Ryan cited the encyclical to argue that the government had a responsibility to assure the welfare of working people. Ryan, an American Catholic priest, was in the forefront of those calling for a minimum wage, an eight-hour workday, protection of peaceful picketing and boycotting, and unemployment insurance. "Some of the opponents of state intervention in industry," Ryan wrote, "may be conveniently classed with the juvenile bully who resents the 'interference' of parent or teacher in his relations with young and weaker boys, and with the burglar or highwayman who objects to the activity of the policeman. These are the possessors of superior bargaining power who realize that if government will only let them alone they will be able successfully to exploit their weaker fellows."

The Methodist Episcopal church also endorsed labor reform with a statement in 1908 calling in part:

For the protection of the worker from dangerous machinery, occupational disease, injuries, and mortality.

For the abolition of child labor.

For such regulation of the conditions of labor for women as shall safeguard the physical and moral health of the community.

For the gradual and reasonable reduction of the hours of labor to the lowest practical point, with work for all; and for that degree of leisure for all which is the condition of the highest human life.

For a release from employment for one day in seven.

For a living wage in every industry.

Few manufacturers responded to the call. Three years after the church's declaration of workers' rights, 146 factory workers, most of them immigrant women, died in the Triangle Shirtwaist fire in New York City. An investigation concluded that the fire and the deaths resulted from criminal negligence. The workers could not flee down the stairways because the factory doors were locked, and there was only one fire escape for the hundreds of people inside.

In New England, a Connecticut mill owner made a notable effort to end the alienation between management and labor. Sidney Blumenthal, owner of Shelton Looms in the Housatonic Valley, was the son of a German immigrant who manufactured silk ribbons. Blumenthal enlarged his father's business, and his Shelton workers created velvets and plushes that decorated ballrooms and hotels. Wealthy young women wore sheer negligees, tea gowns, and kimonos that bore the Shelton Looms label.

Blumenthal did not hesitate to cut his workers' pay when business slowed, and he was unyielding during labor strikes. But in 1915, at the age of fifty-two, he embraced the concept of industrial democracy and gave his workers a voice in running the mill. It was a concept unheard of in most of the country's workplaces.

Shelton Looms had a Cabinet whose members came from senior management, a Senate of department heads and foremen, and a House of Representatives elected by the workers. The House and Senate met weekly on company time to discuss how to make better products and how to improve working conditions. In a small corner of the troubled New England textile industry, Shelton Looms maintained a civilized relationship with its workers while its looms produced profits. The company's future in the region seemed secure.

Few textile workers in New England had bosses like Sidney Blumenthal. In their greatest confrontation with the mill owners—the 1912 Lawrence strike—they turned for help to the IWW. Elizabeth Gurley Flynn, the IWW's star strike organizer, went to Lawrence with a philosophy she carried to every labor crisis in which she was involved: "Nothing was handed on a silver platter to the American working class by employers. All their hard-won gains came through their own efforts and solidarity."

Fifty years after witnessing worker exploitation in his family's mills, Episcopal Bishop William Lawrence still held to the view that the New England textile industry had been blind to its obligations to the mill workers. Although he believed in the capitalist system that brought such great wealth to his family, he wrote that "a finer spirit, a better understanding of the mind of the worker, a [more just] administration and increasing recognition and representation of the workers must come steadily on, or the system will be smashed." It was in the city named for his family that the system came close to being smashed.

7

Fighting for Roses

Thursday, January 11, 1912, was payday at the mammoth Everett Mill in Lawrence, Massachusetts. Weary Polish women stopped weaving ginghams and denims long enough to open their pay envelopes. They counted their money. In unison they turned back to their looms, shut them down, and walked away. "Not enough money," the weavers told the bosses who confronted them. Other women shouted through the workrooms: "Short pay! Short pay! All out!" The women had heard that a pay cut was coming. The news was calamitous to workers who were falling behind as the cost of living was rising and as rents for their slum tenements were going up. Every penny counted. Now the pay cut was in effect, but the women refused to tolerate it. They strode down the aisles of the Everett Mill and out of the doors into bone-chilling winter air. They left behind almost two thousand idle looms. The great Lawrence strike had begun.

More than any other labor battle in the history of the New England textile industry, the Lawrence strike united women workers who vowed that this time their efforts to win fair pay and decent working conditions would not end in futility. This time they would defeat management efforts to create division among the many ethnic groups the workers represented.

This time they would not rely on the American Federation of Labor or its affiliate, the United Textile Workers, because neither had helped them in previous labor battles. The Lawrence workers, aided by the organizing skills of the radical Industrial Workers of the World, conducted the strike themselves. For eight weeks their grievances held the attention of the country. Women immigrants, who did the most demeaning work in the mills and who were scoffed at as "oxen without horns," stepped forward to display leadership talents they never knew they had. They guided and inspired twenty-five thousand of their coworkers, men and women, in the biggest textile strike that had ever been staged in America. They took on powerful mill owners and confronted government forces determined to crush them. Bodies were bruised, blood was spilled, and lives were lost. But this time they won.

Before strike organizers were in place, long-repressed worker anger exploded into uncontrolled rage. The day after the Polish women marched out of the Everett Mill, all the other mills in the city were struck. Strikers reentered the Everett Mill to get all the nonstrikers out of the building. Labor editor Justus Ebert was at the mill as strikers "swept through its long floors, wildly excited, carrying an American flag which they waved amid shouts of 'Strike! Strike! All out!' From room to room they rushed, an enraged indignant mass." Arming themselves with clubs and whatever other crude weapons they could get their hands on, they went from loom to loom, drove away operatives, stopped looms, tore finished cloth, and smashed machines when nonstrikers tried to operate them. "As they swept on, their numbers grew," Ebert wrote, "and with them grew the contagion, the uproar and the tumult."

At the Wood Mill, men abandoned their workstations and sabotaged machinery. The strikers ran through the building wielding guns, knives, and clubs. They ordered other workers to quit and threatened those who hesitated. They pulled women away from their work; several of the women fainted.

Frank Sherman, an executive at the Wood Mill, recalled: "I heard the most ungodly yelling and howling and blowing of horns I ever heard, and the paymaster came rushing into my department and says 'For God's sake, Mr. Sherman, they have broken in the doors...and are loose in the entire mill.' They had him scared white." Sherman telephoned the police.

Earlier on the same morning, C. F. Lynch, the public safety commissioner, was called out of a meeting at City Hall for an urgent telephone message. He was told there was trouble at the Washington Mill and that police were needed. Lynch dispatched patrolmen to the scene and returned to the meeting. He was interrupted again with Sherman's call from the Wood Mill. Another mill manager phoned in the plea: "For God's sake, ring in the riot call."

Mayor Michael Scanlon ordered the riot alarm rung in the City Hall belfry. More police squadrons rushed to the mill district, but the mills stretched for a mile along the Merrimack River, and there were not enough police to control rebellious workers at so many separate locations.

At the Washington Mill, strikers rushed the police who then clubbed them into submission. "The initial violence, the threats of blowing up the mill . . . ," wrote Donald B. Cole, "formed a picture the strike observers could not forget." Terrified city officials closed all the saloons. Mill managers rented every privately owned gathering place in Lawrence, even snow-covered ball fields, to further limit the locations where strikers could demonstrate. But no one could stop them from using their social halls.

The strikers acted at a time when the mill owners were powerful enough and determined' enough to smother labor rebellion. Every Lawrence striker worried about keeping enough food and coal in the house during a long, freezing winter. Every one of them was aware that just eight years before, managers of the eighty-five textile mills in Fall River had dealt with demands for better pay by locking the factory gates for six months, leaving thirty thousand people out of work. The Fall River workers had gained nothing; many of them who left town during the strike to find temporary jobs never returned. Still, the Lawrence workers were willing to gamble that they could defeat mill owners who had rarely experienced defeat at the hands of their workers, especially immigrant workers.

A week before the strike began, Governor Eugene Foss had called for industrial peace in Massachusetts. Foss owned textile mills (none of them in Lawrence) and worried about growing strife in the factories of the state. In his inaugural address, he declared that "willing and well-paid workmen are as necessary to capital as capitalists to labor, and the highest business intelligence now recognizes that the common interests of capital and labor far outweigh their differences." Few people involved in the Lawrence strike paid attention to the governor's message.

In 1912 there was still some evidence of the careful urban planning carried out by the founders of Lawrence. Strikers paraded on broad streets past sturdy elms planted almost a century earlier and past churches and schools built by the mill owners. They passed the Common, a fifteen-acre park in the center of the city, donated by the Lawrence family. They congregated on Appleton Way and Jackson Street, named in honor of the early New England mill barons. They passed by the city library that was filled with books donated by Abbott Lawrence.

The city planners were determined that slums would not disfigure their community. In that spirit, mill executives established a home ownership program for skilled male workers and their families. Lawrence became "the city of homes."

When immigrants from Europe came to work in the Lawrence mills, Robert H. Tewksbury, treasurer of the Essex Company mills, declared: "Sociologists view with great interest the experiment of bringing together here, in one industrial community, representatives of every civilized race and are surprised to find all dwelling in amity, controlled only by prompting patriotism, all alike seeking the rewards of toil. Such an exhibition of the brotherhood of man they see in Lawrence."

Tewksbury's upbeat observation was made in 1905 during a great tide of immigration. By then, however, immigrant families were packed into hundreds of multistory tenement buildings. A citizens' committee, formed to defend the city's name when the 1912 strike began, declared: "There is no brighter looking, more up-to-date industrial city in the country than Lawrence with its 85,000 people. In the last ten-year period it made a thirty-seven percent gain in population." The citizens' group expressed reservations, too. Perhaps, it said, the growth had been too rapid, and perhaps too many unskilled laborers had crowded into the city looking for jobs.

Thirteen thousand people in Lawrence worked for the American Woolen Company, at the time the world's largest manufacturer of worsted and woolen fabrics. The Lawrence workers and their families depended on wages earned at American Woolen for their survival.

The company was founded by William M. Wood, who ruled his realm with a brilliant mind and an iron fist. Strengthened by protective tariffs that fended off foreign competition, the company dominated the domestic wool market. Workers turned out millions of yards of blue serge for Hart Schaffner & Marx, J. C. Penney, and other commercial customers, and millions more yards of fabric for military uniforms. In the decades before the 1912 strike, Wood had shared his prosperity with the workers by granting a series of pay raises. American Woolen operated dozens of mills in the eastern United States, including several in Lawrence: the Ayer Mill, with its giant tower clock giving the time of day to the whole city, the Washington, the Prospect, and the biggest of them all, the Wood Mill.

The Wood Mill was built in 1906, and the absence of strong unions in Lawrence was one reason William Wood decided to go ahead with such a large project. Each of the two wings of the main building stretched a half mile along the Merrimack River and its canals. Seven thousand people worked on thirty acres of floor space that, in contrast to most mills, were well lighted and well ventilated. The mill had modern bath facilities, a cafeteria, a reading room, and a large hall where children of the workers could spend recreation time. The textile industry's first escalators carried the workers between floors. Every week, the mill consumed the wool shorn from one hundred thousand sheep raised on New England farms. The 1,470 thunderous looms and 230,000 humming spindles reaped rich returns for the stockholders. When the strike began, American Woolen was paying annual dividends of 12 percent. Some investors in the Lawrence mills who paid seventy-five dollars a share saw their stock increase in value to thirty-eight hundred dollars a share in just a few years.

In the city of Lawrence, William Wood governed the lives and fortunes of almost everyone. City Hall listened when he spoke, and so did all those who held power in the community. He was influential in the Massachusetts legislature, which wrote the laws regulating factory work and safety conditions. In Washington, Congress usually complied when he asked for higher tariffs on imported textiles. His admirers called him generous. A magazine described him this way: "He had a round face and sleek hair, was short, fat, brusque to impoliteness, wore spats and fancy clothes, surrounded himself with yes-men, and therefore had few intimates." And, the article added, he had a terrible temper.

Although William Madison Wood's name suggested Yankee blue-blood stock, he was the son of a Portuguese-born sailor who had anglicized the family name when he settled on Martha's Vineyard off the coast of Massachusetts. "Billy" Wood, a high-school dropout, began his career as an office boy in the Wamsutta cotton mills of New Bedford. At the age of twenty-eight he went to Lawrence to work at the Washington Mill. The owner was Frederick Ayer, whose family had made a fortune in such patent medicines as sarsaparilla and hair restorers. (The mill women of earlier decades had sought relief from their ailments with Ayer's Pills.) Wood became a star salesman for the Washington Mill, and he was soon earning twenty-five thousand dollars a year, a munificent salary in the 1880s. He married Ayer's daughter, moved into management, and consolidated numerous mills into the American Woolen Company. He had earned his place as a leader of the New England textile industry, and like the real blue bloods—the Lowells, Appletons, and Lawrences—he built a mansion in Boston. When he visited his Lawrence mills, he resided on an eighty-acre estate in nearby Andover called "Arden." He once confided that he owned so many cars that he had lost count of them. During the strike he was taunted with a slogan calling for fewer cars "for the mill owners and more pork chops for the workers."

At the time of the strike, more than four hundred thousand people worked in New England's textile mills. Business was booming, and American Woolen, along with its competitors, had a voracious appetite for workers. Company agents toured the peasant regions of Europe to recruit more people. John Buckley, who grew up in Lawrence and became mayor of the city, remembered that the mill agents told the people in Europe that "the streets in Lawrence were lined with gold, with plenty of money for everybody, and they were completely disillusioned when they got here."

The immigrants saw plenty and had nothing. They soon became aware that there were people in Lawrence whose lives were very different from their own. Prosperous citizens drove by in Model T Fords that cost $850, almost three times the average mill worker's annual wages. The newspapers reported on people like Mary Collins, "who has been spending three weeks with a party of friends at St. Augustine, Ormond Beach and Palm Beach, Fla. [and] who has returned to her home on Winthrop Avenue." After the mills closed for the day, mill executives fled to the suburbs, and the inner city belonged to the workers.

The immigrants took their place in American life and saved some of their earnings to bring younger family members from Europe to Lawrence. They mailed money back home, along with Kodak snapshots of themselves dressed up in their new clothes. Sarah Lena Druckman sent her photo to relatives in eastern Europe and her mother wrote back, "You look like the queen of Rumania."

By 1912, Lawrence was home to dozens of ethnic groups who spoke more than fifty languages and dialects. In a city with a population of 85,000, there were 21,000 people of Irish heritage, 12,000 Franco-Americans, 9,000 English, 8,000 Italians, 6,000 Germans, 3,000 Lithuanians, 2,700 Syrians (mostly Maronite Catholics who were later known as Lebanese), 2,500 European Jews, 2,300 Scots, and smaller numbers of other nationalities. Only 3,000 people were native-born, including a small community of African Americans who had settled in Lawrence before the Civil War, and who, for the most part, did not work in the mills.

Many immigrants brought with them a traditional socialist view of capitalism and labor. Germans had established a Socialist party in the United States as early as 1874; others, including Franco-Belgian and English workers, wanted a strong union movement in Lawrence. They believed, as did the American Socialist Eugene Debs, that "industry, the basis of life, instead of being the private property of the few and operated for their enrichment, ought to be the common property of all, democratically administered in the interest of all." It was a poisonous philosophy to William Wood and his stockholders, to the people riding by in their Model T Fords, and to most Americans.

For those who could afford a few pennies and nickels, there were pleasant ways to spend leisure time in Lawrence and so forget about the mills and tenements. Trolleys took families to the Glen Forest recreation park in nearby Methuen for dancing, boating, bowling, and shows. There were canoe clubs and bicycle clubs and shooting clubs and glee clubs; there were bands and athletic teams sponsored by the mills. Summer excursion boats drifted along the Merrimack, the river that gave life to the city.

German immigrants relished their beer in Turn Hall. In Lyra Hall and Bavarian Hall they harmonized in Mozart and *Liederkrantz* singing societies. The Greeks chatted the hours away in their coffeehouses. The Poles built Paul Chabis Hall at Oak and Short streets, the Franco-Belgian Hall was on Mason Street, and the Portuguese Hall was on Common Street. The English cheered at matches promoted by the Lawrence Cricket Club. Irish Catholics competed in field games organized by the Gaelic Athletic Association. Irish Protestants from Ulster formed Orange societies to remember ancient victories in Ireland. Italians played boccie on courts they built with their own hands and socialized at the Christopher Columbus Benefit Society. When a prosperous neighbor bought a new Victrola, they listened with pride as the arias of Enrico Caruso reverberated through the streets. The Scots reveled at Clan MacPherson picnics, and at their Caledonian Club banquets they lifted a cup of kindness in memory of Robert Burns. There was always music and dancing in the halls of the St. Michael Polish Society, the Sons of Israel Synagogue, the Sons of Lithuania Club, and at numerous other social centers.

The ethnic social halls gave newly arrived immigrants the chance to connect with people from their homeland. Those who could not find solace in these activities and who wanted to blot out their misery, turned to alcohol. There were two hundred saloons, "rum holes," and "kitchen bars" in the city. There was a lot of misery to forget—frequent cases of infanticide, illegal abortions, illegitimate births, child neglect, and prostitution.

At the time of the strike, a housing survey found that in several neighborhoods, six hundred people were living in tenements covering just one acre, about the area of a city block today. "Huddling people together is a disease," the survey report said, with owners of the tenements generating "profits that are a poison, intoxicating the whole community." The long rows of tenement buildings were so close to each other that slumlords who climbed stairs all day to collect rent saved their energy in upper-story dwellings by reaching out alley windows for the neighbor's rent.

"America, everywhere people not healthy," a Lawrence woman said. "No milk, bad water, and so much sadness." A Socialist newspaper, the *New York Call*, described Lawrence as "an industrial blot on the map, a pestiferous industrial city, a place where human beings are ... starved to produce vast wealth for the mill owners, a city of hunger and destitution, of child labor, of women labor ..." William Wood's biographer surmised that the vile smells of the tenements had never reached his Andover estate. He wrote, "It is doubtful that Wood had ever driven, let alone walked, along the pitiful streets and alleys that were home to most of his employees."

In their own neighborhoods, the ethnic groups worked together to deal with problems generated by industrial life. The women, wrote Ardis Cameron, helped each other in such crises as childbirth, illness, domestic violence, and desertion. They repelled attempts of gouging landlords to raise rents without improving conditions in the tenements. They brought with them from Europe a distrust of authority and stood together to confront any police officer who entered their ghettos to arrest one of their own. "On street corners and stoops, in kitchens and markets, at bath houses and public laundries, on walks to and from factories, laboring women shared experiences, offered aid, nursed kin and neighbors, made friends and build alliances," Cameron wrote. "Out of such daily exchange, concrete personal networks emerged, entwining the skilled and unskilled, the homemaker and widow, the midwife and the grocer's wife, the peddler and the consumer, young and old."

Many parents sent their children away from the disease and filth of the slums to earn their board and room with families in outlying towns and brought the youngsters home on weekends. The parents struggled to save enough money to buy a place of their own in the Lawrence suburbs. Most of all, ambitious parents dreamed of having better jobs and better lives. They saved for the day when they could study in commercial colleges and qualify for office jobs. Others hoped to open their own grocery or barbershop or beauty parlor and be free of the mill forever. One of those who won her freedom was Jennie Resnick, the daughter of Jewish immigrants. She went into the mill at the age of twelve to help her family but could not abide the work. She was pretty, intelligent, and vivacious. She married a young businessman named Sam Bernstein, and they moved to suburban Boston. She returned to her mother's house in Lawrence only long enough to give birth to a son, the future composer and conductor Leonard Bernstein. Jennie left behind friends at the looms who could not find their way out of the mills.

For the families of mill workers, saving money was difficult. The average weekly pay was nine dollars. Skilled workers earned eleven dollars a week or more while unskilled mill laborers, who made up most of the workforce, were paid as little as seven dollars. For the working class, the weekly rent averaged three dollars. Twenty pounds of coal cost ten cents. Coffee was thirty cents a pound, bread was three cents a loaf, milk was eight cents a quart, and stew beef was ten to fourteen cents a pound. A pair of shoes cost three dollars; a skirt, five dollars; a cotton dress, three dollars. Several ethnic groups operated cooperative stores that kept prices down, but most families were barely surviving. For the poorest families, a common meal was bread, molasses, and water.

The wage reduction that prompted the 1912 strike came after the Massachusetts legislature mandated that the maximum workweek for women and minors under sixteen years old be lowered from fifty-six to fifty-four hours. Unilaterally, the textile mills then extended the reduced hours to the male workers because without women on duty at the machines, the mills could not fully function. The owners cut everyone's pay by $3\frac{1}{2}$ percent because of the two lost hours of production. Management circulated statements explaining all this to the workers, but communicating with people who spoke so many languages and dialects was difficult. As the *Washington Post* reported, the initial cause of trouble was the "lack of knowledge of the language of America." What the workers did understand was that the pay cut for most families amounted to the price of ten loaves of bread. These people were, as the Poles called themselves, *ze chlebem*, the "for bread" immigrants, and the mills were taking their bread away.

For the workers, mill wages "meant the lowest possible standards of living," reported Ray Stannard Baker, one of several prominent journalists who covered the Lawrence strike. Baker was a member of the muckraking school of writers and, like Lincoln Steffens and Ida Tarbell, he focused on the ills of American society. He had seen the repression of coal miners in Pennsylvania, employer abuses in the New York garment trade, and racial violence. By the time of the Lawrence strike, Baker was called "America's Number One Reporter." With all his experience, though, what he saw on the wintry streets of the mill city stunned him: "Men with large families had to compete with adventurous single men and unmarried girls. No man can support a family on $300 or $400 a year even though he lives in the meanest way. The result was that the wife had to go into the mills, followed by one child after another, as fast as they arrived at the legal age." Baker saw lost chances for dignified lives. Reporting for *American* magazine, he wrote that mill work in Lawrence "meant living in dark tenements; it meant taking in lodgers to the point of indecent crowding." He believed that the Lawrence mill owners were sensitive to the responsibilities of great wealth but unconcerned about the ethics applied while acquiring wealth. They contributed to good causes, "but about conditions in the dark alleys of Lawrence, where their own money comes from, they know very little, nor do they want to know."

Victor Berger, a Socialist congressman from Wisconsin, said if he had to live the way the Lawrence workers did, "I'd be a dangerous man." He persuaded the House of Representatives to hold hearings on the Lawrence strike and its causes. He told Congress that workers "of any nationality will endure a certain degree of slavery, but no more. The limit of endurance seems to have been reached in Lawrence."

The star witness at the hearings was Camella Teoli, a thirteen-year-old worker at the American Woolen Company's Washington Mill. She was among several children who explained to members of the House committee why the strike occurred:

THE CHAIRMAN: Are you one of the strikers?

MISS TEOLI: *Yes, sir.*

THE CHAIRMAN: Why did you do that?

MISS TEOLI: *Because I didn't get enough to eat at home.*

Among those listening to the testimony was Helen Taft, wife of President William Howard Taft. For her and others in the hearing room, the little girl sitting in the witness chair was a symbol of injustice in industrial America. Camella Teoli's voice was small, but in the grand marble congressional chamber she spoke with crystal clarity about factory injuries and about the exploitation of child laborers in the dingy mills of Lawrence:

THE CHAIRMAN: Now, did you ever get hurt in the mill?

MISS TEOLI: *Yes.*

THE CHAIRMAN: Can you tell the committee about that—how it happened and what it was?

MISS TEOLI: *Yes.*

THE CHAIRMAN: Tell us about it now, in your own way.

MISS TEOLI: *Well, I used to go to school, and then a man came up to my house and asked my father why I didn't go to work, so my father says I don't know whether she is 13 or 14 years old. So, the man say you give me $4 and I will make the papers come from the old country saying you are 14. I went to work, and in about two weeks got hurt in my head.*

THE CHAIRMAN: Well, how were you hurt?

MISS TEOLI: *The machine pulled the scalp off.*

THE CHAIRMAN: The machine pulled your scalp off?

MISS TEOLI: *Yes, sir.*

As Camella Teoli writhed in agony on the mill floor, friends working with her had the presence of mind to place the bloody pulp in a paper bag. They carried her to the mill infirmary where doctors managed to restore only part of the scalp. She told the committee she spent seven months in the hospital. She said the company paid her medical bills but suspended her salary until she returned to her mill job. After her testimony, Mrs. Taft and the president invited her and other Lawrence child workers to lunch at the White House. The Tafts contributed one thousand dollars to the Lawrence strike relief fund.

Many other children worked in the Lawrence mills. In 1911, the year before Camella Teoli's testimony, four hundred children had quit grammar school, and 70 percent of them entered the mills. Only the robust lasted. Elizabeth Shapleigh, a physician in the city, made a mortality study among mill workers and found that one-third of them, victims of the lint-filled air of the mills, died before reaching the age of twenty-five. "Every fourth person in line is dying from tuberculosis," she said. "And further, every second person, that is, one alternating with a healthy person, will die of some form of respiratory trouble."

During the House hearings on the Lawrence strike, the detached demeanor of some witnesses puzzled committee members. Congressman Augustus O. Stanley questioned the Reverend Clark Carter, who operated an interdenominational city mission that the Lawrence mills helped support.

> MR. STANLEY: Well, do you think that it is a wholesome or healthy surrounding for a girl of 14 years of age to go to a mill before daylight and to leave it after dark, as they must do in the winter time for six days a week? Do you think that is wholesome or a healthful surrounding for a young girl just developing into womanhood?
>
> MR. CARTER: *There are moral considerations to be taken note of.*
>
> MR. STANLEY: I am not talking about the moral considerations; I am talking about her as a mere animal. Just from the standpoint of her physical condition, do you think that it is conducive to her physical health to be cooped up that way for that many days a week?
>
> MR. CARTER: *I know that it does not seem to hurt a great many people. It may be in some instances too severe on the individual.*
>
> MR. STANLEY: Don't you think it is too severe on the individual when she is 14 years of age?

MR. CARTER: *Not necessarily.*

MR. STANLEY: As a general thing?

MR. CARTER: *I have said all I can say on the subject.*

Congressman William Wilson didn't get anywhere with Carter, either:

MR. WILSON: Are you in sympathy with child labor?

MR. CARTER: *The work the children do in the mills is perfectly proper for children to do.*

Former President Theodore Roosevelt, trying in 1912 to win another term in the White House, ran on a Progressive party ticket that proclaimed the need to change much of American society. Like other reformers, he proposed the eight-hour day, the abolition of child labor, and a workman's compensation law. He lost the fight, and change would have to wait. Children twelve and thirteen years old toiled in the anthracite coal mines of the Shenandoah Valley and many were killed or injured in industrial accidents. Upton Sinclair's novel *The Jungle* described filthy working conditions in the meatpacking industry. New York newspapers reported on state labor board hearings concerning a laundry workers' strike in the city. Workers told of long hours and squalid conditions. Annabel Walker, fourteen years old, timidly approached the witness chair to tell the investigators that she worked fifty-eight hours a week for four dollars. Katherine Murphy, eighteen, said she quit her job because her boss would not let her go home after she fainted at work. Samuel Silverman said simply, "I am a slave."

The Lawrence workers understood that they, too, were falling behind. They knew that sixteen years earlier union printers in Lawrence had won the eight-hour day. They knew that women telephone operators were establishing their first union local in Boston and were achieving solidarity in bargaining for better work contracts. They knew that textile workers in the Amoskeag Mills of Manchester were benefiting from generous employer policies. The New Hampshire workers participated in a stock-ownership plan and a housing-purchase plan. The company provided visiting nurses for mill families and free dental care for their children. It sponsored classes in skill trades to help workers win promotions to better-paying jobs. The mill's chief executive, Frederic Dumaine, no doubt wanted to avoid the arrival of radical union organizers in his mills. Consequently he offered words the Lawrence workers never heard from their own bosses: "We cannot go on making money forever without regard to the welfare and proper development of the rising multitudes without bringing disaster down about our heads."

The men and women who worked for William Wood in 1912 were a multitude of dissatisfied and increasingly bitter employees. There was only one union in the mills, the United Textile Workers. Like most unions affiliated with the American Federation of Labor, the UTW was for skilled workers only. Some immigrant workers had earlier turned for help to the Industrial Workers of the World, and in 1905 the IWW began a membership drive in Lawrence. Like the defunct Knights of Labor, the IWW welcomed as members all mill hands, skilled and unskilled, and all ethnic groups. With the arrival of the IWW in Lawrence, Italians, English, Jews, Franco-Americans, and Franco-Belgians formed their own IWW chapters. By the time the strike began, Lawrence had about one thousand IWW members, representing only 2 percent of the workforce in the mills. They were the Wobblies, so called because a convention speaker with a speech defect uttered a word sounding like "wobbly" when he tried to pronounce the letter *W*. Detractors sneered that IWW stood for "I Won't Work."

When the strike began, the Italian chapter of the IWW asked the national office to send organizers. The Italian workers did so despite pressure from Italian community leaders who opposed the strike and abhorred the violence associated with the IWW in other strikes across the country. Ray Stannard Baker thought it ironic that the Italians made the decision that thrust management against labor in fierce turmoil. "Of all the mingled peoples of Lawrence," he wrote, "none are so humble as the Italians, none so eager for work at any price, and none so ill-paid." Walter E. Weyl of *The Outlook*, a magazine of progressive thought, considered the IWW "pregnant with danger" but wrote that in Lawrence, the workers who placed their trust in the Wobblies were "splendid, earnest, peace-loving men and women of all nationalities and beliefs, men and women with thwarted hopes and crippled aspirations, men and women who have been trodden by us, the cowardly good citizens of America, through our optimistic materialism, which is as ruthless and as blind as is the measureless, undisciplined idealism" of the radicals in the labor movement.

Joseph Ettor, an IWW organizer, went to Lawrence to help conduct the strike. Ettor was soon to be joined by the IWW leader, William (Big Bill) Haywood whose cause was One Big Union for all workers. Haywood's deputy, Elizabeth Gurley Flynn, also arrived in Lawrence. These were the dreaded syndicalists who imported from European labor centers the idea that workers' unions, not the owners, should control the factories, and that the way to success was direct action such as the strike. Syndicalism called the wage system unjust, believed that capitalism exploited the worker, condemned government as a tool of the capitalists, wanted the state to be abolished, and had no use for political means to achieve its goals. Now the most feared enemies of capitalism were in Lawrence at the side of the workers.

Ettor, a native of Brooklyn, was twenty-seven years old when he arrived in Lawrence. He showed a benign, smiling face to workers but used a caustic tongue in his dealings with capitalists. As he walked the city streets, he saw the mills that symbolized great wealth for their owners and chronic poverty for the people who worked in them. He had seen the same disparity between rich and poor during strikes in Pennsylvania steel towns and in New York shoe factories, and he told an interviewer, "No class of people ever gave up the chair of privilege until somebody tipped the chair over."

Ettor had been a worker in California shipyards when he joined the Socialist movement. Elizabeth Gurley Flynn remembered that he always wore a black shirt with a red tie. He lugged around a suitcase packed with IWW membership application forms. Speaking fluent English, Italian, and Polish, as well as passable Yiddish and Hungarian, he was able to address ethnic groups at their rallies and to devise strike strategy with their leaders.

He knew of the ethnic tensions in the mills and told the strikers: "Division is the surest means to lose the strike.... Among workers there is only one nationality, one race, one creed." His speeches in the social halls and on the streets mesmerized the strikers and all others who heard him. Julia Dublin Garbelnick was a child at the time of the strike, but when she reached old age she still remembered hearing Ettor speak and said, "I was spellbound."

Ettor had plenty of work ahead of him to make the strike effective. Four days after the violent beginning of the strike, the mills reopened under the protection of armed guards, and the owners announced that they would welcome anyone who wanted jobs. Some strikers, risking retribution from their coworkers and neighbors, went back to work. Some, particularly English-speaking workers, never supported the strike and stayed on the job. Many unemployed people, including recently laid off municipal workers, also crossed the picket lines. During the two months of the strike, the mills operated at about 50 percent capacity.

The strikers were further tormented by the knowledge that textile workers in nearby North Andover who were not part of the labor dispute were paid twice the wages earned in Lawrence. The North Andover workers, reported the *New York Times*, "are of a higher type, consisting for the most part of Scotch, Irish and English operatives." And so, while others worked and brought home their paychecks and put food on the table, the strikers, hungry and angry, stood on the frigid streets of Lawrence.

Ettor set up IWW headquarters in the Franco-Belgian Hall. He involved representatives of all ethnic groups in strike strategy. He taught strikers the tactics of direct action against management: parades to get the public's attention, picketing in large numbers, and verbal confrontations with scabs trying to enter the mills. Despite the physical attacks and vandalism that had already occurred, the official position of the IWW was against violence because it would distract the public from the strike issues. But there was plenty of talk about violence wherever the strikers gathered. "Anything short of murder and maiming is justifiable to keep a scab from working," one unidentified strike leader said. An Italian language circular suggested how to deal with scabs and other opponents of the strike: "Throw them down the stairs. Break their bones, and leave them a remembrance for life." Donald Cole wrote that the Franco

Belgians were "among the most violent, even to the point of suggesting that all scabs be thrown in the river." In public, Ettor told the strikers, "By all means make this strike as peaceful as possible." And he warned them, "In the last analysis, all the blood spilled will be your blood."

Ettor brought with him to Lawrence another labor organizer, Arturo Giovannitti, to supervise strike-relief operations. Giovannitti had been born near Campobasso, Italy, the son of a doctor. He arrived in the United States at the age of sixteen as an aspiring poet. He renounced his Roman Catholic faith, became secretary of the Italian Socialist Federation, then editor of its newspaper, *Il Proletario*. When he joined the strike, he was twenty-eight years old. People remembered him at strike meetings as trembling and pale and with a cultured manner. But when he took pen in hand, he hurled revolutionary rhetoric:

> *The Mob, the mightiest judge of all,*
> *To hear the rights of man come out,*
> *And every word become a shout,*
> *And every shout a musket ball.*

No public official in Lawrence and no mill manager could read Giovannitti's words without wondering what the outcome of the strike was to be and whether the city would ever be the same:

> *'Twill come, a dazzling shaft of light,*
> *Of truth to save and to redeem,*
> *And—whether Love or Dynamite—*
> *Shall blaze the pathway to your dream.*

Ettor presented the workers' demands: Even with the state-mandated workweek of fifty-four hours, the mills must grant a 15 percent pay increase with double time for overtime, they must pledge not to fire anyone for strike activity, and they must reform the premium system.

Of all the punishing policies inflicted on the textile workers, the premium system was the most hated. Premium pay was designed to reward efficient workers, but the system deteriorated into exploitation. Workers who operated on a piecework basis earned straight pay by producing a minimum quota of finished textiles each month. To earn extra, or premium pay, they produced a set amount of additional cloth in the same month.

They were forced to participate in the premium system whether they wanted to or not. If they did not meet the premium quota, they did not receive premium pay. Most frustrating of all, when they failed to reach the premium quota, they were not paid anything for the extra cloth they had produced, which sometimes represented 95 percent of the premium goal. One day's illness, or mechanical failures beyond their control that halted the looms, or unfair treatment by supervisors could jeopardize a whole month's struggle to reach the goal of premium pay. Alluding to the debilitating effects of menstruation at the time, Ray Stannard Baker wrote, "Many women, especially, who are likely to be ill a day or two a month complained bitterly that they had no fair chance." Instead of earning eleven or twelve dollars a week, the penalized workers took home only eight dollars or so.

All the extra cloth produced for no pay reaped golden profits for the mill owners. As for the workers, Baker wrote, they were trapped in "an exhausting, yes killing, struggle." The *Lawrence Tribune* reported that few were immune from tears "when difficult work was given to them when they were so near to winning a premium that they thought they would surely get." William Wood insisted on keeping the premium system.

When the IWW came to town, it found powerful enemies. Father James T. O'Reilly regarded the IWW leaders as threats to religion and to social order. O'Reilly, whose parishioners at St. Mary's Catholic Church were mostly Irish Americans, was an influential clergyman in a city that, because of immigration, had become overwhelmingly Catholic. He controlled ten other churches in Lawrence and adjacent Methuen. Most of them consisted of ethnic congregations he had helped to establish, including Sts. Peter and Paul for the Portuguese, St. Francis for the Lithuanians, and St. Anthony's for Maronite Catholic Syrians. He had been the pastor of St. Mary's for more than a quarter century when the strike began. He did not hesitate to use his power to endorse political candidates from the altar or to attack any action in Yankee New England that he perceived to be anti-Catholic or to speak out for an Ireland free of British rule.

In past labor troubles O'Reilly had been sympathetic to the workers' cause. He had told Wood and the other mill owners that if they could afford to pay 12 percent dividends to their stockholders, they could afford to pay fair wages to their workers. During a mill strike in 1894, he donated money to the workers to tide them over and to protest "the inhumanity of those who would rather lose one hundred thousand dollars in defeating you than allow it to you as fair compensation for your labor."

During the 1912 strike, O'Reilly again supported a wage increase for the strikers, but he also held that the IWW and what it stood for was a greater threat to order than the greed of the owners. These were, in his view, the Socialists, the anarchists, the godless, the enemies of the church, and he would have no part of any strike in which they participated.

Irish-American businessmen and professionals in the city shared O'Reilly's view, and so did most of the mill workers who belonged to St. Mary's parish. Many of them continued to work during the strike, and few of those who did stay out played significant roles in the walkout. Throughout the strike, pickets shouted the invective "Irish scabs" at O'Reilly's parishioners.

The Italians' pastor was Father Mariano Milanese, whose Holy Rosary Church on Union Street faced the gate of the Everett Mill. Milanese, an immigrant himself, helped many newly arrived Italians secure mill jobs; in return he often kept their first week's pay. Like O'Reilly, he was unnerved by the IWW, and by the anticlerical radicals who had joined it. He supported the workers but tried to minimize the role of the Wobblies by urging his striking parishioners to come to him for food and other necessities rather than resort to the union's relief programs. Ten days after the Polish women walked out of the Everett Mill, he read a letter to his congregation from Wood, who asked the strikers to return to work. Milanese read the letter as a courtesy to Wood, but the priest told his parishioners to stand firm in their strike demands. When strikers demonstrated on Union Street in front of the Everett Mill, they often turned to Holy Rosary to cheer Milanese.

Franco-American pastors, by contrast, spoke against the strike, as they had in many other labor battles over the years. As happened in those old troubles, some Franco-Americans left Lawrence to find mill jobs in other cities or returned to Quebec for the duration of the strike. Members of other congregations pressured their clergymen to support the strikers' cause.

During the first weekend of the strike, there was a snowstorm and the temperature dropped to ten below zero, but two thousand Polish workers struggled through the drifts to Paul Chabis Hall. Their leaders told them they faced hunger, police beatings, and jail if the strike continued. The workers reaffirmed their decision to stay out.

There were similar meetings and the same results at the Franco-Belgian Hall and the Portuguese Hall. For the first time since they had arrived in America, the immigrant laborers learned how to fight for themselves. They found translators to help ethnic groups work with each other as they coordinated relief programs for thousands of families. They organized workers to stand on the picket lines. They wrote appeals for public support. They used their economic power to intimidate their enemies or to win the help of people not directly involved in the strike. Russians pressured landlords not to rent to opponents of the strike, Polish bakers and Armenian merchants cut prices for the strikers, and Armenian boardinghouse owners provided free food to them. A Franco-American clothing store donated part of its receipts to their strike fund, and numerous other stores offered liberal credit to them. Neighborhood barbers refused to let scabs enter their shops. People all over the city wore badges with the legend, "Don't be a scab." Many also wore IWW badges and as a consequence were denied admission to movie theaters and were banned from city trolleys.

A *Lawrence Tribune* report of a typical strike day told readers the workers were unified:

The Germans reported they will meet Monday afternoon in Lyra Hall.

The Polish delegate reported that he has received a communication from [nearby] Amesbury stating that the workers there are desirous of forming a branch of the IWW and want three speakers from Lawrence.

The Greek delegate said that his people were out on the picket line Monday morning and stopped seven "scabs" from going to work.

The Jewish reported that they have arranged for a banquet for Haywood and the rest of the leaders.

Leadership talents blossomed among the women. Josephine Lis, a twenty-one-year-old mender in the mills, was quickly recognized by the others as a born leader. Lis, who was of Polish and Austrian heritage, spoke several languages. The city court routinely asked her to interpret at proceedings involving arrested strikers. She counseled the accused on their rights and arranged for their bail. She also ingratiated herself with court officials and then spied for the strike leaders, warning them of upcoming moves by police and prosecutors. She soon joined the IWW, and her tenement home became a center of militant strategy.

With all the unifying forces that existed, taking on the powerful mill bosses was still a new and daunting challenge for the women. Their only symbol of unity was the American flag, which they carried when they marched through the streets of Lawrence.

The IWW organizers introduced music to bridge the language barriers among the strikers. "Lawrence was a singing strike," reported Mary Heaton Vorse, another muckraking journalist who covered the strike. "The workers sang everywhere: at the picket line, at the soup kitchens, at the relief stations, at the strike rallies. Always there was singing." For Ray Stannard Baker, "it was the first strike I ever saw which sang! . . . there was in it a peculiar intense, vital spirit—a religious spirit, if you will— that I never felt before in any strike." Among the workers' songs was the *Internationale*, the anthem of European radicals:

> *Arise, ye prisoners of starvation!*
> *Arise, ye wretched of the earth,*
> *For justice thunders condemnation,*
> *A better world's in birth*

Reporter Al Priddy described a musical demonstration: "A wheezy Italian band furnished the music; a droning, blaring, strumming collection of trombones, guitars, pipes and drums. They played the *Internationale*, and the vibrant, laughing men and women sang it in a Pentecostal merging of languages and dialects."

James Oppenheim was a thirty-year-old poet at the time of the strike. His compassion for workers who struggled for justice was reflected in lines he wrote which became linked with the 1912 Lawrence strike. His poem, "Bread and Roses," was based on an old Italian labor phrase, *Pane e rosa*. Labor historians of later years referred to the Lawrence rebellion as the "Bread and Roses" strike, a time when women sought to persuade America that their strike was not just about fair wages, but about social justice as well:

> *As we come marching, marching, we bring the greater days*
> *The rising of the women means the rising of the race.*
> *No more the drudge and idler—ten that toil where one reposes,*
> *But sharing of life's glories: Bread and roses! Bread and roses!*

Police, under orders from flustered city officials, kept the women moving along sidewalks and picket lines by jabbing their clubs into ribs, stomachs, and kidneys. The police took careful aim; they had been ordered not to hit the women in the face or to inflict other visible wounds. Newspapers around the world reported on the confrontations.

City officials seethed because of the publicity, but Police Chief John J. Sullivan defended the violence of his patrolmen, saying the women had it coming to them. He said they "held up everybody who was going in the direction of the mills, men and women, and stopped them and turned them back; and when they were approached by the police [who] asked them to go along and stop that sort of thing they would either drop down on the sidewalk and stay there and insist on being arrested or continue the assaults." Sullivan concluded they wanted to be "martyrs, heroines . . . they wanted to be brought to the police station," and wanted to be jailed for their actions.

The striking women used IWW cameras to photograph scabs entering the mills, and posted the pictures and names of the offenders in grocery stores, shops, and the social halls. When they confronted strikebreakers, who were easily identified by the lunch pails they carried, the most militant strikers threatened them with bowling pins, cordwood, iron pipes, and scalding water.

Lawrence newspaper headlines increasingly focused on the women:

"MAN INTIMIDATED BY WOMEN PICKETS,"
"WOMAN FINED $20 FOR ASSAULTING OFFICER,"
"JENNIE RADSIARLOWITZ CONVICTED OF INTIMIDATING MAN."

Big Bill Haywood said "the women strikers were as active and efficient as the men and fought as well." An exasperated prosecutor, Douglas Campbell, called the IWW cowardly for putting women, some of them pregnant, on the front lines. "Let the men come out," he declared, and "keep the women out of it. It has been truly said that it takes but one man to overcome ten men, but it requires ten men to manage a single woman." He urged judges to impose harsh sentences on women offenders so the strike committee "will understand that they cannot send their women and children out when the men won't come out themselves." Judge Jeremiah J. Mahoney was angry at the IWW, too. "The pity is that they are putting forward the women and children to go on the streets each morning," Mahoney said, "to continue a sort of reign of terror."

Elizabeth Gurley Flynn recalled that "there was considerable male opposition to women going to meetings and marching on the picket line. We resolutely set out to combat these notions. The women wanted to picket. They were strikers as well as wives and were valiant fighters. We knew that to leave them at home alone, isolated from the strike activity, a prey to worry, affected by the complaints of tradespeople, landlords, priests and ministers, was dangerous to the strike."

In Boston, a worried Governor Eugene Cox established a legislative reconciliation committee that sought to end the strike through mediation; its chairman was Calvin Coolidge, a freshman member of the state senate from Northampton.

As the demonstrations grew in size, and as worker anger intensified, Ettor worked to ensure maximum unity among the strikers. He insisted that the ten-member workers' committee have representatives from the major ethnic groups participating in the strike. Josephine Lis was on the committee and assumed enormous responsibility for such a young woman.

Another committee member was Annie Welzenbach, twenty-four years old. Welzenbach followed her parents into the mills when she was fourteen. By the time the strike began, she was one of the most skilled fabric menders in the city. She earned twenty dollars a week, much more than most of the workers. Her husband also was a highly skilled textile worker, so the family income equaled that of most middle-class households in the city.

The Welzenbachs were profiled by a young reporter, Harry Emerson Fosdick, who chose not to identify them by name for the likely reason that the mills would blackball them permanently once the strike was over. Neither of them had a personal grievance with employers, but Annie Welzenbach expressed hatred for mill overseers' abuse of unskilled immigrant workers. "I have been getting madder and madder for years at the way they talked to those poor Italians and Lithuanians," she said.

She spoke German, Polish, and Yiddish besides English and became a popular speaker at strike meetings. Almost every day during the strike, Welzenbach, a woman of stately physique, led a parade of pickets through the streets of Lawrence. Always drawing a huge throng of admiring women strikers, she was a shining star guiding them through their first social rebellion in America. After one rally, two thousand women walked behind her as she returned to her home. They were ready to pounce on any authority figure who accosted her. When police decided to arrest her for a picketing violation, they went to her home in the middle of the night so they would not have to face her protectors. Later in the day Welzenbach was released on bail and immediately addressed another rally. "They say that she could tie up three of the largest mills in Lawrence by a word," Fosdick wrote in an article for *The Outlook*. "The other day an Italian [woman] shambled up to her and said . . . 'If any hurt you, I die for you.' "

To those who hesitated to take on the mills, Welzenbach's stock command was, "Get on the picket line!" She worked to persuade skilled workers to support the strike; in previous walkouts they had never perceived common interests with mere laborers. While the strikers idolized Welzenbach, the scabs were terrified of her. She embodied the spirit of Sarah Bagley, Jennie Collins, and the other pioneers who tried to improve the working lives of women in the New England textile mills. Like them, her spirit was made of steel.

When Welzenbach and other members of the strike committee went to Boston to meet with William Wood, she told him of the deprivations suffered by the unskilled workers and their families. She told him his workers were hungry. She lectured him on the oppressive premium system. Wood listened but vowed he would not deal with the IWW. "You are being advised, so I am informed," he later told his thousands of workers, "by men who do not live in this state and are strangers to you . . . they do not know the history of your relations as employees with this company." But the IWW was all that the workers had. The city braced for a long winter during which most of its residents would have no work and little food other than what was offered in the soup kitchens. The fear of hunger was seeping into the minds of tens of thousands of people. Timothy Riley, a city overseer of the poor, said some people "are worked up to such a pitch that it is almost dangerous to speak to them."

Mayor Scanlon, fearing that the strikers would overwhelm his one hundred member police force, requested the National Guard, and Governor Foss ordered one thousand two hundred troops to the city. The commanding officer, Colonel E. LeRoy Sweetser, housed his troops in the mills and installed searchlights and machine guns in the buildings. He stationed his forces at the mill gates and on patrol wherever the pickets marched or gathered. Sweetser told unit commanders to "charge bayonets" if their troops were in danger and ordered the militia members not to salute the American flag when it was carried by strikers. But as for the women's leadership in the strike, Sweetser told a reporter, "If I learn that any one of my men has been unnecessarily rude to a woman I shall punish him as severely as I can." The sight of armed troops in their blue uniforms on the streets of Lawrence would remain an indelible image for those who experienced the strike.

Some militia troops were mill workers called to National Guard duty; some were Harvard University students who volunteered for guard assignments with the approval of the university president, A. Lawrence Lowell of the textile family. The young men of Harvard earned academic credits for their tours of duty. A member of the Coolidge reconciliation committee told Lowell, "Nothing could be done that would intensify class hatred more than this." *The Outlook* quoted a captain in the militia as saying of the Harvards, "They rather enjoyed coming down here to have a fling at those people [the strikers]." The *New York Call* reported, "Insolent, well-fed Harvard men parade up and down, their rifles loaded... their bayonets glittering."

Reporter Walter Weyl had a different impression of the militia: "These soldiers—tin soldiers, the strikers call them—were for the most part mannerly, pleasant-faced boys. They were the sort of boys that you see at a baseball match, and they had joined the militia for the reason that boys go to baseball matches and strikers go to moving-picture shows. The militia boys were always stamping their feet, not from rage but because their feet were cold, and they yawned behind their bayonets because they did not sleep well in the uncomfortable quarters in the mills."

The militia was tested at once. On Monday, January 15, about eight thousand picketers marched through a snowstorm to the Washington and Wood mills and stopped nonstriking workers from entering. By the time the crowd moved on to the Prospect Mill, it was fifteen thousand strong. The strikers shattered the Prospect Mill windows with stones and chunks of ice and then moved on to the Atlantic and Pacific mills where the militia stopped them with high-pressure fire hoses. Summoning reporters, Ettor issued a statement aimed at the Lawrence authorities: "You may turn your hose upon the strikers but there is being kindled in the heart of the workers a flame of proletarian revolt which no fire hose in the world can ever extinguish." The local and national press from this point on relied on Ettor for colorful quotations and rarely interviewed the strikers on the front lines, probably because most of them did not speak English. The IWW and its leaders began dominating the headlines.

While the fire hoses were being turned on the strikers, violence claimed a life in another part of the city. A young Syrian man who was not a striker was stabbed during a skirmish between demonstrators and National Guardsmen. John Ramey, twenty years old, was a musician in a Syrian band that was marching and playing during the demonstration. The troops ordered the group to move along. In the pushing and shoving that ensued, a militia bayonet cut deep into Ramey's back. Ramey lingered in a hospital for two weeks, then died of internal hemorrhaging. No one was charged in the death; police said no one filed a complaint with them. Hundreds of strikers attended Ramey's funeral at St. Anthony's Church as the militia stayed on alert.

Joe Hill, the poet of the IWW movement, wrote:

> *The preachers, cops and money-kings were working hand in hand,*
> *The boys in blue, with stars and stripes were sent by Uncle Sam,*
> *Still things were looking blue, 'cause every striker knew*
> *That weaving cloth with bayonets is hard to do.*

As tension increased throughout the city, the mill managers took more steps to exacerbate the situation. They imported private detectives to spy on the strike leaders, brought in professional strikebreakers, and armed their loyal workers with clubs. An electric fence was erected around the Arlington Mill. At night, searchlights atop mill buildings swept adjoining neighborhoods as nervous troops, looking for gunmen, scanned open windows. Lawrence was a city under siege.

The strike committee, responding to Wood's contention that outside agitators did not know the history of Lawrence labor relations, published a statement questioning whether "the militia, the special policemen, and the Pinkerton detectives recently brought into this city know anything about the textile industry, except to bayonet and club honest workingmen into submission."

John Golden, head of the United Textile Workers, arrived in town on January 16. He charged that the mills were exploiting the workers, but he showed no sympathy for a strike led by the radical IWW. He was a disciple of Samuel Gompers, president of the American Federation of Labor, and, like Gompers, he detested the IWW and its leader, Big Bill Haywood.

Golden could not tolerate the idea of workers seizing property from capitalists. He declared that "any time class consciousness is put above justice to the employer, I am ready to hand in my union card." His position reflected the deep divisions in American labor at the time of the strike. "Between the American Federation of Labor and the Industrial Workers of the World," Walter Weyl wrote, "there is an antagonism more irreconcilable than that between the mill owners and textile workers."

Golden, a Lancashire Irishman who was blackballed by the mills in England because of his union activity, followed other Irish labor agitators to Fall River. He had become president of the United Textile Workers nine years before the Lawrence strike, and he had little interest in recruiting unskilled immigrant workers, especially the militant workers of Lawrence. He told the press "they are foreign to our institutions and unacquainted with the spirit of Massachusetts. Teaching them our methods is a slow process and their ignorance makes them susceptible to the influence of unwise leaders." Of skilled workers, he said: "I find them the most intelligent and easiest to organize. They are also of more value to us than the unskilled workers." So with the approval of his members, Golden preserved the tradition of "the weaver for the weaver" and "the spinner for the spinner," with no one speaking for the unskilled workers.

Golden tried to break the strike; he told his members to cross the picket lines and report for work, and many of them did. When some leaders of the Women's Trade Union League disagreed with his harsh anti-immigrant attitude, Golden tried to order them to leave the city. Among the women who challenged him was Margaret Dreier Robbins. "Many of those in power in the AFL," she said, "seem to be selfish and reactionary and remote from the struggle for bread and liberty of unskilled workers."

Mary Kenney O'Sullivan, who had been an AFL organizer for two decades before the 1912 strike, also went to Lawrence on behalf of the Women's Trade Union League. She was an established champion of skilled women workers in the trade unions, but urged the labor movement to recognize the great changes under way because of the tide of immigration. Labor, she maintained, must speak for all workers. Of Golden and his role in Lawrence, she said, "This is the first time in the history of the [AFL] movement that a leader failed the people in his industry." She argued that the AFL's narrow view of the needs of workers only strengthened the IWW in Lawrence, and declared: "Catholics, Jews, Protestants, and unbelievers—men and women of many races and languages—were working together as human beings with a common cause. The American Federation of Labor alone refused to cooperate. As a consequence, the strikers came to look upon the federation as a force almost as dangerous to their success as the force of the employers themselves." O'Sullivan said that members of the strike committee had "more respect for the mill owners than for the leaders of this antagonistic element within their own ranks." During the strike, she resigned from the league and stayed in Lawrence to help feed the strikers' families.

Shortly after Golden arrived in Lawrence, there was a crucial turning point. Thousands of skilled workers who were members of the United Textile Workers, many of them German weavers, defied their union leader and joined the strike. When they took their places on the picket lines, solidarity was finally established among skilled and unskilled workers. Golden no longer played a significant role in the strike.

A week after the strike began, a peculiar incident diverted everyone's attention and accelerated fears of revolutionary menace. The *New York Times* reported that a large amount of dynamite had been shipped from Boston to Lawrence and was "in the hands of an anarchistic element among the mill workers." In Boston, a twenty-four-hour bodyguard detail was ordered to protect Governor Foss because, an aide said, "certain interests" had hired thugs to attack Foss and other officials.

Lawrence police, acting on a tip from John Breen, son of a former mayor of Lawrence, found dynamite in a shop owned by a Syrian who was an active supporter of the strikers. The police found more dynamite in another home in the Syrian neighborhood and in a cemetery. The most sensational discovery was dynamite found in a shoe store next to the printing office where Joseph Ettor picked up his mail. Ettor and Giovannitti were arrested. The mills doubled the number of guards. Sharpshooters were stationed at mill windows. At the Atlantic Mill, tons of cotton bales were rolled up behind the gates to block any saboteurs.

Ettor and Giovannitti were quickly cleared of any role in the dynamite affair. Breen, who had served as an alderman and on the city board of education, was convicted of trying to frame them and was fined five hundred dollars. Many people believed that William Wood was involved in the frame-up scheme. He was eventually indicted for conspiracy to plant the dynamite but was acquitted. The case was never fully solved, but during the strike it demonstrated that the IWW leaders had mortal enemies in Lawrence.

The mill managers, hoping to break the morale of hungry strikers, tried to create the impression that production was not crippled. They sometimes went to ridiculous lengths, as a *New York Times* reporter found when he went to the Washington Mill at Canal and Mill streets. As the reporter approached the building he heard the din of a busy factory, but when he entered he discovered an elaborate management deception. "In the spinning room, every belt was in motion," the reporter wrote. "The whir of machinery resounded on every side, yet not a single operative was at work and not a single machine carried a spool of yarn." Strikers who no doubt wanted to close down what they thought was a functioning mill were kept away by the militia. The *Times* reporter moved on to the Arlington Mills at Broadway and Park Street where four thousand weavers had worked before the strike. He found only sixteen employees in the cavernous buildings, but many machines were running, and "in the spooling room the empty spools were bobbing without a single operative or a yard of yarn in sight."

On January 24, almost two weeks into the strike, the IWW's presence in the city became complete with the arrival of Haywood and Elizabeth Gurley Flynn. Fifteen thousand people greeted them at the train station. Strikers sang the *Internationale* as they raised the hefty Haywood on their shoulders and marched through snow squalls down Essex Street. They brought the IWW leaders to midtown where thousands more people had gathered to hear them speak. The workers of Lawrence believed their hour of deliverance was at hand and that these two Socialists were their saviors.

"I have read in the newspapers that Lawrence was afraid of me," Haywood told the strikers. "It is not the people of Lawrence who are

fearful of me; it is the superintendents, agents, and owners of the mills."
Looking across the throng and through leafless trees to the distant streets
where the militia stood guard, Haywood played his audience for cheers,
shouting, "I have been in other strikes where soldiers were at hand, but
I never saw a strike defeated by soldiers." He won the cheers.

Big Bill Haywood, a forty-two-year-old giant, had an extraordinary
ability to communicate with workingmen and -women. He believed in
class conflict and was proud of the IWW's basic tenet: "It is the historic
mission of the working class to do away with capitalism." Such pronouncements carried an extra measure of intimidation because of Haywood's appearance; a childhood accident had resulted in the puncture of
his right eye, giving it a milky glaze. Whenever practical, he offered his
left profile for the news cameras that followed him through his labor
battles.

Haywood promised the working class a new society free of tension
between capitalists and workers, with every citizen having access to land
and its resources. "In that day," he wrote, "there will be nonpolitical
government, there will be no States, and Congress will not be composed
of lawyers and preachers as it is now, but will be composed of experts
of the different branches of industry, who will come together for the
purpose of discussing the welfare of all the people." And that change, he
said, would end industrial exploitation.

Haywood was a veteran of bitter union-organizing battles in Western
states on behalf of workers in steel, agriculture, lumber, and mining. In
Idaho, he and several other labor agitators were charged with the 1905
murder of an antiunion former governor, Frank Steunenberg. Haywood's
renowned lawyer, Clarence Darrow, won his acquittal. President Theodore Roosevelt, reformer that he was, nevertheless disapproved of Haywood's militant unionism and called him an "undesirable citizen."
Workers across the country who supported Haywood responded to Roosevelt's attack by wearing buttons bearing the legend "Undesirable Citizen."

With his arrival in Lawrence, "many feared that Haywood, having
thrown the Western mines into a turmoil, would now upset the textile
world," wrote Donald Cole. "Take a character like this," Ray Stannard

Baker wrote, "hard, tough, warped, immensely resistant, and give him a final touch of idealism, a Jesuitical zeal, and you must not expect to find him patient of obstacles, nor politic, nor withholding a blow when there is power to inflict the blow, nor careful of means when ends are to be gained."

Haywood, like Ettor, warned the Lawrence workers to beware of the mill owners' tactics. "Do not let them divide you by sex, color, creed or nationality, for as you stand today you are invincible," Haywood told them at every rally. "Billy Wood can lick one Pole, in fact he can lick all the Poles, but he cannot lick all the nationalities put together." Lecturing the workers on their need to unify, he raised his big hand, counted off with fingers spread apart, and bellowed, "The AFL organizes like this: Weavers, loom-fixers, dyers, spinners." Then he joined his fingers, made a beefy fist, shook it at the audiences and declared, "The IWW organizes like this!" The crowds cheered for One Big Union.

At twenty-one, Elizabeth Gurley Flynn was the rising star of the IWW when she arrived in Lawrence. Her job was to organize women strikers and to teach them picket strategy. The women she came to help suffered all the injustices Flynn had battled for years: They had no right to vote, no legal rights concerning their children, and their fathers or husbands controlled their wages.

Flynn was born in Concord, New Hampshire, of Irish-Catholic parents who were Socialists. She recalled in her autobiography that Yankee Protestants ridiculed the Irish "Papists" for their big families, their fighting, and their drinking. She spent part of her childhood in the mill towns of Adams, Massachusetts, and Manchester, New Hampshire. "Once, while we were in school in Adams, piercing screams came from the mill across the street," she remembered. "A girl's long hair had been caught in the unguarded machine and she was literally scalped." She remembered a young woman mill worker who showed her a hand with two fingers lost in a mill accident, a sight that "shocked me immeasurably." She remembered women workers who earned a dollar a day in the mills and who wore shabby clothes. Flynn developed a hatred for the rich, for "the trusts they owned, the violence they caused, the oppression they represented."

After her school days she worked in the labor movement, and she joined the IWW when she was sixteen. She honed her ability to address large crowds by studying the styles of masters. She wrote with admiration of Maud Malone, a fighter in the woman suffrage movement at the turn of the century. Flynn was there when Malone, speaking at a New York City rally, dealt with a male heckler who yelled at her, "How would you like to be a man?" Malone replied, "Not much. How would you?"

Haywood was Flynn's most influential tutor. He showed her how to command the attention of workers who spoke in many tongues and who comprehended little English. "They all understood his down-to-earth language, which was a lesson to all of us," Flynn wrote. "I learned how to speak to workers from Bill Haywood in Lawrence, to use short words and short sentences, to repeat the same thought in different words if I saw that the audience did not understand. I learned never to reach for a three-syllable word if one or two would do."

Flynn was called labor's Joan of Arc. Mary Heaton Vorse wrote that when Flynn spoke in Lawrence, "the excitement of the crowd became a visible thing. . . . She stirred them, lifted them up in her appeal for solidarity. Then at the end of the meeting, they sang. It was as though a spurt of flame had gone through the audience; something stirring and powerful, a feeling which had made the liberation of people possible, something beautiful and strong had swept through the people and welded them together."

Flynn's first goal in Lawrence was to convince English-speaking workers not to cross the picket lines. "In this struggle it is the foreigners who have taken the lead," she told them. "We must prove we have the same fighting timber to these doubting foreigners. It is up to you to make good before the working class of the world."

She worked with the immigrants to bolster the ethnic unity that made the strike possible. "Mainly we carried on simple agitation," she said. "We talked of their own experiences, how they had come from Europe, leaving their native villages and fields, their old parents, sometimes wives and children. Why had they come to a faraway strange land where a different language was spoken and where all the ways of life were different? . . . Was it to be called 'Greenhorns' and 'Hunkies' and treated as inferiors and intruders? Heads nodded and tears shone in the eyes of the women.... We talked Marxism as we understood it—the class struggle, the exploitation of labor, the use of the state and armed forces of government against the workers. It was all there in Lawrence before our eyes.... We said firmly: 'You work together for the boss. You can stand together to fight for yourselves!' This was more than a union. It was a crusade for a united people—for 'Bread and Roses.' "

On the day Haywood and Flynn arrived in Lawrence, the strike committee wrote to Wood and expressed a willingness to meet with him. "Many operatives are beginning to feel the pinch of hunger, and the severe cold which has gripped the city almost every day since the trouble began has added to their suffering," the *New York Times* reported, "so that toward the latter part of last week there were desertions from the ranks of the strikers." Joseph Ettor suggested that the hunger could breed violence: "If the mill men intend to use the wolf of hunger as an argument," he told a rally on Friday, January 26, "it may break the limitations of men, women and children, and destroy lives. It may be necessary that they go back to work in the mills, but we will cripple their machinery." Never one to miss an opportunity to terrify the mill owners with metaphors, Ettor added, "We may use dynamite that has been planted, the dynamite of class solidarity, the fuse of working-class rebellion."

Catholic diocesan newspapers focused their wrath on the young IWW organizer. The papers carried a statement from the Citizens' Association of Lawrence that charged that from the time of Ettor's arrival, "terrorism, undefined, widespread, all-pervasive, spread through the city." The statement declared that the IWW used the tactics of the Mafia while trying to shut down the mills, and added, "But in all the news printed about the Lawrence strike there was not a word of sympathy for the thousands of workers, most of them women, many of them widows, who, not believing in the anarchistic and revolutionary doctrines [of the IWW], felt that they still lived in a free country and had a right to work if they wanted to."

Annie Welzenbach never let up on those who continued to work. Speaking on picket lines and in ethnic halls, she delivered the strike committee's message: "See all who are still at work and induce them to stay out. Show them that their action means increased misery to them

205

selves and their children, and that scabs in this strike are traitors to their families and class. The strike cannot be lost. Who will come here to replace strikers at six dollars a week? Attend meetings. Don't be a scab."

Sympathy for the strikers and their hungry families was demonstrated by simple acts of charity. Teachers in the Lawrence public schools brought breakfast food to their classrooms to share with their pupils. The IWW, the Salvation Army, and the city's churches and synagogues opened soup kitchens to serve fifty thousand people. More help came from the Socialist party and from union workers across the country. Polish mill workers in North Adams, Lowell, and Manchester sent money. A Polish priest in Nashua delivered seventy dollars in gold collected by mill workers at St. Stanislaus' parish. Portuguese workers in New Bedford and Lowell offered support. Five hundred Lithuanians at St. Rocco's Church in Brockton raised three hundred dollars.

First Lady Helen Taft visited the city and toured the tenement districts with a group that included the Reverend Adolph Berle of Tufts College. As they walked the streets and viewed the squalor, Mrs. Taft was appalled. Berle said, "Somebody is doing a satanic wrong." President Taft launched a federal investigation of conditions in mill towns throughout the country.

January 29 was another day of freezing temperatures, but the cold did not discourage those bent on violence. On Broadway, a mob attacked twenty trolley cars that were carrying scabs to the mills. The attackers hurled rocks and ice at trolley windows as passengers cringed. The attackers beat them, ripped off their work clothes, and smashed their lunch pails until police came to the rescue. Some observers later expressed suspicions that the mills hired hoodlums to stage the violence.

At Union and Garden streets, the second violent death of the strike occurred. This time the victim was a woman striker. The trouble started in the Italian and Portuguese neighborhoods when a group of women, claiming they had a right to assemble on city streets, began resisting the police. The dozen policemen were quickly surrounded by a crowd that had grown to about one thousand. During the pushing and shoving, someone stabbed policeman Oscar Benoit. The other officers fought their way to safety by beating off the crowd with nightsticks. Then, said a news account, "the crisp, short bark of a revolver broke in upon the cries and shouting. The flare of that signal unsheathed hundreds of guns. Knives flashed from hidden sheaths, bullets screamed through the filling darkness and in an instant, riot took the place of law and armed warfare the place of peace." An eyewitness said four or five shots rang out and that the wounded Benoit was the shooter. One of the shots hit Annie Lopizzo, a striking weaver, as she stood on the edge of the crowd. The bullet shattered her shoulder blade, killing her. She was thirty-four years old.

That night, a blinding snowstorm and a morbid silence descended on the workers' neighborhoods. The strikers held meetings to mourn Lopizzo's death while the mill searchlights scanned the streets and corporate properties. It was as if, the *Lowell Sun* reported, the guards were "awaiting the coming of a hostile force."

The whole city was aware of the strikers' wrath. Colonel Sweetser of the National Guard issued a proclamation virtually establishing martial law. He ordered citizens not to mingle with the strikers and banned parades and mass meetings. "This order is interpreted that the soldiers today will shoot on the slightest provocation," the *Sun* told its readers. "Discipline, as rigid as that in war, is being enforced." Sweetser also sent for twelve more companies of infantry and two more cavalry units. When the reinforcements arrived at the railroad station on January 30, a crowd was there. Strikers muttered invectives as the troops stepped off the trains. The young part-time soldiers, eyes straight ahead, marched to their barracks in silence.

The Women's Progressive Club of Lawrence, whose wealthy members worked to improve the lives of immigrant families, denounced authorities for their "treatment of innocent women whose only crime was being in the wrong place at the wrong time." Police Chief Sullivan maintained that Officer Benoit did not kill Lopizzo. He said Benoit was armed with a .32-caliber pistol and that the woman was killed with a .38-caliber. Sullivan suggested that someone in the crowd was aiming at Benoit but missed and hit Lopizzo instead.

Ettor blamed city authorities for the death and declared they wanted only "the peace of the cemeteries." The Lopizzo shooting and the violent attack on the trolley cars were followed by a new wave of arrests. Strikers were charged with carrying concealed weapons, intimidation, or refusing police orders to move along on the picket lines. A *New York Times* account of the violent day was headlined, "Real Labor War Now in Lawrence."

Police arrested Joseph Caruso, a striker, and charged him with the murder of Annie Lopizzo. They arrested Ettor and Giovannitti as accessories and charged them with inciting the violence, although they were not at the scene of the shooting. All three remained in jail for the rest of the strike as they awaited grand-jury proceedings. Ettor stayed in touch with the strike committee and with the press through those who visited his cell. When Harry Emerson Fosdick stopped by, Ettor reprised his Socialist song: "They tell us to get what we want by the ballot. They want us to play the game according to the established rules. But the rules were made by the capitalists. *They* have laid down the laws of the game. *They* hold the pick of the cards. We never can win by political methods. The right of suffrage is the greatest hoax of history. Direct action is the only way."

The body of Annie Lopizzo was taken to the DeCaesere funeral parlor on Common Street. Colonel Sweetser marched his troops to the scene at double-time pace. As Lopizzo's family, friends, and coworkers stood in silence by the casket, they could hear the militia outside shouting orders at a large crowd of mill workers. The throng remained orderly and people were allowed to enter and pay their respects. Ettor issued a jailhouse statement to the strikers: "Tomorrow will be the funeral of our sister who was dreaming the same dreams and aspiring to the same hopes to which you aspire but she is one of the victims of the struggle. . . . We will gather and escort our fellow worker to her last resting place. We meet . . . to pay our last sad tribute to our comrade who has parted with her life blood in the struggle."

The IWW organized ten thousand people to march behind the horse-drawn hearse carrying the body of Annie Lopizzo to a winter tomb at Immaculate Conception Cemetery. At Ettor's request, Colonel Sweetser had agreed to the march but then prohibited it on grounds it could set off more violence. Ettor urged his followers to obey Sweetser's order. Annie Lopizzo would have a quiet service, but it was marred by a momentary lack of grace. "In taking the body from the hearse," a reporter wrote, "one of the bearers slipped on the edge of the sidewalk, causing him to let go of his end of the casket and allowing it to fall partially to the ground. It was lifted immediately and placed in the hearse, which hurried off for the cemetery." A single vehicle followed, carrying one relative and several friends. Among the floral tributes placed at the tomb was a large arrangement, "From the Polish Workers to a Victim of Capitalism." The strike committee issued a statement: "They have murdered our fellow workers, they have broken our heads and arms, but they cannot break our spirit."

Huge demonstrations in support of the strikers were held in several European cities, including London, Rome, Bern, and Budapest. Eugene Debs, speaking for the American Socialist movement, sent a message to the jailed Ettor: "Victory is in sight. The working class will back you up to a finish in your fight against peonage and starvation. The slave pens of Lawrence under protection of America's Cossacks are a disgrace to American manhood."

As the strike entered its third week, some families began sending their children out of the city to stay with relatives, friends, and strike sympathizers. The exodus followed a custom born in Europe during labor confrontations, but it further embarrassed city officials who worried that it showed the world that Lawrence could not take care of its own problems.

In mid-February, the strike organizers sent a group of 150 children to New York City where IWW supporters and their families took them into their homes. Thousands of people greeted the children at Grand Central Station, and a welcoming parade was staged for them.

The New York Women's Socialist Committee in charge of the children was headed by Margaret Sanger, a young registered nurse who two years later would establish the National Birth Control League. Sanger testified before Congress that the Lawrence children "were very much emaciated; every child showed signs of malnutrition." She said almost all of them had swollen adenoids and enlarged tonsils.

Thirty-five more children set out on the same day for Barre, Vermont, home of many Italian-born granite workers who supported the Lawrence strikers. About one thousand six hundred people went to the train station to greet them. A parade with several bands marched down Main Street to the Socialist Hall where a banquet was held for the children. The Italian drama society raised money to support their stay by staging a show at the Barre Opera House.

The Lawrence city marshal issued an order prohibiting the strikers from sending away any more children. Questions were raised about his legal authority to prevent the exodus; nevertheless, when another group of children was assembled at the train station on Washington's Birthday, police forcibly prevented them from leaving.

During the days surrounding the train station episode, there was the appearance of concord and order. The *Lawrence Telegram* reported that City Hall was the "scene of splendor last night" as the Elks Club held its annual concert and ball. "This event is looked forward to as the most brilliant social function of the season, and the affair last night was un-paralleled by any preceding successes." On the evening of Washington's Birthday, while strikers and their families gathered in soup kitchens, the Lawrence Street Church quartet entertained members of Company K, Fifth Regiment, in the Arlington Mill. Pastor Robert W. Beers lectured the militia troops on "Washington and his influence upon American cit-izens." In the Wood Mill, Company M, Fifth Regiment, staged a minstrel show. A news report said a Private Tucker was the interlocutor, Corporal White performed a clog dance, and Private Kenney sang "Brotherly Love." The press reported that "officers from headquarters, visitors from other companies and a large number of ladies were present." In adjacent Me-thuen, more than five hundred people attended the Canoe Club's minstrel show. People who were not directly involved in the labor war seemed to be saying they wanted to get on with their lives despite the impact of the strike on everyone. But still more trouble was in store.

On Saturday, February 24, the Boston and Maine Railroad's regularly scheduled train to Boston was due to depart from Lawrence at 7:11 A.M. At the rail depot, about two hundred police and mounted militia troops watched as a group of strike sympathizers from Philadelphia led forty children into the station. The children ranged in age from five to twelve years old. Their parents, all on strike, had signed consent forms putting the children in the temporary care of the Philadelphia group headed by Jane Bock.

Police and parents inside the station watched as Bock and the others assembled the children in two orderly lines. When the children were led to the train, police moved in to stop them from boarding, citing the city marshal's order banning further departures of children. The purpose of the order was to preserve what was left of the city's image; instead, there was chaos, and Lawrence became an even greater symbol of class warfare.

"In a moment I saw nothing but one terrible mass of children and women and policemen, all in the greatest confusion," Tema Camitta of the Philadelphia committee testified before Congress. "I was pushed up against the wall. I did manage to cry out, 'Be careful of the children, you are killing them.' "

Police fought off parents, and "were compelled to use their clubs," the *Lawrence Telegram* reported. The officers hauled the children to militia vehicles; they wrestled mothers into the trucks as well. Officer Michael Moore boarded one of the trucks, and, according to a news report, "no sooner had he gotten aboard than four or five of the enraged women set upon him. Another officer went to his aid but in trying to get aboard was slapped in the face several times by the women on the truck."

The violence continued at the police station where some of the children were being held. "Both sides went the limit of their power and the police prevailed," said the *New York Times*. "Fifty arrests were made, many of them women who had fought the police savagely, and several heads were broken by the clubs of the officers.... Later in the day the wailing of fourteen of the children as they were being led... to the City Home drove a crowd of 500 foreigners frantic, and a riotous scene followed. From all directions people gathered... and such a stubborn fight was made by the excited crowd that the police found themselves practically unable to keep their hands on the children." After a twenty-minute battle, the police managed to get twelve of the children to a city shelter. The other two were taken from the scene by their father.

Jane Bock described the scene at the train station to the congressional committee during hearings on the strike: "I was standing there helpless.

When the police began clubbing and the children were screaming and thrown to the floor, they hastily grabbed them and carried them to a military truck that was standing a few paces from the platform and threw them in without regard for their screams or where they were throwing them."

Congressman Thomas Hardwick wanted to know more about the incident but, in the spirit of the times, when cities teemed with immigrants, was suspicious about Bock herself:

MR. HARDWICK: Were you born in this country?
MISS BOCK: *No, sir.*
MR. HARDWICK: What country?
MISS BOCK: *Russia.*
MR. HARDWICK: Hebrew by nationality?
MISS BOCK: *Hebrew by nationality.*

Hardwick pressed Bock on a charge made by many strike organizers that police clubbed children as well as adults, a charge denied by city officials:

MR. HARDWICK: Did the policemen beat them?
MISS BOCK: *The policemen beat them.*
MR. HARDWICK: It struck me as awful to think about a thing like that.
MISS BOCK: *It strikes me the same way.*
MR. HARDWICK: Did it happen: Of course the children may have been thrown to the ground, but did the policemen actually strike them?
MISS BOCK: *They did.*
MR. HARDWICK: With their hands or with their clubs?
MISS BOCK: *I should say with clubs; that was the handiest thing.*
MR. HARDWICK: Let us try to be very careful about that. You say the policemen did strike the little children with clubs that way?
MISS BOCK: *Yes, sir; I do say the policemen struck the little children with clubs.*

"It was a day without parallel in American labor history," said Elizabeth Gurley Flynn. "A reign of terror prevailed in Lawrence which literally shook America." William Dean Howells, a prominent figure in American letters, said of the train station violence, "It is an outrage—could anyone think it was anything else?" The conservative *New York Sun* condemned "the attempt to put an embargo on the movements of residents of an American community." Senator William Borah of Idaho, who had prosecuted Haywood in the Steunenberg murder case, joined the protest. Borah said the Lawrence police violated the constitutional rights of the children. Solicitor General Frederick Lehman, President Taft's chief legal adviser agreed, saying, "it is the right of any parent to send his children anywhere if he is guided by parental forethought and is acting for their welfare." The *New York Tribune* said the actions taken by the Lawrence officials were "as chuckle-headed an exhibition of incompetence to deal with a strike situation as is possible to recall." But the *Tribune* also suggested the IWW wanted violence and that the events at the train station were "intended to be only a part of a nationwide, if not a worldwide strike in the textile trade, and thus, as the plotters hoped, the beginning of a social revolution."

Mayor Scanlon declared that "an incipient revolution is in progress in Lawrence." Father O'Reilly told his congregation at St. Mary's on the day after the violence: "It is now a war against society—the abolition of the wage system, the destruction of the present social order. It is a war against lawfully constituted authority, against religion, against the home, against the people. It is a worldwide war of class against class."

As O'Reilly spoke, the war continued. All the ethnic groups held Sunday strategy meetings in their social halls. A few days later, the strike committee accused police of brutality during another confrontation, this one involving about fifteen women who, the committee said, were returning home peacefully from a meeting. About fifty police officers surrounded the group. The committee said that under orders from a police commander, patrolmen clubbed the women. Bertha Crouse, a pregnant striker, was beaten unconscious and subsequently lost her child. New waves of hatred for all authority swept through the neighborhoods and the picket lines. "We will remember," the strike committee said in a letter to Governor Foss. "We will never forget, and never forgive."

Coincidentally, on the same day that the police beat the women, American Woolen and the other mills proposed a wage hike of 5 percent and announced that they were willing to negotiate with the strike committee. William Wood said the offer of the raise was being made even though "the mills at Lawrence pay wages as high as are given for the same kind of work anywhere else in the country."

The Arlington Mill placed an advertisement in the newspapers saying it was offering the pay hike despite financial setbacks. "During the past two years our business has yielded no profit," the mill said. "Less than one half of our machinery has been operated. During this period of depression wages were not reduced." A few days later, American Woolen announced a surplus of $11.5 million for the year and a dividend of 8 percent for the stockholders. The strike committee held out for a 15 percent raise.

A state of near anarchy continued. Hundreds of strikers turned out before sunrise to picket at the gates of the Prospect Mill. Women strikers were harassing women strikebreakers when police driving a horse and buggy arrived. The *Lawrence Tribune* reported that "the entire crowd of howling women started after the vehicle on the run, all clamoring to be arrested." In the confusion, the horse bolted and raced down a railroad track until it stumbled on the ties and fell. Rescuers got the horse back on its feet.

Father O'Reilly tried again to break the IWW's hold on the strikers. He invited a former Socialist, David Goldstein, to speak in St. Mary's parish hall. Goldstein told the audience that socialism was undermining the church and the home; its followers, he said, were atheists who engaged in free love. A news account said that O'Reilly "went to the very root of the matter and proved the futility of reconciling Catholic faith and socialist principles. The Catholic who insists upon being a socialist must go counter to the mandates of the church itself."

From his pulpit during Sunday Mass on March 3, O'Reilly urged parishioners who were still on strike to cross the picket lines. News reports noted that other priests and ministers told their congregations that returning to work was an individual choice. The choice, they preached, was between socialism and traditional American values. After a Franco-American priest delivered such a sermon, a crowd of eight thousand formed on Broadway and paraded to his home. The police said the demonstrators "stood out there and booed at him and called him vile names. They threatened to pull his house and church down. . . . They called it a procession, but it was a wild, unorganized mob." Joseph Ettor intervened from his jail cell and sent word to the IWW organizers to draw the crowd away from the scene. The priest and church property were saved.

Elizabeth Gurley Flynn said the IWW told the antistrike clergymen to stay out of the strike. "We did not attack their religious ideas in any way," she wrote, "but we said boldly that priests and ministers should stick to their religion and not interfere in a workers' struggle for better conditions, unless they wanted to help."

At Holy Rosary Church, Father Milanese declined to join the anti-strike clergy. He publicly disagreed with O'Reilly's statement urging the workers to accept the mills' wage offer and end the strike.

There was growing talk that negotiations were going well between the mill managers and the strike committee. Management had good reason to settle. The mills' most important customers, the manufacturers of clothing and other finished textile goods, needed fabrics for the spring trade. More important, a settlement would end a public-relations nightmare. The House hearings on the strike were still under way in Washington and continued to focus national attention on the plight of the workers. There was still widespread anger because Ettor and Giovannitti were in jail on what strikers considered trumped-up charges. Among those joining the campaign for their release was Helen Keller, a renowned blind and deaf lecturer and author who was sympathetic to Socialist causes. The real offense of those like Ettor and Giovannitti, Keller said, was "helping strikers in their assault on the pocketbooks of the owners."

On March 13, after two long months of hate and hunger, the strike ended. The workers won. Annie Welzenbach, Josephine Lis, and the rest of the strike committee negotiated the settlement with the mills. The owners agreed that even with the reduced hours mandated by the state, there would be wage increases ranging from 5 to 20 percent. Unskilled workers would receive larger increases, overtime pay would be increased, the reviled premium system would be changed to eliminate the abuses that had robbed workers of their extra earnings, and there was to be no retribution against strike leaders. The strike committee tried but failed to negotiate the release of Ettor, Giovannitti, and Caruso, but the Coolidge legislative conciliation committee promised to pursue the case.

Mary Kenney O'Sullivan, the veteran of countless labor wars across the country, said of the workers' negotiators that it was "the most unselfish strike committee I have ever known. With two exceptions its members are skilled workers in the Lawrence mills. It was at the suggestion of these skilled workers that the lowest paid, unskilled workers of Lawrence received the largest advance in wages and the highest skilled workers received the smallest." For at least this brief period, Lawrence symbolized One Big Union.

The day after the settlement, twenty five thousand men, women, and children gathered at the Lawrence Common to celebrate. Bill Haywood told them: "This is the first time in the history of labor movements that a strike has been conducted like this one. It has been entirely in the hands of the strikers themselves." Looking out at the throng of people, the big man roared out his perpetual message for the final time in Lawrence: "You are the heart and soul of the working class. Singlehanded, though, you are helpless; united you can win everything."

A few days later, Haywood told a New York audience: "It was a wonderful strike, the most significant strike, the greatest strike that has ever been carried on in this country or any other country. Not because it was so large numerically, but because we were able to bring together so many different nationalities. And the most significant part of that strike was that it was a democracy."

After the Lawrence settlement, textile mills in dozens of other New England cities and towns granted pay raises to some 250,000 workers, most of them also immigrants. "For these people," Donald Cole wrote, "Lawrence was a famous city, not a notorious one."

In their *History of Labor in the United States,* Selig Perlman and Philip Taft wrote that the strike taught the AFL that it had to pay more attention to the needs of powerless workers. "To the young American *intelligentsia,*" they added, "Lawrence was proof that a revolutionary American labor movement, which had been forecast as inevitable in the theoretical socialistic writings, was here at last, and deepened its dissatisfaction and impatience with the leadership of the American Federation of Labor."

For Harry Emerson Fosdick, who left journalism to become a leading American clergyman, the strike of 1912 offered America the opportunity to seek new solutions to the ceaseless differences between management and labor. As he concluded his reporting days, he told his readers: "When a thoughtful man leaves Lawrence he is not concerned to sit in judgment on mill owners or strikers. They are all caught in the same net. But he wishes that Lawrence might be a summons, which all the country would hear, to unselfish, progressive social-spirited citizenship."

By the end of March, all the children who had been sent away for the duration of the strike were back in their Lawrence homes. Joseph Ettor and Arturo Giovannitti, along with Joseph Caruso, had to wait until November before they were acquitted of all charges in connection with the death of Annie Lopizzo. No one else was ever arrested for the shooting.

The strike committee went out of existence two weeks after it won the settlement, but not without a farewell message to the mill owners: "The class struggle will end only when the working class has overthrown the capitalist class and has secured undisputed possession of the earth and all that is in and on it."

The IWW was unable to build on its role in Lawrence; it failed to recruit a significant membership among the mill workers after the strike. "By temperament and conviction," wrote labor historian Herbert Harris, the IWW leaders "were crusaders for times of crisis" who were more interested in winning converts to their revolution than in organizing and collective bargaining. Elizabeth Gurley Flynn agreed: "Most of us were wonderful agitators but poor union organizers."

In 1917, Haywood and other IWW leaders were arrested for sedition as America entered World War I. The charges came after they called the war a capitalist ploy to exploit workers. Haywood and the others were convicted by the capitalist system they had always condemned. Haywood was sentenced to twenty years in prison. In 1921, while free on bail, he fled to the Soviet Union. He died there in 1928 when he was fifty-nine years old.

Elizabeth Gurley Flynn, like Haywood, clung to her ideals of social justice all her life. She helped found the American Civil Liberties Union and later became a leader of the American Communist party. During the Cold War in 1952, hysteria generated by congressional Red hunters culminated in her trial for Communist activity, and, in her sixties, she was sentenced to prison. She was released in 1957 after twenty-eight months behind bars. Seven years later, she was on vacation in the Soviet Union and died there at the age of seventy-four. The Soviets honored her with a state funeral.

Joseph Ettor vanished from the labor scene in the late 1920s after inheriting enough money to open a winery in Cucamunga, California. He led a quiet life far from labor strife until his death in 1948. Arturo Giovannitti, striving for what he called "the emancipation of human kind," stayed in the labor movement until his health failed in the 1940s. He died in New York in 1959. His funeral was held in the auditorium of the New York headquarters of the Amalgamated Clothing Workers of America. Those who came to mourn his passing surely recalled his revolutionary poetry:

> *Aye, think! While breaks in you the dawn,*
> *Crouched at your feet the world lies still.*
> *It has no power but your brawn,*
> *It has no wisdom but your will.*

The symbol of solidarity in Lawrence, Annie Welzenbach, made one more effort to achieve justice for the workers. She returned to the Washington Mill after the strike only to find that many of the jobs there were still held by scabs. She led two hundred other workers in a walkout; it was ineffective, and the scabs kept their jobs. Gradually, Welzenbach,

Josephine Lis, and the other women who led the strike bowed out of their activist roles after their brief but fierce quest for bread and roses on behalf of those trapped in "the slave pens of Lawrence." Workers who did not strike, many of them of Irish and English stock, won better-paying jobs for their company loyalty.

A year after Camella Teoli testified before Congress, the Massachusetts legislature enacted a law limiting the workday to eight hours for children under sixteen. The new law also increased the number of days working children were required to attend school. Camella Teoli returned to the mills and worked for several more years. She married and brought up a family in the Lawrence area. A newspaper recounted in 1990 that for years, Josephine Catalano began each day brushing and combing her mother's hair into a bun that hid a bald spot six inches in diameter. The old woman's disfigurement was a constant reminder of the scalping she had suffered in the mill. Today, a street in downtown Lawrence is named Camella Teoli Way. She is one of the few women of the Lawrence strike whose names are remembered.

William Wood became a changed man after the strike. His son, William Junior, was an executive at American Woolen and worked to improve management-labor relations. He organized company recreation programs, a day-care nursery, a home-loan program, and summer camps for workers' children. The company took care of its managers, too. It built a model community called Shawsheen Village in nearby Andover, with lovely homes and executive offices. A strike-embittered labor newspaper called Shawsheen the home of "Lawrence lickspittles."

The younger Wood's efforts to humanize American Woolen appeared to mellow William Senior, who soon was calling the ex-strikers in his mills "my fellow workers." In time, the old man became a popular boss, known to one and all as "Captain Billy." He also became richer. His son helped him to win $102 million in federal contracts to manufacture the army's new khaki uniforms. Then, affliction clouded the life of William Madison Wood.

In 1920, he was tried in federal court, charged with war profiteering, but won acquittal. Two years later, he was distressed by his son's decision to leave the mill business. Soon after that, the son was killed in an automobile accident. William Senior became mentally unbalanced. He also suffered a stroke that impaired his speech. In 1924, under doctors' orders, he resigned as president of American Woolen, a company with forty thousand workers, fifty-nine mills throughout New England, and annual sales of $175 million. In his retirement years, he was plagued by financial setbacks. One day in Florida in 1926, he asked his chauffeur and his valet to accompany him to the shores of Daytona Beach. He left them waiting at the limousine, walked out of their sight, raised a .38-caliber pistol to his mouth, and fired. He died a suicide at the age of sixty-eight.

Calvin Coolidge's political career was enhanced by his role in the Lawrence strike. As chairman of the special legislative committee that dealt with both sides, he had, a biographer noted, "handled his part tactfully and, although his solution did not meet all the strikers' demands, it was generally conceded that he had been fair and dispassionate." Coolidge went on to become governor of Massachusetts and president of the United States. President Taft's call for an investigation into mill conditions did not bring significant reform; long after he left the White House, the exploitation of mill workers remained a scandal.

Seven months after the strike was settled, there was a disruptive postscript that infuriated city leaders who thought the awful chapter in their history was over. The anarchist Carlo Tresca led about three thousand mill workers through the streets in a pouring rain in what was supposed to be a tribute to the slain Annie Lopizzo. But from under their umbrellas, the marchers pulled out red flags and waved them defiantly. They carried a banner proclaiming: "Arise! Slaves of the World! No God! No Master! One for All and All for One!" Elizabeth Gurley Flynn, who had a romance with Tresca during the strike, wrote decades later that she suspected the banner display was a deliberate act of provocation aimed at the IWW. "A committee in charge should have had the authority to yank it out of the line of march, as would happen in any other labor parade," she said, but the parade leaders granted too much freedom to the marchers "and this was one unfortunate manifestation of it."

Father O'Reilly was outraged by what he considered a sacrilegious and unpatriotic episode. Enlisting the aid of clergymen from other denominations as well as business and community leaders, he organized a counterdemonstration. On October 12, Columbus Day, thirty two thousand people, including many children of the strikers, marched in the "God and Country" parade. They created a mosaic of red, white, and blue as they waved small American flags. Their uniforms were emblazoned with patriotic emblems. Their banner read: "For God and Country! The Stars and Stripes Forever! The red flag never!" Thousands of spectators cheered as if to say Lawrence had no place for anarchists and socialists.

"The city is waking up," Father O'Reilly declared. "But it was not until the rodents got at the foundations and threatened to tear it down and then did we awaken to our position. We are on the map and have given them the answer that all cities must if the Constitution and the country are to live."

As spring approached in 1912, news stories suggested that life was back to normal. At the Broadway Theater, the vaudeville bill included the Vannersons, comedy gymnasts "whose clown antics on the bars will bring tears of merriment to the eyes." Employees of the city parks department won a raise in daily wages from $2 to $2.25. The children of St. Mary's parish gave a St. Patrick's Day concert at the Lawrence Opera House. John McGraw was getting his New York Giants ready for the new baseball season. Walter Johnson seemed anxious to leave the Washington Senators and to pitch instead for a pennant contender like the New York Yankees but in the end stayed put. William Jennings Bryan, like Theodore Roosevelt, pondered another run for the White House. An Essex Street paint store, H. J. Stanchfield & Co., advertised: "Get Ready for Spring Painting." Marian French was in court to divorce Otis French because "she objected to one woman with whom he kept company particularly." There was growing belief that Marie Curie's discovery of radium would provide enough radioactive energy to produce "a growth of new, healthy hair on even the baldest head." The Reverend A. W. Moulton preached at Grace Episcopal Church, "If you are bringing up children, do not allow them to feed on the ideas that they are to despise and hold aloof from the children of the foreigners, but teach something of the love Jesus had for the foreigners."

O'Reilly remained the most influential clergyman in Lawrence for more than a decade after the strike and ministered to his people's needs from the day of their baptisms to the day of their funerals. He was their priest for forty years. Wherever he traveled in the city, he saw the truth of Proverbs: "The fruit of the righteous is a tree of life." There were the churches he had built, and the convent, and the schools. The IWW and Bill Haywood and Joseph Ettor and Elizabeth Gurley Flynn were gone. So was their revolutionary rhetoric. His people were back to work. For him, Lawrence was what it should be, an American place.

The people still struggled to survive, even with the wage increases they had won. Many of them never escaped from their slum tenements. Julia Garbelnick, who as a child was entranced by the oratory of Joseph Ettor, said almost eight decades after the strike: "No bread and roses came out of that. Bread and blood came out of it." Perhaps she was right when it came to the strikers themselves. But there *were* roses for the children and grandchildren of those who braved the picket lines for two long months. The new generations bear many of the same names as the strikers--Zapenas, Scarito, Ritvo, Guerrea, Pettoruto, Gurka—but they do not answer to mill overseers, do not fear hunger and cold, do not pass their lives in squalor and despair. They are doctors and nurses, lawyers and educators, judges and mayors.

Visitors to the city see the Ayer Mill tower clock, restored with contributions from the descendants of mill workers, still giving the time of day to all. The visitors also see the hustle and bustle of small industries that operate in some areas of the massive, mostly empty mill buildings. They tour an old mill that houses the Lawrence Heritage State Park and learn the story of the textile workers. Some stop by the Immigrant City Archives on Essex Street, searching for information about ancestors who worked in the mills.

In a city that endured much trouble, one old man brought good will. He was Aaron Feuerstein, the owner of the Malden Mills, one of the few textile firms still operating in New England. In 1995, just before Christmas, fire destroyed three of the nine mills Feuerstein operated. Thirteen hundred employees would have to be out of work all winter until the mills were rebuilt. At great personal cost, Feuerstein kept the idled workers on the payroll, and he kept them covered by health insurance. He did the same for three hundred other employees at a satellite mill in Bridgton, Maine, when production there also had to halt because of the fire.

Such a man attracted attention. Ten thousand people wrote admiring letters to him. Colleges and civic organizations honored him. Feuerstein insisted that he was simply practicing good business. "I think that a corporation should operate with a set of principles, ethical values, which permeate the entire organization," he told the press. "If a worker feels he's getting double-crossed, he'll see to it that the quality of what you make is not what it ought to be. In the long run you'll lose your profit. But if that worker has a feeling of loyalty and belonging to a company, you'll have a better quality product."

Eighty-three years earlier, the Lawrence strikers had fought against many abuses imposed on them by mill owners who barely considered them human beings. Because Aaron Feuerstein ran his business with a simple sense of decency, the people of Lawrence came to revere a mill owner. The strikers of 1912 never would have believed it.

8

───◆───

Last Bells

On Saturday, November 15, 1924, Frederic Dumaine, chief executive officer of the giant Amoskeag textile mills in Manchester, New Hampshire, opened his diary book and made this entry: "The outlook for textiles in New England is, to my mind, most uncertain and to such an extent that, feeling as I do today, should a reasonable bona fide offer be made for the property, I am sure I would recommend its sale."

Had the admission become public it would have disheartened the eighty four thousand people of Manchester. Dumaine had made Amoskeag into one of the largest textile manufacturers in the world. It employed seventeen thousand people whose variety of skills were used in seventy four departments. Many workers shared with Dumaine family roots in Quebec. And as the most powerful Franco-American in textile management he was responsible for their economic well-being. A decade earlier, believing that the industry could survive in New England, Dumaine had expanded operations. Now he was ready to close shop and sell out or, if there were no buyers, to auction off the real estate to speculators and the machinery to junk dealers.

In 1922, two years before he despaired in his diary about the future of the industry, Dumaine asked his workers to take a pay cut, telling them it was the only way the Amoskeag Mills could stay open. He proposed to increase work hours while cutting wages by 20 percent. The workers rejected his plan and struck. From February through spring and summer and until Thanksgiving Day, the city of Manchester languished as thousands of looms stood in silence. In 1912, the Lawrence strikers had envied the Amoskeag workers because they were paid more and their company benefits were more generous. Now, a decade later, it was Manchester's turn to endure hunger, strife, and fear of the future.

In the end the Amoskeag workers came back. While they had to accept the longer hours, they did manage to force the company to cancel the pay cut. Tamara K. Hareven wrote that the 1922 strike permanently changed the relationship between management and labor. Despite its enormous size, the Amoskeag had earned the loyalty of the workers with its paternalistic policies. "We were like family," one of them told Hareven. But after the strike there was uneasiness between the bosses and the mill hands.

The company, whose baseball team was good enough to play against the Boston Red Sox in exhibition games, ended its sponsorship of numerous recreational, social, educational, and health programs for employees. Dumaine invested less in plant improvements and used company assets to pursue profits in other industries. Gradually, the Amoskeag workforce was reduced. In the middle of the Great Depression, the lights went out for the last time in the cavernous Amoskeag mills that for a century had given economic life to the city of Manchester.

Amoskeag was one of the last of the giants in New England to stagger, crumble, and die. Textile executives at other mills in the region stared at corporate ledgers riddled with red ink. Their mills were decrepit hulks with leaky roofs, broken windows, and obsolete machinery. The mills were, an industry observer said, "an insult to those who worked in them." Workers lost morale and looked with contempt on the Brahmins of State Street in Boston who ruled their lives. "Why should the mills modernize?" asked a worker in Biddeford, Maine. "When things fall apart in Biddeford, the companies will just move South."

In Lowell, people walked past the silent buildings that had once displayed famous mill names—Middlesex, Hamilton, Massachusetts, Suffolk,

Tremont, Appleton. The Boott and Merrimack mills survived in Lowell until the 1950s and then they finally closed, too. Once, there had been 111 mills in Fall River. Eventually, every one of them went out of business. "The city of the dinner pail no longer woke at six a.m. or rang with the sounds of the army of industrial workers," wrote John T. Cumbler. "Fall River had receded into obscurity. Its workers, who had once created a proud community of operatives and the strongest union movement in textiles, now fought desperately for the few remaining jobs and blamed their unions for the situation." Workers watching the industry desert them asked, "How are we going to stop it?" There was no answer.

Community leaders wearied of the crises and the disruption of local economies. In Saco, Maine, across the river from Biddeford, political leader Sam Lord asked the public to judge whether the York Mill was of any economic or social value. "If it is not," Lord said, "let it pull up stakes and get out, and make room for some other industry that will be a benefit to the city." Eventually, the owners of the mill did pull out and headed south. A local newspaper wondered "whether the mills are to be torn down and the bricks packed in cotton and shipped along with the machinery." The company took its looms and other machines but left behind the barren brick buildings as daily reminders to everyone of the town's economic troubles.

Those who still had jobs in the doomed industry continued to battle for labor justice. They struck again in Lawrence in 1919 for a shorter workweek. The Industrial Workers of the World had left the city, but the women remembered the lessons of 1912 and united the ethnic groups for a punishing strike that lasted fifteen weeks. They won again.

Women workers in New Bedford fought back in 1928 when the mills, citing competition from nonunion Southern mills, cut their pay by 10 percent. Thirty-five thousand mill workers, mostly women, went on strike, and while they failed to achieve most of their demands, women became leaders as they had in Lawrence. Portuguese and Polish women became principal figures in the strike as they devised picketing strategy, spoke at rallies, and staged public protests. They did all this despite ethnic cultures that disapproved of public roles for women. Strike organizer Sophie Melvin remembered how union activism generated domestic violence. "I actually saw the husbands become vicious against their wives who took a meaningful position in the union," she said. "I stayed with one family where one night, the wife, the two daughters and myself in the midst of winter had to get dressed and run out of the house because the husband came back drunk and he lashed out at his wife, primarily because she was at a meeting that night and spoke. It was horrible."

The increasing role of women in labor disputes attracted the attention of social activists who sponsored education programs for them. Those gifted with leadership were invited to attend summer school on college campuses. They studied history and economics. They learned labor law, how to organize workers, and how to negotiate with management. Some became shop stewards in textile unions that had long been dominated by men. They often won better labor contracts for their members, but time was against them. For one hundred years, women in the New England mills had fought for their rights and had almost always lost those fights. Now, as they were finally coming into their own in the mills, the industry was perishing before their eyes. Their struggle was a futile effort against a manufacturing system whose time in New England was at an end. It was time for the rising of the textile industry in the South.

Ever since the Civil War and the repressive economic policies imposed by a vengeful North, the South had been the poorest section of the country, with blacks and whites chained together in poverty. Former slaves and their children and grandchildren worked on the land as they had always done, and were mired in a hopeless existence as they had always been. Their labor continued to supply cotton to textile mills from Maine to Alabama. The cities and towns of the South teemed with people who had no land, no education, and no future. Now the region was ready to inherit the textile industry from the tired mill managers of the North. By the 1920s, more than a million poor whites in the South were working in textile factories. In later years, after the walls of segregation crumbled, blacks also began working in the mills.

Southern towns wooed Northern mill investors who had had their fill of the never-ending demands of their immigrant workers. The chamber of commerce in Macon, Georgia, flaunted the town's charms: "Abundant supply of labor. Thrifty, industrious, and one hundred per cent American." Community leaders in Spartanburg, South Carolina, drawled: "Labor of purest Anglo-Saxon stock. Strikes unknown." The goal of boosters in Gastonia, North Carolina, was to see one new mill begin operations every week. By 1923, the Gastonia area had 105 mills. Six years later it was the leading textile center in the South and third in the nation.

Historian Page Smith concluded that the campaign to persuade New England mills to move south was motivated by vindictiveness. "By pushing the Northern cotton manufacturers into bankruptcy, by beating them at their own game," Smith wrote, "the South could exact a measure of revenge for its defeat in the war, for, according to Southern mythology, it was the Northern greed for Southern cotton that had been the real and efficient cause of the War Between the States." The building of Southern mills became a matter of patriotism, wrote M. D. C. Crawford. For the South, he said, "the terrible years of Reconstruction had burned the lesson deeply into all minds that independence could best be won through the conversion of its principal raw material into yarns and fabrics. . . . It is not too much to describe the first decade of building as a political venture, almost a crusade."

In the Southern mill towns, people believed that at last they were on their way to Easy Street. Towns cast off dusty facades and took on a spic-and-span sparkle. Fresh coats of paint brightened old buildings. There were new churches, schools, hospitals, town halls, and movie houses. Shiny new cars cruised the streets, and people wore fashionable clothes instead of threadbare denims. Merchants, professionals, suppliers, and contractors, all of them serving the new mills, became prosperous. Their benefactors were the country's new textile giants—the Dan River Mills, the Burlington Mills, J. P. Stevens, Deering-Milliken, and Cannon.

Southern mill executives and community leaders detested unions. They kept the workers in place as long as possible with union busting, which was often carried out by the Ku Klux Klan. Although the Klan had only a brief resurgence in New England in the 1920s, it remained strong in the South. In many Southern mill towns, KKK members ruled in the police station, in the sheriff's office, and in the mill itself. Police and mill guards used violence to break up workers' groups that wanted to unionize, and company spies working in the mills sniffed out insurrection. Agitators were evicted from company-owned shacks.

Even as Northern textile interests closed their New England mills, they invested profitably in Southern mills. When business slowed at the Loray mill in Gastonia, the company cut the workforce from three thousand five hundred to two thousand two hundred, then imposed the stretchout on the remaining workers to maintain the same production level. The mill managers acted at the direction of their owners, the Manville-Jenckes Company of Rhode Island. Mattie Hughes, the mother of three, had earned $7.47 for sixty hours of work at the Loray mill in March 1929. The next month, her pay for the same hours was down to $5.53. The $1.94 difference that she lost went to the stockholders of Manville-Jenckes. Pay cuts and speedups forged common bonds between mill workers in the snow-covered cities of New England and the sun-baked towns of the South.

The Pacific Mills of Lawrence operated in several Southern towns. The Nashua Manufacturing Company had a mill in Cordova, Alabama. American Thread of Willimantic, Connecticut, built mills in the Carolinas and Georgia. When Elizabeth Glendower Evans, a Boston socialite who was concerned about the welfare of mill workers, saw for herself the appalling conditions in Southern mills, she was dismayed to find that as a stockholder of the Massachusetts Mills of Lowell, her family's investments helped finance textile factories in Lindale, Georgia.

Northern investors who had profited from child labor in New England did so again in the South. A minister who visited a mill in Columbus, Georgia, owned by Boston interests, said, "I have never seen as many children in any one mill as there were there." The children he saw worked twelve hours a day. Sarah Northcliffe Cleghorn, a poet, social reformer, and Socialist, went to South Carolina in 1913 and saw children working in a cotton factory. The building was adjacent to a golf course, a juxtaposition that led her to lament:

> *The golf links lie so near the mill*
> *That almost every day*

LAST BELLS

The laboring children can look out
And watch the men at play.

The Depression of the 1930s hastened the industry's demise and left tens of thousands of people in the mill cities, as it left millions of Americans everywhere, with little hope. President Franklin D. Roosevelt's New Deal programs to revitalize the American economy took many years to turn the country around, but he could not save the New England textile industry. Roosevelt set up a government board whose principal task was to reduce the considerable difference in wage levels in Southern and Northern mills by raising the pay of Southern workers. The result was a federal minimum wage of twelve dollars a week in Southern mills and thirteen dollars a week in Northern mills—too low, the workers said—and the outlawing of child labor under the age of sixteen. The board was also supposed to end employment abuses in both regions, but organized labor charged that the board was dominated by textile executives who favored company unions over independent unions and sided with the mills in other management-labor disputes. In 1934, the result was a month-long strike in twenty states by five hundred thousand textile workers. Textile towns in both the North and the South erupted in violence.

In Georgia, Governor Eugene Talmadge's National Guard rounded up hundreds of striking women and held them in camps surrounded by barbed wire. In Honea Path, South Carolina, mill guards shot and killed seven picketers. Four New England governors called out the National Guard as strikers clashed with company guards and police in Saylesville and Woonsocket, Rhode Island; Danielson, Connecticut; Lewiston, Maine; and Ludlow and Pittsfield, Massachusetts. The workers were no match for machine gun nests and shotguns. When the strike was over, they had accomplished little.

During the Depression, reporter Louis Adamic of *Harper's* magazine toured New England mill communities that reeked of economic death. He arrived in Lawrence in early morning and "saw hundreds of shabby, silent, hollow-eyed men and women, native and foreign-born, going toward the immense, dark mills. I discovered later that very few of them

281

were going to work; the others were seeking work." There were no jobs for most of them, Adamic wrote, and there had been no jobs for years.

He saw similar misery in Fall River and New Bedford; in Dover and Somersworth, New Hampshire; in Waterville, Lewiston, and Biddeford, Maine. While Roosevelt and his allies in Congress were sponsoring labor-reform legislation, Adamic was reporting on girls in Somersworth who were working at thirty looms each from sunrise to sunset. A Lithuanian priest in Lawrence told Adamic of parishioners who cried, "What is going to become of our children?"

In New Bedford, a jobless man told of a brother who had recently murdered his wife and child, and then committed suicide. "I don't blame 'im," the man said to Adamic. "I'd do the same, only I ain't got the guts. I'd have to kill four of 'em. And I couldn't . . . I couldn't. Christ, ain't it awful?"

Like vultures descending on carrion, entrepreneurs alighted in the mill cities, scenting the prospect of quick profits. Dress manufacturers who had fled union militancy in New York City opened for business in New England. City officials eager to help their unemployed people gave the shop owners tax breaks and rent-free space in empty mills. "If any industry will guarantee to employ a certain number of people for a period of years," the mayor of New Bedford announced, "I will sell them the Butler mill, the Pemaquid mill, or the Whitman mill for one dollar." In the initial excitement of being hired again, the workers, mostly women, felt a surge of hope that they might make it through hard times after all. It was not to be. The garment shop operators proved to be among the most vicious employers in the history of the region.

John T. Cumbler described the garment shops of Fall River as "gypsy" factories. The owners installed sewing machines and hired women as "learners." The "learners" did not qualify for even minimum wages. After an owner had enough finished garments for a profitable sale in New York, he loaded his trucks and left Fall River for good. The jobless women had no choice but to find work in another garment shop. Some owners who stayed in Fall River longer than the fly-by-night operators found another way to cheat on wages. Once the women in their shops had achieved enough skills as "learners" and had qualified for better pay, the owners fired them and replaced them with new "learners."

Cumbler recounted the history of one company in Fall River that employed one thousand seven hundred workers, most of them Portuguese and Franco-American women. "The practice of hiring 'learners' and firing experienced workers was so extensive," Cumbler wrote, "that over two hundred a year were fired and hired. The company ran a school which gave it a continual supply of new learners. And it was always ready to repress any union movement. Guards were hired to watch over the employees to prevent in-shop associating. Floor ladies were assigned . . . to prevent the women from learning each others' names and becoming friendly." Ten thousand people in Fall River worked in garment shops that were as brutal as the sweatshops of New York.

President Roosevelt visited the area in 1935. When he returned to Washington he told White House reporters of a woman garment worker in New Bedford who fought her way through the crowd and past security officers to hand him a note that read: "I wish you would do something to help us girls. You are the only recourse we have left. We are working in a garment factory, and a few months ago our minimum wages were $11. Today they have been cut down to $4 and $5 and $6. Please send someone from Washington to restore our minimum wage so that we can live." Three years later the women did win a wage increase, but it was war that helped them escape poverty.

The New England textile industry made a significant, if temporary, comeback during World War II when mills turned out mountains of military supplies. Day and night shifts of workers produced uniforms, blankets, parachutes, tents, jungle hammocks, and hundreds of other items. The mills won more time when American Air Force bombers obliterated Japan's industries, including textile mills that had exported many products to U.S. markets. After the war, the American mills reconverted to the production of conventional fabrics. The Japanese cleared away the rubble and ashes of war, built modern mills, and once more exported their products to the United States. The Southern textile industry continued to grow, and the New England industry continued its inexorable decline.

As the end approached, some owners of failing mills lost all sense of compassion for their employees. Work conditions regressed to the darkest days of the mills in England that so repulsed William Blake and Charles Dickens. James Ellis was nineteen years old and working in the dye house of a Lowell mill when he saw a sixty-five-year-old coworker, the father of seven, stricken with a heart attack and lying on the floor. "I went to his assistance, and my boss immediately came forward and instructed me to get back to my machine," Ellis told Mary H. Blewett. "He would not let me administer first aid to a man who at that moment was dying. It was at least a half an hour before the nurse came down with the doctor, who then declared the man dead." Ellis fulfilled a vow he made to himself that day and became a union organizer.

When Sidney Muskovitz, another dye worker, saw a man's hand trapped in machinery, he shut down the machines and struggled without success to free the hand. Other workers managed to do so, and after the ambulance took the injured man away, Muskovitz remembered, "the boss says to me, *Why did you shut your machines down? ... You should have called the next room and got help and keep the machines going.*'" Other workers recalled that when anyone died on the job, an undertaker arrived to remove the body in a burlap bag while the work of the mill went on.

Financial buccaneers found that with the help of the federal tax code they could enrich themselves by presiding over the death of the Northern textile industry. William F. Hartford noted that "the federal tax code made liquidation a profitable undertaking for the former owners. Many ... made substantial profits during the war years, but had little interest in using them to undertake needed modernization programs; nor did they wish to pay the high personal income taxes that would be levied upon these earnings if they were distributed as dividends. By selling out, owners paid only a capital gains tax and buyers acquired the firms at what were in effect fire-sale prices."

On State Street in Boston, the word among investors was that selling out was the way to go; there was scant discussion about the impact on people who worked in the mills, or on the communities where they lived.

Buyers waited in line to take over the old mills. Royal Little, a long-time manufacturer of rayon for women's "intimate apparel," formed the

Textron Corporation in Rhode Island after the war and within a few years bought seventeen old mills. Among them was the Nashua Manufacturing Company, which the Boston Associates had built in the 1820s. The Nashua mills were the lifeblood of the local economy. Four thousand people were working there when Little assumed control. On September 13, 1948, Textron announced that by the end of the year, the mills would close. People with fear in their eyes spoke of the news throughout the city, from the Miss Nashua Diner, to the grocery stores, to the banks, and to the country club. Royal Little told the Nashua people that he was shifting some mill operations to the union-free South and that he was building a mill in Puerto Rico. Nashua was no longer a viable location for textiles, he explained. As he left town, he nonchalantly offered unsolicited advice: "New Englanders must go back to work and stop living in the past."

Dorothy Hayward was among those who had worked in the Nashua mills, along with her father, two sisters, and two brothers. She remembered the closing's devastating effect on the workers. "That was their home—their livelihood—and they didn't know where to turn," Hayward said. "Some people didn't speak English. They were hurt the most. They came to the mill young, and that was all they knew."

Fred Dobens, managing editor of the *Nashua Telegraph*, remembered that for months after the closing, long lines formed at the unemployment office. The people were waiting to collect a weekly benefit check of twenty-two dollars, half the amount they had earned as mill workers. They meditated on how to pay the bills that came in the mail every day, and on what the future held for them and their families. Who needed them? The mill had been their livelihood and now it was gone. "I'll never forget their faces," Dobens said.

Emil Rieve, president of the Textile Workers of America, estimated that Royal Little's mill closings in several New England towns threw seven thousand people out of work. As for the shutdown of the Nashua Manufacturing Company, Rieve added: "Mr. Little hasn't used Nashua as a mill—he has used it as a mine. He has mined it and stripped it . . . he is an undertaker."

Whenever Little took over a failed or dying mill, he assumed liability for the losses being sustained and so, like the sellers, reaped generous federal tax benefits. Little moved on to Lowell where he bought out the Newmarket silk mill, closed it, and left hundreds of unemployed people behind. He moved on to Lawrence, bought out William Wood's company, American Woolen, and shut down those operations, too. Once, the Lawrence mill workers had battled William Wood with the help of Annie Welzenbach, Josephine Lis, Big Bill Haywood, and Elizabeth Gurley Flynn. In the years after World War II, when their antagonists were Royal Little and the puzzling new economics of the textile industry, no one could help them. For all his faults, "Billy" Wood operated his mills to produce goods for the American economy. Royal Little made it clear his only reason for buying American Woolen was to gain tax benefits. He said if the company "hadn't been such a God-awful mess, I couldn't have picked it up." Eventually, Congress closed the tax loopholes that allowed Little and other financiers to enrich themselves, but by then most of the mill jobs had vanished.

Mill worker Blanche Sciacca, recalling all the jobless workers Little abandoned in Lawrence, told an interviewer: "We thought the shoe shops were beneath us. We thought only people without any education went to the shoe shops. But once the mills closed we gladly went to the shoe shops."

A few industry leaders in New England wanted to stand and fight against the dissolution of the mills. Among them was Seabury Stanton who headed the Hathaway Manufacturing Company in New Bedford. In 1951, as mills in the region were giving up and closing, Stanton tried to rally managers of the surviving mills. "Our roots are deep in New England soil," he reminded them. "Most of our mills were established way back in the last century; those of us who still remain have stood fast during the thirty years of general exodus from this area. From a standpoint of character and personality, we are, I guess, stubborn men who like a fight and who refuse to give up under competitive difficulties."

Even in its dying days, the industry had some good bosses. Mary H. Blewett interviewed Lowell workers about their days at the Wannalancit Mill owned by Alan Larter. They remembered that Larter was never in a hurry to give them raises, but that he paid them decent wages, helped many of them through their financial troubles, and during a time when so many of his competitors acted like monsters toward their employees, treated them with dignity. John Neild did the same for his workers at the Neild Mill in New Bedford, and when he faced bankruptcy in 1937, the workers willingly took a 10 percent pay cut to save the mill.

Greek immigrant workers in Lowell had a similarly enlightened boss at the Merrimack Mill. Jake Ziskind was a mill liquidator and a buyer and seller of textile machinery. But he also provided his employees with decent working conditions and fair wages. Tarsy Poulous told writer Nicholas V. Karas that Ziskind regularly walked through the mill to talk with his employees. "The workers were glad to see him," Poulous said. "They respected him. Even when he became seriously ill, he visited the floors even though he was in a wheelchair." When Ziskind died, his workers established a scholarship in his name. "Imagine," Poulous said, "doing that for a boss."

Such instances of mutual respect were unusual in a time of economic turmoil. Men and women all over New England scrambled to find jobs as the mills disappeared. When the jobs were not to be found, people joined assemblies of the damned on the unemployment lines. Private lives collapsed. Personnel managers in the mills counseled workers who were dealing with depression, alcoholism, spousal abuse, abortions, and unwanted pregnancies.

The industry continued to stumble into oblivion. The giant Bates Manufacturing Company, newly acquired by New York financier Lester Martin, shut two mills in Lewiston and Saco, Maine. A few miles from Saco, people in the town of Sanford woke up one morning to learn that the Southern-based Burlington Mills had taken control of the mill that Thomas Goodall had established in Sanford eighty-seven years before. Burlington Mills moved the Sanford looms to its Southern plants and closed the mill. The statue of Thomas Goodall stood in the center of a town that was left with three thousand six hundred jobless people and two million square feet of empty mills. The evidence of the Goodall presence was still everywhere—the hospital, the library, the ballfield— but people in Sanford knew that their lives had changed forever.

In Shelton, Connecticut, managers closed the Shelton Mills, and Sidney Blumenthal's dream of industrial democracy for his workers was dead. The company moved on to North Carolina. New owners of Alan Larter's Wannalancit Mill shut it down. The same thing happened to Jake Ziskind's Merrimack Mill. John Neild's mill in New Bedford vanished. Union negotiators in surviving mills focused on winning severance packages for their members rather than on pension plans, because the workers had no faith the textile companies would be around to provide pensions. A Franco-American song summed up New England's fate:

> *I don't hear the bells ringing anymore*
> *From every direction, from everywhere*
>
> *I don't hear the bell ringing anymore*
> *Calling us every morning.*

In 1951, during the peak of the mill closings, those who no longer heard the bells could read startling conclusions in *Fortune* magazine: "Fifty years ago American capitalism seemed to be what Marx predicted it would be and what all the muckrakers said it was—the inhuman offspring of greed and irresponsibility, committed by its master, Wall Street, to a long life of monopoly. It seemed to provide overwhelming proof of the theory that private ownership could honor no obligation except the obligation to pile up profits...but American capitalism today is actually nothing of the kind." Indeed, *Fortune* declared, Big Business showed great responsibility by working for the benefit of stockholders, employees, customers and the general public. Clearly, *Fortune* did not gather its observations in the mill towns of New England.

Today, unions fight for workers' rights in the Southern mills that are still doing business. They fight child labor and worker exploitation in American sweatshops. They fight the abuses of textile plants in Latin America and Asia whose workers are in a virtual state of bondage. For pitiful wages, the workers produce garments that carry famous labels and the endorsements of American sports and entertainment stars. American apparel corporations and celebrities periodically express shock that their names are attached to products made at such a shameful cost. The overseas mills keep running and running.

Four hundred thousand men and women once worked in the New England mills. By 1954, more than half of the jobs had vanished, and the decline never stopped. Senators and congressmen from the region tried to stanch the bleeding with a variety of ultimately futile congressional proposals. John Buckley, a mayor of Lawrence in the 1950s, recalled the day that President Dwight D. Eisenhower told a crowd on the Common that "this is the forgotten city." The president invited Buckley and other Lawrence officials to a White House conference to discuss the depressed economy of the region. "It ended up," Buckley said, "with his saying that this is a local problem that should be solved locally."

Mill communities like Nashua and Manchester, New Hampshire, and Sanford, Maine, succeeded in attracting new industries that gave work to their people. Other cities and towns were not as successful. A citizens' group in New Bedford said in a 1970 report, "New Bedford is, for a very large part of our population, an absolutely miserable city, a city where many can't make a decent living, can't get a decent house to live in, can't get a good education for their kids, can't find a decent place for their kids to play." Jonathan Kozol, whose books call attention to the worst of America's social ills, visited Lawrence and called it "one big ghetto." Jack Kerouac remembered St. John de Baptiste Church in his hometown of Lowell as the "ponderous Chartres Cathedral of the slums."

Urban renewal cleared away many of the slums in the mill communities. Along with the old tenements and the *Petit Canadas* and other ethnic enclaves, the wrecking balls demolished some of the boarding-houses that once were home to the thousands of hopeful young women who first worked in the mills. Preservationists had wanted to save them in the 1950s, but for textile workers, embittered by hard times, the boardinghouses symbolized corporate paternalism. Mary H. Blewett called the destruction of the houses "working-class revenge."

Some boardinghouses escaped demolition and still stand in Lowell, and tourists walk through old rooms rich in history. The houses are part of the Lowell National Historical Park, operated by the National Park Service. A museum in an old brick mill commemorates early factory life in America. Its exhibits tell the story of the Lords of the Loom who built the mills and of those who worked in them.

There are artifacts of the New England farm women who led the way to the Lowell mills and re-creations of their bedrooms and dining tables and parlors. The furniture and wallpaper and quilts cannot convey the trepidation the women felt as they stepped forward to claim their place in American society. No museum curator can gauge their influence on succeeding generations of women who asked that in their work they be granted simple justice. But the museum visitor does come away with a sense that these New England farm women, most of them teenagers, did, on their own, win a lasting place in the story of their country.

Throughout her life as a teacher and poet, Lucy Larcom never forgot the women she worked with in Lowell. Summing up her life, she said: "I regard it as one of the privileges of my youth that I was permitted to grow up among these active, interesting girls, whose lives were not mere echoes of other lives, but had principle and purpose distinctly their own.... They gave me a larger, firmer ideal of womanhood." To those women, she said simply, "I am glad I have lived in the world with you!"

The museum exhibits also hint at the rich history of those who left many lands to pursue their modest dreams in the mills. There are precious possessions the immigrants brought with them to America: shawls from Ireland, songbooks from Quebec, ornate candlesticks from Russia, religious icons reflecting many faiths, and family photographs. The images of aged immigrants holding infant grandchildren tell of people who came to America to stay, to survive, and to succeed.

A museum wall is filled with names representing the ethnic groups that came to Lowell to find work. There are English and Irish names: Abbott, Casey, Shattuck, Wyman. Then the Franco-Americans and Germans came: Allard, Bergeron, Courchaine, Dubois, Schemmehorn, Vansteenberg. Greeks and Jews and Italians and Poles and others came: Agelakis, Antonio, Glowinski, Goldenberg, Hirsch, Warshawsky. Now in Lowell, as in so many other New England towns, the newest names are Chin, Cruz, Pham, Tran.

There is the loom room, a vast space where tourists see eighty-eight pounding looms weaving cloth. A few park employees tend the automated machines. Visitors can imagine the time when women stood amid the industrial pandemonium. They can imagine how terrified the women were of the speeding leather belts turning the shafts and gears, how the workers feared that the belts might break and whip into their bodies, maiming them for life. The park visitor who can no longer tolerate the loudness leaves the room. The mill women withstood years of peril among the howling machines.

From the time of Lucy Larcom to the final days of the industry, men and women all over New England have come away with conflicting views of mill life. A few years ago, the American Textile History Museum, now located near the Lowell Historical Park, asked the public to become members. Ray Fremmer declined. In a letter to the *Lawrence Eagle-Tribune*, Fremmer wrote: "I saw my grandparents, great-grandparents, and parents, all their brothers and sisters, dehydrated of every creative human impulse by giving their working lives to the very same mills the museum now seeks to glorify. The mills were hellholes, purgatories that tortured the human mind into submission. The mills never elevated the human spirit; they degraded it to the level of mules harnessed to machines for life."

Madalyn Stahley Donahue wrote in reply that the struggles of those earlier times inspired people of her generation. She wrote of the grandchildren of immigrants who graduated from Harvard and Holy Cross, and who are now part of America's middle class. Remembering those who worked so long and so hard in the mills, Madalyn Donahue said that she believed that their spirit never died. "No, Mr. Fremmer," she wrote, "their spirit lives on."

When classes let out at Lowell High School on Kirk Street, children of the newest immigrants pass by some of the well-preserved boardinghouses. They pass granite and steel memorials to the mill women and the silhouette bust of Francis Cabot Lowell who started it all. They follow in the footsteps of men and women, rich and poor, native and immigrant, who left behind so much history, as well as the most visible evidence of their lives, the enormous empty mills.

At Immaculate Conception Cemetery on the outskirts of Lawrence, thousands of mill workers rest under modest gravestones that reflect their lives and the great tides of immigration that made possible the New England textile industry. The engraved names are of Ireland and Quebec and Europe. John Ramey, a young victim of violence during the 1912 labor strife, is buried there. So is Annie Lopizzo, who was shot to death during the strike. For almost ninety years, her grave had no stone. Now her name is heralded on a solid block of granite carved and donated by the granite workers of Barre, Vermont, whose ancestors had harbored Lawrence children during the strike. John Ramey and Annie Lopizzo rest with workers who were bruised by adversity as they fought for every dollar they earned and for every measure of respect and fairness that was their due in the mills and in American society. In an adjacent cemetery, there is a memorial to unknown victims of the 1860 Pemberton Mill disaster who never got their due.

The Lords of the Loom are with their own kind in Mount Auburn Cemetery, a robin's flight away from their hallowed Harvard University. Generations of Boston Brahmins lie with them under heavy stones in stately garden settings that are shaded by sugar maples and pines. The cemetery silence is softly broken by the summer song of mockingbirds and wood thrushes.

The names on the granite monuments symbolize New England history: Wendell Phillips, the blue-blood reformer who condemned worker exploitation; Edward Everett, the statesman who believed that Irish immigrants were inferior but suitable for mill work; Henry Cabot Lodge, the old senator who worried about immigrants coming to America; and Henry Cabot Lodge Jr., who followed his grandfather into the Senate with the help of immigrants' votes.

Nathan Appleton is there with his daughter Frances Appleton Long-fellow, and her husband, Henry Wadsworth Longfellow. Many Lowells rest at Mount Auburn, including Amy and James Russell Lowell, and their illustrious relative by marriage, Isabella Stewart Gardner.

The Lawrence family plot is enclosed by a wrought-iron fence. Some fifty family members are buried there, including old Amos Lawrence, his son, Amos A. Lawrence, and *his* son, Bishop William Lawrence. Towering above their stones is a marble column on the more imposing tomb of Abbott Lawrence, the most venerated of all the Lawrences.

Across the cemetery path, a stone sphinx reposes on a memorial to those who died in the Civil War to preserve the Union and to end the slavery that supplied cotton to the mills of Abbott and Amos Lawrence and their associates. A short stroll away is the grave of Senator Charles Sumner, whose thunderous antislavery speeches tormented the consciences of the New England cotton lords. All sleep in the beauty of what Emily Dickinson called "the city of the dead."

There is a deathly silence, too, in many of the mills the Brahmins and their successors built. "We Weave the World's Worsteds," the workers of Lawrence once proclaimed to the world. Then the owners took away their looms. The great novel experiment that Nathan Appleton was so proud of was at an end.

The rivers of New England long ago ceased to generate power for the mill machines that clothed the world. Now, on warm, sun-filled days, the rivers carry people in canoes and kayaks as they explore the old industrial waterways. They are people who work in sleek technology plants and gleaming skyscrapers. They shop at L. L. Bean and in glittering malls, and do not worry about bread money. In the distance, they see the deserted mills, with weeds reaching up to shattered windows and gloomy interiors. They wonder about the past, about ghosts, about broken dreams. They turn away and drift downstream, searching for scenery more pleasing to the eye.

NOTES

1. A Place in the Universe

3. Women who could not afford: Stephen Winship, *A Testing Time*, 39.
3-4. "The tender breasts of ladies": June Sochen, *Herstory*, 73.
4. "Let the woman be satisfied": Sara M. Evans, *Born for Liberty*, ??
4. It was the sons: Thomas Dublin, *Farm to Factory*, 40.
4. Before 1840: Harriet H. Robinson, *Loom and Spindle*, 42.
4. "in social meetings": Evans, *Born for Liberty*, 73.
4. "The thought that I am living": Ann Swett Appleton Letters, 1847-1850, typescript edited by Priscilla Ordway 1953. Manchester (N.H.) Historic Association, Miscellaneous Person Papers, Box 1, Folder 7.
4. Some were unmarried: Bernice Selden, *The Mill Girls*, 90.
4, 5. A mill worker wrote: Benita Eisler, *The Lowell Offering*, 61.
5. "The cotton factory was a great opening": Robinson, *Loom and Spindle*, 42.
5. "I had no hope": Laura Nichols Bridgman manuscript, Houghton Library, Harvard University, ABC Individual Biography, Box 10. From the American Board of Commissioners for Foreign Missions Archive. By permission of the Houghton Library, Harvard University.
5. In the western Massachusetts town: Kathleen Barry, *Susan B. Anthony*, 15-18.
6. By 1850: Steve Dunwell, *The Run of the Mill*, 51.
6. "Will it wash?": Philip G. Hubert, "The Business of a Factory," 321.
6. His New England mill workers: Louise Hall Tharp, *The Appletons of Beacon Hill*, 189.
7. The image of a dragon: *An Introduction to Biddeford History*, 44.
7. An Indian head: Winship, *A Testing Time*, 48.

7. "from the Emperor": exhibit, Lowell National Historical Park.

7. "American cotton manufacturers": ibid.

7. The mills had commercial customers: Theodore Steinberg, *Nature Incorporated*, 61.

7. "One of the most beautiful": Ferris Greenslet, *The Lowells and Their Seven Worlds*, 231.

7. "a city springing up": Dunwell, *Run of the Mill*, 40.

7, 8. "Acres of girlhood": Robinson, *Loom and Spindle*, 45.

8. "I went in among": *Davy Crockett's Own Story*, 202.

8. "Out of so large a number": Charles Dickens, *American Notes for General Circulation*, 73.

8. "It is for this class": *Dictionary of American Biography*, Vol. 6, 531.

9. "Steamboat to Hartford": Bridgman manuscript.

2. The Glory of the Nation

11. The women chatted: Hannah Josephson, *Golden Threads*, 66.

11. They had whimsical names: Edith Abbott, *Women in Industry*, 273; exhibit, Lowell National Historical Park.

11. In the new mill city: exhibits, Lowell National Historical Park.

12. "I tell you Sarah": Ann Swett Appleton letters.

12. "After the first payday": Robinson, *Loom and Spindle*, 42.

12. "It is difficult to imagine": *America and the Americans*, Vol. 1, 251-66.

12. "What amongst us": John Coolidge, *Mill and Mansion*, 161.

12. A mill executive told: Josephson, *Golden Threads*, 4.

13. In Dover, New Hampshire: brochure, "Walking Tour in Dover," 1985. Dover, New Hampshire, public library.

13. "Young ladies": *The Factory Girl's Garland*, Vol. 1, no. 19, September 14, 1844.

13. "mate themselves with the pride": Nathaniel Hawthorne, *Mosses from an Old Manse*, 277.

13. "If you should be blessed": Dublin, *Farm to Factory*, 22.

13. "The most intelligent": "Farming Life in New England," *Atlantic Monthly*, August 1858, 341.

14. In Derry, New Hampshire: exhibit, Lowell National Historical Park.

14. The call of the mills: Thomas Dublin, *Transforming Women's Work*, 78.

14. In 1831: Caroline F. Ware, *The Early New England Cotton Manufacture*, 215.

15. "Here was in New England": Nathan Appleton, *Introduction to the Power Loom and Origin of Lowell*, 15.

15. Boott built mills: Dunwell, *Run of the Mill*, 37.

15. He built the Merrimack: Frances W. Gregory, *Nathan Appleton Merchant and Entrepreneur*, 191.

15. "be remembered till": Frederick W. Coburn, *History of Lowell and Its People*, 143.

15. "the peaceful hum": Josephson, *Golden Threads*, 4.

16. Lowell, he wrote: George F. Kennegot, *The Record of a City*, 13.

16. "The price of such a woman": Eisler, *Lowell Offering*, 59.

16. Charlotte Hilburn recounted: exhibit, Lowell National Historical Park.

16. A skeptical woman worker: Eisler, *Lowell Offering*, 74.

17. Their common experiences: Evans, *Born for Liberty*, 74.

17. "scarcely any rest": exhibit, Lowell National Historical Park.

17. "They don't give us time": Eisler, *Lowell Offering*, 75.

17. The mills paid: Stephen A. Mrozowski, Grace H. Ziesing, and Mary C. Beaudry, *Living on the Boott*, 52.

17. "these small luxuries": ibid., 55.

18. "When the lecturer entered": Eisler, *Lowell Offering*, 32.

18. "They subscribed to the British reviews": Van Wyck Brooks, *The Flowering of New England*, 176.

18. In Saco, Maine: Roy P. Fairfield, *Sand, Spindles and Steeples*, 71.

18. "Gain, and not bread": Ware, *Early New England Cotton Manufacture*, 217.

18. "As Kirk Boott was an Episcopalian": Coolidge, *Mill and Mansion*, 42.

19. "This is unprincipled conduct": Ware, *Early New England Cotton Manufacture*, 250.

19. Workers raised money: exhibit, Museum of Work and Culture, Woonsocket, Rhode Island.

19. The workers had large parties: *Introduction to Biddeford History*, 26.

19. "No persons can be employed": Dunwell, *Run of the Mill*, 43.

20. "This moral poppycock": Josephson, *Golden Threads*, 74.

20. "It was a rigid code": Lucy Larcom, *A New England Girlhood*, 180.

20. "though regulation in practice": Thomas Dublin, *Lowell*, 52.

20. *And if one broke:* Robert Frost, "A Lonely Striker."

21. "You know that people": Eisler, *Lowell Offering*, 52.

21. "In the sweet June weather": Larcom, *New England Girlhood*, 182.

22. "but aside from the talking": Eisler, *Lowell Offering*, 63.

22. "The daughter leaves": Abbott, *Women in Industry*, 125.

22. "as snow falls in winter": Charles A. Scontras, *Collective Efforts Among Maine Workers*, 263.

23. "I have been called": Philip T. Silvia Jr., "The Position of Workers in a Textile Community."

23. Eventually, 70 percent: Laurence F. Gross, *The Course of Industrial Decline*, 64.

23. "The conscientious among them": Robinson, *Loom and Spindle*, 44.

23. *Despite the toil:* Greenslet, *The Lowells*, 224.

24. *Speed on the light:* John Greenleaf Whittier, "The New Year".

24. "Are we torn from our friends": Robinson, *Loom and Spindle*, 116.

24. "if the vote of": Larcom, *New England Girlhood*, 255.

25. *When I've thought:* Selden, *Mill Girls*, 65.

25. "The superior capabilities": Gregory, *Nathan Appleton*, 188.

25. *O sing me a song:* Arthur M. Schlesinger Jr., *The Age of Jackson*, 272.

26. Jackson took time out: ibid., 311.

26. "Very pretty women": Josephson, *Golden Threads*, 60.

26. "the ambition of women": Ware, *Early New England Cotton Manufacture*, 216.

26. "a propensity among those": Dublin, *Transforming Women's Work*, 111.

26. "They were all well dressed": Dickens, *American Notes*, 72.

27. "I hope sometime": Dublin, *Farm to Factory*, 99.

27. "I have earned enough": Loriman Brigham, "An Independent Voice: A Mill Girl from Vermont Speaks Her Mind."

27. "I am making three dollars": Dublin, *Farm to Factory*, 102.

27. "I went out and bought": Ann Swett Appleton letters.

28. With support from the public: Paul Buhle, Scott Molloy, and Gail Sansbury, *A History of Rhode Island Working People*, 3.

28. "a control over the lives": Ware, *Early New England Cotton Manufacture*, 297.

28. "The mob of great cities": Schlesinger, *Age of Jackson*, 310.

28. "A general turnout": *Dover* (New Hampshire) *Enquirer*, December 30, 1828.

29. "The late strike": Scontras, *Collective Efforts Among Maine Workers*, 83.

29. "The operatives are well-dressed": *Boston Quarterly Review*, July 1840, 366-95, quoted in *The Annals of America*, Vol. 6, 536.

29. "This afternoon": Thomas Dublin, "Women, Work, and Protest in the Early Lowell Mills," in *The Continuing Revolution*, ed. Robert Weible, 86.

29. In Nashua, where the mills imposed: Winship, *A Testing Time*, 51-52.

30. "riotous combinations": *Dover* (New Hampshire) *Gazette* and *Strafford Advertiser*, March 4, 1834.

30. "to reduce the females": Josephson, *Golden Threads*, 235.

30. They pooled their money: Laurie Nisonoff, "Bread and Roses."

30. "Curtis was a strange": Robert Whitehouse, "Dover History," Vol. 1, 81.

31. While riding one of his trains: Foster's *Daily Democrat*, September 4, 1987.

31. "the mistaken impression": Abbott, *Women in Industry*, 130.

31. "As our fathers resisted": Josephson, *Golden Threads*, 237.

31. This time the women used: Dublin, "Women, Work, and Protest," 88.

31. "manifest *good spunk*": ibid.

32. "Girls of fifteen to eighteen": *New-York Weekly Tribune*, August 14, 1847.

32. A Boston newspaper: Dunwell, *Run of the Mill*, 91.

32. A doctor at Lowell Hospital: Abbott, *Women in Industry*, 125.

32. Another medical survey: *Report on Condition of Woman and Child Wage-earners in the United States*, 103.

32. Yet another doctor: Scontras, *Collective Efforts Among Maine Workers*, 93.

32. Henry David Thoreau visited: Dunwell, *Run of the Mill*, 93.

33. "That there is sickness": Miles's observations are all from *Lowell As It Was, and As It Is*.

34. In 1845, women at the Dwight: Josephson, *Golden Threads*, 267.

34. Eliza Adams, who had journeyed: exhibit, Lowell National Historical Park.

34. "morally reprehensible": Josephson, *Golden Threads*, 74.

34. Despite all their disadvantages: Barry, *Susan B. Anthony*, 5.

35. The most strident: Helena Wright, "Sarah Bagley," *Continuing Revolution*, 97-113.

35. "Is anyone such a fool": *Voice of Industry*, September 18, 1845, exhibit, Lowell National Historical Park.

36. "*If I must*": Selden, *Mill Girls*, 137.

36. "The morals of the operatives": Foster Rhea Dulles, *Labor in America*, 85.

36. Bagley visited prisons: Wright, "Sarah Bagley."

37. The women were described: Nisonoff, "Bread and Roses."

37. "Labor is intelligent": Josephson, *Golden Threads*, 260.

37. The women accused: Dulles, *Labor in America*, 85.

37. Although women did not have the vote: Dublin in *The Continuing Revolution*, 91.

37. The New Hampshire workers: Winship, *A Testing Time*, 53.

37. By this time: Selden, *Mill Girls*, 173.

38. Bowing to public pressure: Josephson, *Golden Threads*, 285.

38. The women argued: ibid., 213.

38. Women shoe workers: Dublin, *Transforming Women's Work*, 121.

38. Samuel Rodman, treasurer: Seymour Louis Wolfbein, *The Decline of a Cotton Textile City*, appendix.

39. "The girls were afraid": Josephson, *Golden Threads*, 220.

39. "Mine," wrote Harriet Hanson Robinson: Robinson, *Loom and Spindle*, 45.

39. Henry Miles cited: Miles, *Lowell As It Was*.

39. Other reasons included: Carl Gersuny, "A Devil in Petticoats."

40. "There have been a good many": Josephson, *Golden Threads*, 225.

40. Thomas was editor: Ware, *Early New England Cotton Manufacture*, 296.

40. Whittier was an editorial adviser: Eisler, *Lowell Offering*, 35.

41. "Susan" wrote: ibid., 209.

41. Another worker publication: *Woman and Child Wage-earners*, 103.

42. The *Voice* charged: ibid., 107.

42. The *Voice* confronted: Dulles, *Labor in America*, 75.

42. "And amidst the clashing": *Woman and Child Wage-earners*, 102.

42. Women slaves in the cotton states: Kenneth M. Stampp, *The Peculiar Institution*, 303, 306.

43. "Frederick, is God dead?": *Encyclopedia of African-American Culture and History*, (Simon and Schuster, 1996), Vol. 5, 2675.

43. Some joined: Stewart H. Holbrook, *The Yankee Exodus*, 74-75.

43. The mills hired men: Abbott, *Women in Industry*, 282.

43. One driver who transported: *Woman and Child Wage-earners*, 80.

43. A Portland, Maine, newspaper: Scontras, *Collective Efforts Among Maine Workers*, 96.

43. "You could not count": Josephson, *Golden Threads*, 227.

44. "a mouthpiece": Robert F. Dalzell Jr., *Enterprising Elite*, 68.

44. She denied that: Abbott, *Women in Industry*, 131.

44. "I have never felt": Selden, *Mill Girls*, 158.

44. "was a pivotal figure": Wright, "Sarah Bagley," 109.

45. Mary Paul returned: Dublin, *Farm to Factory*, 121.

45. Other women took: Josephson, *Golden Threads*, 193.

45. Lucy Larcom, who had pasted: Larcom, *New England Girlhood*, 193.

45. Eliza Adams of Derry: exhibit, Lowell National Historical Park.

3. *The Lords of the Loom*

47. He had known only success: C. David Heymann, *American Aristocracy*, 4.

48. One of the few known: Cleveland Amory, *The Proper Bostonians*, 67.

48. "almost alone": George Sweet Gibb, *The Saco-Lowell Shops*, 6.

49. Factory owners circulated: Eisler, *Lowell Offering*, 15.

49. What age are you? John Carey, *Eyewitness to History*, 295-98.

50. Lowell was a brilliant: Greenslet, *The Lowells*, 156.

50. On his way back: Gregory, *Nathan Appleton*, 146.

51. Moody, the son of: Coburn, *History of Lowell*, 139.

51. "I well recollect": Gibb, *Saco-Lowell Shops*, 8.

51. Samuel Slater, under the patronage: ibid., 7.

52. 1 family with 8 members: Ware, *Early New England Cotton Manufacture*, 199.

52. Corporal punishment for: Abbott, *Women in Industry*, 347.

52. A contemporary said: Coburn, *History of Lowell*, 139.

52. "hoped to find": Gibb, *Saco-Lowell Shops*, 3.

53. "to perpetuate their names": Brooks, *Flowering of New England*, 5.

53. "a harmless, inoffensive": Oliver Wendell Holmes, *Elsie Venner*.

53. *My Grandpa lives:* Amy Lowell, "The Painted Ceiling."

54. "He was," wrote Nathan Appleton: *Dictionary of American Biography*, Vol. 6, 456.

54. In 1815, the first full year: Richard D. Brown, *Massachusetts, a History*, 136.

54. He wrote of "the horrid sight": Tharp, *The Appletons*, 35.

54. "He may have been": Dalzell, *Enterprising Elite*, 60.

54. "In fact, good conditions": Gregory, *Nathan Appleton*, 188.

55. Appleton shared his wealth: ibid., 272.

55. "the feudal curse": *The Poems of Henry Wadsworth Longfellow*, Modern Library edition, 459.

55. Patrick Tracy Jackson, like Lowell: *Dictionary of American Biography*, Vol. 5, 552.

55. "a silver cascade": Henry David Thoreau, *The Concord and the Merrimack*, 77.

55. The valley covered: Steinberg, *Nature Incorporated*, 50.

56. The pristine river: ibid., 207.

56. The corporate structure: Dublin, *Lowell*, 33.

57. "Confucius would have recognized": Greenslet, *The Lowells*, 220.

57. "Five thousand dollars a year": Coburn, *History of Lowell*, 169.

57. They had some small mills: Stampp, *Peculiar Institution*, 65.

58. "That we have cultivated": *Annals of America*, Vol. 5, 226.

58. "There could be no mistaking": John F. Kennedy, *Profiles in Courage*, 62.

58. The Boston Associates rewarded: Greenslet, *The Lowells*, 220.

58. To his dying day: Robert V. Remini, *Daniel Webster*, 200.

59. They looked to the day: Tharp, *The Appletons*, 249.

59. While he was the editor: *Complete Poetical Works of John Greenleaf Whittier*, 262.

59. "Let Southern oppressors": *The Liberator*, January 1, 1831.

59. "fanatical monomaniac": *Dictionary of American Biography*, Vol. 1, 331.

59. "The wheels of the cotton factories": Brooks, *Flowering of New England*, 172.

59. Among those who fought: Myron O. Stachiw, "For the Sake of Commerce."

59. Mill fever broke out: Gibb, *Saco-Lowell Shops*, 111.

60. Abbot Lawrence's competitive: Dalzell, *Enterprising Elite*, 148.

60. "it is no less the duty": Hamilton Andrews Hill, *Memoir of Abbott Lawrence*, 107.

61.   "tend to create mechanics": Donald B. Cole, *Immigrant City*, 24.

61.   "a certain mad haste": Josephson, *Golden Threads*, 168.

61.   "Business before friends": Amory, *Proper Bostonians*, 64.

61.   "There is one thing": Bernard A. Weisberger, "The Working Ladies of Lowell."

61.   The letter was from: Ware, *Early New England Cotton Manufacture*, 270.

61.   Decades later, John D. Rockefeller: Dalzell, *Enterprising Elite*, 230.

62.   "If my vote": *Dictionary of American Biography*, Vol. 6, 47.

62.   "He still grasps at money": Dalzell, *Enterprising Elite*, 148-49.

62.   *Yet shame upon them*: Whittier, "The New Year."

63.   "I am for the Union": Kinley J. Brauer, *Conscience versus Cotton*, 23.

63.   "covered old Massachusetts": ibid., 168.

63.   "There is something better": Heymann, *American Aristocracy*, 75.

63.   "We are not only destined": *Letters from the Hon. Abbott Lawrence to the Hon. William C. Rives of Virginia*, Boston, 1846, 8-23, quoted in *The Annals of America*, Vol. 7, 329.

63.   "the word *liberty*": Remini, *Daniel Webster*, 677.

63.   "lost archangel": Milton Rugoff, *The Beechers*, 316.

64.   *So fallen!*: Whittier, "Ichabod."

64.   "a colossus holding": Carl Sandburg, *Abraham Lincoln*, Vol. 1, 100.

64.   When he was elected: Dalzell, *Enterprising Elite*, 202.

64.   "There *is* no other side": *Dictionary of American Biography*, Vol. 9, 213.

64.   "I am in morals": Sandburg, *Abraham Lincoln*, 103.

64.   *My dear Sir*: Andrew Hilen, *The Letters of Henry Wadsworth Longfellow*, 204.

65.   Sumner had once condemned: Tharp, *The Appletons*, 265.

65.   *Dear Sumner*: Hilen, *Letters of Longfellow*, 204.

65.   "an unholy alliance": David Donald, *Charles Sumner and the Coming of the Civil War*, 166.

65.   "Hit him again!": William Lee Miller, *Arguing About Slavery*, 486.

66.   "The Union cannot be touched": Hill, *Memoir of Abbott Lawrence*, 79.

66.   *sail on, O Ship of State*: Longfellow, "The Building of the Ship."

66.   "dying with everything": Hill, *Memoir of Abbott Lawrence*, 122.

66-67.   "How many, many thousands": Josephson, *Golden Threads*, 177.

67.   "Accident and not effort": *Dictionary of American Biography*, Vol. I, 331.

67.   "I am not afraid": Amory, *Proper Bostonians*, 93.

67.   "She has gone": *Dictionary of American Biography*, Vol. I, 331.

67.   "it was during": Josephson, *Golden Threads*, 117.

67.   "We went to bed": Stachiw, "For the Sake of Commerce."

68.   The family's roles: Lawrence Lader, *The Bold Brahmins*, 196.

68.   "Old Brown hanged": Dalzell, *Enterprising Elite*, 286.

68.   "nine of the great corporations": Abbott, *Women in Industry*, 142.

69.   "the pride of the family": Heymann, *American Aristocracy*, 34.

69.   "If every dollar earned": Dalzell, *Enterprising Elite*, 54.

69.   "as each rich man": Jennie Collins, *Nature's Aristocracy*, 142.

69.   "desired dividends more": Herbert Harris, *American Labor*, 313.

70. "Americans stopped thinking": Coolidge, *Mill and Mansion*, 74.

70. Oscar Wilde was a guest: Amory, *Proper Bostonians*, 280.

70. "Mrs. Jack," as she was known: ibid., 129.

71. They helped establish: Heymann, *American Aristocracy*, 178.

71. Percival Lowell, a prominent astronomer: ibid., 51.

72. "before our individuality": ibid., 130, 151, 345.

72. "blinded by privilege": Amory, *Proper Bostonians*, 324.

72. "the most homogeneous": ibid.

72. When John F. Kennedy: Stephen Birmingham, *Real Lace*, 186.

72. In 1946, when Godfrey Lowell Cabot: Amory, *Proper Bostonians*, 346.

73. In private, Amy Lowell viewed: Heymann, *American Aristocracy*, 240.

73. "going from tenement": William Lawrence, *Memories of a Happy Life*, 47.

4. From Across the Irish Sea

75. They were willing to work: George Potter, *To the Golden Door*, 340.

75-78. Much of the material on the early Irish settlers in Lowell is from *The Irish Catholic Genesis of Lowell* by George F. O'Dwyer, and *The Paddy Camps* by Brian C. Mitchell.

76. "an Irish village": exhibit, Lowell National Historical Park.

76. "were one of the first signs": Coolidge, *Mill and Mansion*, 39.

78-79. Material on John Burns in Dover is from Foster's *Daily Democrat* (Dover, New Hampshire), March 17, 1990.

79. When Beecher preached: Potter, *To the Golden Door*, 248.

79. Among the students: Edward T. James, *Notable American Women*, 439.

79. On the night before: Howard Mumford Jones and Bessie Zaban Jones, *The Many Voices of Boston*, 180.

79. Delivering his own sermon: Potter, *To the Golden Door*, 286.

80. In Fall River: Orin Fowler, "An Historical Sketch of Fall River 1841."

80. "If a humane measure": Ralph Waldo Emerson, "The Young American," 363-95.

80. *Out of Ireland:* William Butler Yeats, "Remorse for Intemperate Speech."

81. "These memories will never die": William Cardinal O'Connell, *Recollections of Seventy Years*, 32.

81. "to give full effect": Thomas Keneally, *The Great Shame*, 105.

82. He commented on the folly: Hill, *Memoir of Abbott Lawrence*, 222.

82. In one case: Oscar Handlin, *The Uprooted*, 27.

82. Pope Adrian IV: Edmund Curtis, *A History of Ireland*, 45; Swinford (County Mayo) Historical Society, *Famine in the Swinford Union*, 9.

83. "The priest was banned": Seumas MacManus, *The Story of the Irish Race*, 458.

83. The British banned: Robert Kee, *The Green Flag*.

83. "with the spirit of shopkeepers": Curtis, *History of Ireland*, 298.

84. "Ireland is a conquered country": Hill, *Memoir of Abbott Lawrence*, 222.

84. Agricultural experts tried: Cecil Woodham-Smith, *The Great Hunger*, 409.

84. A government report: Keneally, *Great Shame*, 9.

84. British Prime Minister John Russell explained: Potter, *To the Golden Door*, 453.

84-85. "The influence of *laissez faire*": Woodham-Smith, *Great Hunger*, 54, 410.

85. In August 1845: Patricia Fitzgerald and Olive Kennedy, *The Great Famine in Killala*, 10.

85. All over Ireland: Potter, *To the Golden Door*, 450.

85. Scientists were unable: Michael Coffey, editor; Terry Golway, text, *The Irish in America*, 4, 5.

85. "There is no cause for alarm": MacManus, *Story of the Irish Race*, 602.

85. "God sent the blight": Tom Hayden, *Irish Hunger*, 80.

85. An eyewitness described: Kee, *Green Flag*, 174.

85-86. *Oh, well do I remember*: Coffey and Golway, *Irish in America*, 14.

86. Queen Victoria asked: MacManus, *Story of the Irish Race*, 603.

86. "Would to God the government": Woodham-Smith, *Great Hunger*, 137.

86. After the famine struck: Fitzgerald and Kennedy, *Great Famine*, 12.

86. Along the shore: Keneally, *Great Shame*, 126.

86. "They ate dogs and rats": John Leo, newspaper column, Universal Press Syndicate, published in the *Sarasota* (Florida) *Herald Tribune*, March 18, 1997.

86. *On highway side*: MacManus, *Story of the Irish Race*, 633.

86-87. "We must stop": Swinford Historical Society, *Famine in the Swinford Union*, 42.

87. "I am a match for anything": Woodham-Smith, *Great Hunger*, 155.

87. Protestant congregations: ibid., 131.

87. "whose body had swollen": ibid., 194.

87. They lost their voices: Fitzgerald and Kennedy, *Great Famine*, 47, 57.

87. On stately Georgian squares: Woodham-Smith, *Great Hunger*, 299.

87. In daylight, passengers saw: Birmingham, *Real Lace*, 14.

87. A priest told of visiting: ibid., 13.

87. A contemporary writer: Hayden, *Irish Hunger*, 113.

88. John Mitchel, the Irish patriot: Keneally, *Great Shame*, 124.

88. *"Are we living"*: ibid.

88. Quakers opened food stations: Coffey and Golway, *Irish in America*, 15.

88. The sultan of Turkey: MacManus, *Story of the Irish Race*, 605.

88. "Ladies Work Associations": Woodham-Smith, *Great Hunger*, 156.

88. Although Queen Victoria: Fitzgerald and Kennedy, *Great Famine*, 25.

89. "The moment the very name": Woodham-Smith, *Great Hunger*, 411.

89. "Here were wild crowds": Hayden, *Irish Hunger*, 25.

89. After the famine: Potter, *To the Golden Door*, 453.

89-90. "The most striking modern objects": Hill, *Memoir of Abbott Lawrence*, 223.

90. *They are going*: MacManus, *Story of the Irish Race*, 608.

90. "Even now," she told: Edward Laxton, *The Famine Ships*, 248.

90. "Those who governed": Associated Press report, June 1997.

91. "Your sons in Ireland": Potter, *To the Golden Door*, 365.

91. "were as numerous as maggots": Coffey and Golway, *Irish in America*, 18.

91. British shipping firms: Richard O'Connor, *The Irish*, 179.

91. It is believed: Woodham-Smith, *Great Hunger*, 238.

91. Their fate in Black 47: MacManus, *Story of the Irish Race*, 610.

92. "I saw many marble feet": Henry David Thoreau, "The Shipwreck," in *Cape Cod*, 853.

93. For a person to be happy: Potter, *To the Golden Door*, 71.

93. "Their inferiority as a race": Jeanne Schinto, *Huddle Fever*, 101.

93-94. The arrival of huge numbers: James H. Mundy, *Hard Times, Hard Men*, 136, 154.

94. "Popery," Morse wrote: *The Annals of America*, Vol. 6, 158.

94. The Know-Nothings appointed: Potter, *To the Golden Door*, 583, 587.

94. In Ellsworth, Maine: Dorothy G. Wayman, *Cardinal O'Connell of Boston*, 99.

94. "Our progress in degeneracy": John Gabriel Hunt, *The Essential Abraham Lincoln*, 93.

95. "The Factory operatives must work": Scontras, *Collective Efforts of Maine Workers*, 95.

95. "Their chief work and task": O'Connell, *Recollections*, 12.

95. "no standards": Josephson, *Golden Threads*, 216.

95. "a downward tendency": Abbott, *Women in Industry*, 139.

95-96. "Deal gently with them": Winship, *A Testing Time*, 53.

96. the three things most difficult: Hasia R. Diner, *Erin's Daughters in America*, 16.

96. "Were I asked to say": Potter, *To the Golden Door*, 525.

96. In Lowell, arrest records: Kennegott, *Record of a City*, 91.

97. Mathew went to Lowell: Mitchell, *Paddy Camps*, 72.

97. "In the process": ibid., 153.

97. Hasia R. Diner's study: Diner, *Erin's Daughters*, 57.

97. In 1881, Massachusetts prisons: ibid., 111.

97. Single women, including: Scontras, *Collective Efforts of Maine Workers*, 94.

97. The bosses, when short of labor: Diner, *Erin's Daughters*, 76.

98. "The amount once in possession": *Godey's Lady's Book and Magazine*, March 1859.

98. At the turn of the century: Diner, *Erin's Daughters*, 90.

98. These "Situation Wanted" ads: *New York Times*, February 25, 1912.

98. "Contemptible toadies": O'Connell, *Recollections*, 9.

99. "have a great deal of guano": "Fate," *The Works of Ralph Waldo Emerson*, Vol. 3, 11.

99. *The Pilot* condemned: Potter, *To the Golden Door*, 607.

100. Details of the Pemberton disaster, unless otherwise noted, are from *An Authentic History of the Lawrence Calamity* and *History of Lawrence, Mass.*, by Maurice B. Dorgan.

100. They installed their looms: Weisberger, "Working Ladies of Lowell."

102. "Headless, armless, crushed": Collins, *Nature's Aristocracy*, 165.

104. "With blanching cheeks": quoted by Mari Jo Buhle and Florence Howe in afterword to Phelps's novel *The Silent Partner*.

104. *My Father's house*: Collins, *Nature's Aristocracy*, 166.

105. *A curse on ye*: Kenneth Fones-Wolf and Martin Kaufman, *Labor in Massachusetts*, 84.

106. The press and the public: ibid., 81.

107. He sensed when to press: William F. Hartford, *Where Is Our Responsibility?*, 16.

107. "The heart sickens": John T. Cumbler, *Working-Class Community in Industrial America*, 114.

107. "If our manufacturers": Silvia, "Position of Workers in a Textile Community."

108. "Let it not be said": Carol Polizotti Webb, "The Lowell Mule Spinners' Strike of 1875," in *Surviving Hard Times*, ed. Mary H. Blewett, 17.

108. By this time: Josephson, *Golden Threads*, 297.

108. The women argued: Ardis Cameron, *Radicals of the Worst Sort*, 41.

108. "tall, with a commanding presence": James, *Notable American Woman*, 102.

108. Barry became a schoolteacher: Diner, *Erin's Daughters*, 100.

108. "have acquired, as a sort of": Barbara Mayer Wertheimer, *We Were There*, 188.

109. By the beginning: Diner, *Erin's Daughters*, 96.

5. Voyagers South

111. "America's attic": Lansing Lamont, *Breakup*, 226.

112. Because of the emigrants: Gerard J. Brault, *The French-Canadian Heritage in New England*, 1.

112. "I suffered and I cried": Michael J. Guignard, *La Foi-La Langue-La Culture*, 81.

112. "Country folk do not die": Louis Hemon, *Maria Chapdelaine*, 175.

113. *Born French:* Lamont, *Breakup*, 110.

113. *Dear Basile:* exhibit, Museum of Work and Culture, Woonsocket, Rhode Island.

114. "La revanche": *Immigrants from the North*, James W. Searles, Kent Morse, and Stephen Hinchman, eds., 39.

114. "Nothing hurts me more": "Portrait of a Franco-American Grandmother," American Life Histories: Manuscripts from the Federal Writers' Project, 1936 1940, New Hampshire Writers' Project #1801.

115. The priests and the government: Guignard, *La Foi*, 4.

115. They warned that: Philip T. Silvia, in *Steeples and Smokestacks*, Claire Quintal, ed., 149.

115. "Let them go": Guignard, *La Foi*, 5.

115. *Where are you going?:* Quintal, *Steeples and Smokestacks*, 438.

115. People in the Richelieu Valley: Brault, *French-Canadian Heritage*, 56.

115. So many left: Quintal, *Steeples and Smokestacks*, 91.

115. "My grandmother and grandfather": Searles, Morse, and Hinchman, *Immigrants from the North*, 9.

116. "the Sunday evening train": Dane Yorke, *The Men and Times of Pepperell*, 74.

116. Nine out of ten: Abbott, *Women in Industry*, 349.

116. In her novel *Canuck:* quoted in Quintal, *Steeples and Smokestacks*, 392.

117. "represented thirty-nine percent": Frances H. Early, "The French-Canadian Family Economy and Standard-of-Living in Lowell, Massachusetts, 1870," 186-99.

117. "It is said that American parents": Eva Shorey, "Annual Report of the Bureau of Industrial and Labor Statistics for the State of Maine, 1908."

117. "is a crime to her offspring": Carroll D. Wright, "The Factory System as an Element in Civilization."

117. The Catholic bishop: Roby, in *Steeples and Smokestacks*, 562.

117. "We have seen": Guignard, *La Foi*, 158.

117. "If a woman's place": Cameron, *Radicals of the Worst Sort*, 66.

118. "endured them stoically": Normand R. Beaupré in forword to Guignard, *La Foi*, viii.

118.   "When we came we didn't know": Searles, Morse, and Hinchman, *Immigrants from the North*, 11.

118.   "Oh, God, yes it was": "Factory Island: Bricks, Mortar and Hope," oral history conducted by Normand R. Beaupré, on file at the York Institute, Saco, Maine.

118.   "Transplanted to the": Shorey, "Annual Report," 43.

119.   "the process of acculturation": Brault, *French-Canadian Heritage*, 86.

119.   "In the middle of February": Searles, Morse, and Hinchman, *Immigrants from the North*, 14.

119.   "they laugh at us": Guignard, *La Foi*, 76.

119.   In Maine, the bishop allowed: ibid., 105.

119.   *Le Progrès*, a French-language: Cole, *Immigrant City*, 89.

120.   In Rhode Island: Brault, *French-Canadian Heritage*, 88.

120.   As the bishop in Maine: Guignard, *La Foi*, 103.

121.   "The men's French societies": Dyke Hendrickson, *Quiet Presence*, 207.

121.   "You were a wreck": Tamara K. Hareven and Randolph Langenbach, *Amoskeag*, 197.

121.   Girls were forbidden: ibid., 240.

121.   Some Franco-Americans cannot recall: ibid., 163.

121.   "The fathers, invoking": Roby, in *Steeples and Smokestacks*, 553.

122.   "My last pay day": ibid., 549.

122.   They didn't want: Early, in *Steeples and Smokestacks*, 125.

122.   "an insult and an affront": exhibit, Maine Historical Society.

123.   "The future America": Jack Beatty, *The Rascal King*, 242.

123.   "become a strong and valuable": Guignard, *La Foi*, 7.

124   As a last resort: Roby, in *Steeples and Smokestacks*, 557.

124.   *Pas de croix*: Brault, *French-Canadian Heritage*, 59.

125.   Mortality rates in the tenements: ibid., 60, 37.

125.   When illness struck: Guignard, *La Foi*, 13.

125.   On the other side: ibid.

125.   "Has a crisis arrived": William N. Locke, "The French Colony at Brunswick, Maine."

125.   "They are quiet": Paul Downing, *Brunswick, Maine*, 82.

125-126.   "The Canadians came to the city": Marsden Hartley, *Androscoggin*, 6, 7.

126.   They saw children: Guignard, *La Foi*, 122.

126.   "A passerby can appreciate": Shorey, "Annual Report," 24.

126.   After coal-fed boilers: Hareven and Langenbach, *Amoskeag*, 198.

126.   In Lewiston in the 1880s: Yves Frenette, "Understanding the French-Canadians of Lewiston."

126-129.   Many details of the Brunswick diphtheria epidemic, unless otherwise cited, are from the files of the *Brunswick Telegraph* during the summer of 1886.

127.   The Cabot Mill's dividends: Edward Chase Kirkland, *Brunswick's Golden Age*, 13.

127.   "a man from the Middle Ages": ibid., 15.

129.   By 1887, there were: Guignard, *La Foi*, 29.

129.   "French-Canadians' unwillingness": Lamont, *Breakup*, 63.

129.   the "French hospital": Frenette, "French-Canadians of Lewiston."

130. "With some exceptions": Guignard, *La Foi*, 90.

130. "He who loses": ibid., 4.

130. "Learn the history": James Hill Parker, *Ethnic Identity*, 27.

131. If an unmarried woman: Hendrickson, *Quiet Presence*, 43.

131. A Franco-American woman who required: Hareven and Langenbach, *Amoskeag*, 256.

131. To send Franco-American children: Guignard, *La Foi*, 14.

132. "I felt bad": Hareven and Langenbach, *Amoskeag*, 267.

132. "I had looked through": Larcom, *New England Girlhood*, 156.

132. In some areas: Yves Frenette, "Coping with Uncertainty," in Richard W. Judd, Edwin A. Churchill, and Joel W. Eastman, eds., *Maine*.

132. "There is such a thing": *Annals of America*, Vol. 10, 570.

132. "An exclusively bookish": Cumbler, *Working-Class Community*, 153.

132-133. "If someone wasn't": Searles, Morse, and Hinchman, *Immigrants from the North*, 22.

133. "It came to a point": ibid., 25.

133. "I lost my eyes": Hareven and Langenbach, *Amoskeag*, 68.

133. "When she was home": Hendrickson, *Quiet Presence*, 199.

133. "steal our money": Searles, Morse, and Hinchman, *Immigrants from the North*, 27.

133-134. "Let's say this girl": Mary H. Blewett, *The Last Generation*, 251.

134. Other workers curried: Henry DeSousa interview, "Shifting Gears," oral history, Massachusetts Foundation for Humanities and Public Policy.

134. When ordered to do so: Lawrence Spitz, filmed interview, Museum of Work and Culture, Woonsocket, Rhode Island.

134. During a series: Guignard, *La Foi*, 94.

134. In Fall River: Silvia, in *Steeples and Smokestacks*, 152.

134. "I was proud of them": *Portland (Maine) Sunday Telegram*, May 9, 1926.

134. Franco-Americans have told: Hareven and Langenbach, *Amoskeag*, 209.

134. During a major 1922 strike: Philip Dexter Arnold, "A Row of Bricks," 788.

135. Details of union activity in Woonsocket are from Carl Gerstle, "The Mobilization of the Working Class Community."

136. "Then it was": Hemon, *Maria Chapdelaine*, 281.

136. "I want to see": C. Stewart Doty, *The First Franco-Americans*, 17.

136. *Oh; how deep:* Donald Deschenes, in *Steeples and Smokestacks*, 444.

136. "Canada made me rich": Guignard, *La Foi*, 38, 39.

137. "You are tired of life": ibid., 39.

137. In 1910, Berubé led: Guignard, in *Steeples and Smokestacks*, 134.

137. "My father never said": American Life Histories.

137. "Now Francos began": Searles, Morse, and Hinchman, *Immigrants from the North*, 46.

138. President Franklin D. Roosevelt approved: Lamont, *Breakup*, 208.

138. "I haven't taught": Guignard, *La Foi*, 135.

139. *the stars like:* Paul Marion, in *Continuing Revolution*, 408.

139. The political and community leaders: *Portland (Maine) Sunday Telegram*, September 17, 1961.

140. "When the looms were running": Hendrickson, *Quiet Presence*, 204.

140. "When I think about it": Beaupré, "Factory Island" oral history.

6. *Wretched Refuse*

141. "While the workingmen": *The Bee Hive*, London, January 7, 1865, quoted in *Annals of America*, Vol. 9, 543.

141. A State Department aide: Sandburg, *Abraham Lincoln*, Vol. 1, 380.

141. She toured New England: Buhle, Molloy, and Sansbury, *Rhode Island Working People*, 5.

142. "We affirm": Wendell Phillips, *Speeches, Lectures, and Letters*, 152-53.

142. "Men die of starvation": Henry George, *Progress and Poverty*, 8.

142-145. Quotations and details of Collins in Dover and Fall River are from her book, *Nature's Aristocracy*.

143. "The physical, intellectual": *Report of Commissioners on the Hours of Labor*, 1867, Massachusetts House Document 44.

145-146. Mary Wheelwright details are from Emiline Burlingame Cheney, "The Story of the Life and Work of Oren B. Cheney."

146-148. Details and quotations relating to the Lowell celebration are from *Semi-Centennial of Lowell*.

148. Agents for the mills: film, Lawrence Heritage State Park.

148. "No one goes hungry": Cameron, *Radicals of the Worst Sort*, 76.

148. Priests and ministers: ibid., 82.

149. "The peasants dreaded": Handlin, *Uprooted*, 203.

149. Emily Greene Balch wrote: Emily Greene Balch, *Our Slavic Fellow Citizens*, 107, 183.

150. They met men with familiar names: Mary Blewett, *Last Generation*, 306.

150. "I thank God": Kennegott, *Record of a City*, 227.

150. In Scotland, village ministers: Hareven and Langenbach, *Amoskeag*, 18.

151. "speak English only": Blewett, *Last Generation*, 52.

151. "This family is not": Handlin, *Uprooted*, 283.

151. "drew a sharp distinction": Oscar Handlin, *Race and Nationality in American Life*, 75.

151. "In forty-two volumes": Handlin, *Uprooted*, 294.

152. "This type, as it has shaped itself": Balch, *Our Slavic Fellow Citizens*, 11.

152. "Communism means": Scontras, *Collective Efforts Among Maine Workers*, 386.

152. "Even enlightened employers": Jacques Downs, *The Cities on the Saco*, 59.

152. "It's God's work": Nicholas V. Karas, *Greek Immigrants at Work*, 1.

153. "What a magic word": ibid., 7.

153. Parading Germans carried: Eartha Dengler, Katharine Khalife, and Ken Skulski, *Images of America*, 101.

153. "French and kindred nationalities": Shorey, *"Annual Report,"* 24.

153. Newspaper coverage of them: Arnold, *"A Row of Bricks,"* 109.

154. Luigi Nardella remembered: Paul Buhle, *Working Lives*, 23.

154. "we did not think": Cameron, *Radicals of the Worst Sort*, xiii.

154. "The one belief": Walter Lord, *The Good Years*, 6.

154. "everyone knows everyone": Balch, *Our Slavic Fellow Citizens*, 59.

154-155. "Make the hearts": Cole, *Immigrant City*, 99.

155. "There are many skilled mechanics": Coburn, *History of Lowell*, 344.

155. Jewish immigrants did find: ibid.

155-156. "The immigrant woman": Abbott, *Women in Industry*, 144.

156. "Dirty faces, torn dresses": Collins, *Nature's Aristocracy*, 146.

156. "brought with them": Barry, *Susan B. Anthony*, 315.

157. "had not forgotten": ibid., 315-16.

157. Emily Greene Balch noted: Balch, *Our Slavic Fellow Citizens*, 8.

157. In 1904, management: Herbert J. Lahne, *Labor in Twentieth Century* America, 73.

157. "A loom fixer could": Hareven and Langenbach, *Amoskeag*, 120.

158. "The following is a fair example": Rosalyn Baxandall and Linda Gordon, *America's Working Women*, 98-100.

158. "There are four sins": Buhle, Molloy, and Sansbury, *Rhode Island Working People*, 29.

159. "But is not a dollar": Rugoff, *Beechers*, 504.

159. Beecher's weekly income: ibid.

159. William Graham Sumner also opposed: William Graham Sumner, *What Social Classes Owe to Each Other*, quoted in *Annals of America*, Vol. 10, 594.

159. "the depravity of the business classes": Milton Meltzer, *Bread and Roses*, 43.

159. Mary Langevin of Chicopee: Baxandall, Gordon, and Reverby, *America's Working Women*, 86.

160. "What shall I say": Collins, *Nature's Aristocracy*, 182.

160. "I regard my work people": Dunwell, *Run of the Mill*, 101.

161. "The mule spinners are a tough crowd": Carol Polizotti Webb, in *Surviving Hard Times*, Mary H. Blewett, ed., 14.

161. *Clickity-clack*: Cumbler, *Working-Class Community*, 185.

161. "They are always": Kennegott, *Record of a City*, 20.

162. "They are dwarfed": *Annals of America*, Vol. 10, 573.

162. "I asked the ages": Meltzer, *Bread and Roses*, 122.

162. "And their children's children": Louis Adamic, "Tragic Towns of New England," *Harpers*, May 1931.

162. "Thousands of men": Lawrence, *Memories*, 50.

163. "Indeed, there could scarcely": Gibb, *Saco-Lowell Shops*, 39.

163. "From an economic": Philip Hubert, "A Piece-Rate System," *Transactions of the American Society of Mechanical Engineers*, 1895, 856-903, quoted in *Annals of America*, Vol. 12, 16.

163. "each man's interest": ibid.

163-164. "despised the time-study men": Dunwell, *Run of the Mill*, 147.

164. "So profound was this feeling": Gibb, *Saco-Lowell Shops*, 395.

164. "His leaving marked the end": Roy P. Fairfield, "Labor Conditions at the Old York: 1831-1900"; Fairfield, *Sands, Spindles and Steeples*, 99.

164. Unfortunately for the York workers: Fairfield, "Labor Conditions at the Old York."

165. The Biddeford-Saco community: ibid.

165. "Young man," Lincoln said: George Waldo Browne, *Amoskeag Manufacturing Company of New Hampshire*, 157.

165. His son, Herman: Hareven and Langenbach, *Amoskeag*, 101.

165. During a strike: ibid., 246.

165. Straw supported his workers: ibid., 109, 253.

166. Roy Fairfield wrote: Fairfield, *Sands, Spindles and Steeples*, 94.

167. "Some wear caps": Shorey, "Annual Report," 10.

167. Shorey wrote about a woman: ibid., 27, 28.

168. "there can be no peace": Meltzer, *Bread and Roses*, 118.

168. "Organized labor knows": *Proceedings of the National Association of Manufacturers*, New Orleans, 1903, quoted in *Annals of America*, Vol. 13, 76.

168-169. "Some of the opponents": ibid.

169. The Methodist Episcopal church: ibid., 142.

169-170. Information on Sidney Blumenthal and the Shelton Looms is principally from the *Museum of American Textile History Newsletter*, Vol. 3, no. 1, Winter 1994.

170. "Nothing was handed": Elizabeth Gurley Flynn, *The Rebel Girl*, 21.

170. "a finer spirit": Lawrence, *Memories*, 49.

7. Fighting for Roses

Note: Numerous details of day-to-day activities during the Lawrence strike are from the files of several area newspapers that covered the events.

172. "oxen without horns": Cameron, *Radicals of the Worst Sort*, 172.

172. "swept through its long floors": Meltzer, *Bread and Roses*, 119.

172. "I heard the most ungodly": U.S. House of Representatives hearings, May 2-7, 1912, 439.

172. "For God's sake": ibid., 264.

173. "The initial violence": Cole, *Immigrant City*, 179.

173. Every one of them: Dunwell, *Run of the Mill*, 152.

174. "willing and well-paid workmen": *Lowell Sun*, January 4, 1912.

174. "Sociologists view": Dengler, Khalife, and Skulski, *Images of America*, 8.

174. "There is no brighter looking": House hearings, 418.

175. The Wood Mill was built: Cole, *Immigrant City*, 177.

175. Each of the two wings: Weible, *Continuing Revolution*, 206.

175. Every week, the mill consumed: Schinto, *Huddle Fever*, 123.

175. When the strike began: Ray Stannard Baker, "The Revolutionary Strike."

176. "He had a round face": *Fortune*, April, 1931, 71-112.

176. He once confided: Arnold, "A Row of Bricks," 234.

176. "The streets in Lawrence": "Shifting Gears" oral history.

177. The newspapers reported: *Lawrence Telegram*, March 6, 1912.

177. "You look like the queen": exhibit, Lawrence Heritage State Park, "Celebrating American History. The Jewish Presence in Lawrence."

177. In a city with a population: House hearings, 341.

177. Only 3,000 people: Ken Skulski, *Images of America*, Vol. 2, 59.

177. "industry, the basis of life": *The World's Greatest Speeches*, 196.

178. There were two hundred saloons: Dengler, Khalife, and Skulski, *Images of America*, 126; Cameron, *Radicals of the Worst Sort*, 66.

178. There was a lot of misery: Cole, *Immigrant City*, 107.

178. At the time of the strike: Schinto, *Huddle Fever*, 128.

178-179. "Huddling people together": ibid.

179. The long rows: Cole, *Immigrant City*, 70.

179. "America, everywhere": Cameron, *Radicals of the Worst Sort*, 164.

179. "an industrial blot": "Work and Wages in Lawrence," *Literary Digest*, July 20, 1912, 89.

179. "It is doubtful": Edward G. Roddy, *Mills, Mansions and Mergers*, 71.

179. They repelled attempts: Cameron, *Radicals of the Worst Sort*, 107.

180. They saved for the day: Skulski, *Images of America*, 38.

180. One of those who won: Meryle Secrest, *Leonard Bernstein*, 8, 9.

180. As the *Washington Post* reported: "A Labor Law That Caused a Strike," *Literary Digest*, January 27, 1912, 148-49.

181. The "for bread" immigrants: Sean Dolan, *The Polish Americans*, 39.

181. "Men with large families": Quoted in Meltzer, *Bread and Roses*, 122.

181. "but about conditions": Baker, "The Revolutionary Strike."

181. "I'd be a dangerous man": House hearings, 28, 11.

181. The star witness: ibid, 169-70.

183. In 1911, the year before: Edward F. Pierce Jr., "The Lawrence Strike of 1912 and the Role of the Industrial Workers of the World," 18.

183. "Every fourth person": ibid., 17.

183. Congressman Augustus O. Stanley: House hearings, 402.

184. Congressman William Wilson: ibid., 396.

184. Workers told of long hours: *New York Times*, January 20, 1912.

184. They knew that sixteen years: Skulski, *Images of America*, 47.

184. They knew that women telephone operators: Philip S. Foner, *Women and the American Labor Movement*, Vol. 2, 83.

185. "We cannot go on making money": Arnold, "A Row of Bricks," 182.

185. With the arrival of the IWW: Pierce, "The Lawrence Strike," 43.

185. Detractors sneered: Schinto, *Huddle Fever*, 16.

185. The Italian workers did so: Cole, *Immigrant City*, 188.

185. "Of all the mingled peoples": Baker, "The Revolutionary Strike."

185. "pregnant with danger": Walter E. Weyl, "The Strike at Lawrence."

186. "No class of people": Harry Emerson Fosdick, "After the Strike in Lawrence."

186. Elizabeth Gurley Flynn remembered: Flynn, *Rebel Girl*, 86.

186. "Division is the surest means": William Cahn, *A Pictorial History of American Labor*, 214.

187. "I was spellbound": "Shifting Gears" oral history.

187. "are of a higher type": *New York Times*, February 1, 1912.

187. "Anything short of murder": Fosdick, "After the Strike."

187. "Throw them down the stairs": Cole, *Immigrant City*, 187. ·

188. "among the most violent": ibid., 188.

188. "By all means": Cahn, *Pictorial History*, 214.

188. People remembered him: Cole, *Immigrant City*, 7.

188. *The Mob, the mightiest judge:* Arturo Giovannitti, *Arrows in the Gale*, 66.

188. *'Twill come:* ibid., 30.

189. "Many women, especially": Baker, "The Revolutionary Strike."

189. "when difficult work": *Lawrence Tribune*, February 12, 1912.

189. He did not hesitate: Schinto, *Huddle Fever*, 140; Hartford, *Where Is Our Responsibility?*, 49.

190. "The inhumanity of those": Hartford, *Where Is Our Responsibility?*, 50.

190. Many of them continued: Cole, *Immigrant City*, 184.

190. "Irish scabs": ibid., 226.

190. Milanese, an immigrant himself: Schinto, *Huddle Fever*, 143.

190. Milanese read the letter: *New York Times*, January 21, 1912.

190. When strikers demonstrated: Cole, *Immigrant City*, 268.

191. Russians pressured landlords: Arnold, "A Row of Bricks," 297.

191. Neighborhood barbers refused: Cole, *Immigrant City*, 189.

191. People all over the city: Samuel Yellen, *American Labor Struggles*, 188.

191. Many also wore: Cameron, *Radicals of the Worst Sort*, 142.

191. The Germans reported: *Lawrence Tribune*, March 11, 1912.

192. Lis, who was of Polish-Austrian heritage: Cameron, *Radicals of the Worst Sort*, 128.

192. "Lawrence was a singing strike": Mary Heaton Vorse, *A Footnote to Folly*, 12.

192. "it was the first strike": Baker, "The Revolutionary Strike."

193. "A wheezy Italian band": Al Priddy, "Controlling the Passions of Men in Lawrence."

193. They "held up everybody": House hearings, 302.

194. The striking women used: Cameron, *Radicals of the Worst Sort*, 128.

194. "the women strikers": William D. Haywood, *Bill Haywood's Book*, 249.

194. "Let the men come out": *Lawrence Telegram*, February 23, 1912.

194. "The pity is: ibid., February 26, 1912.

194. "there was considerable": Flynn, *Rebel Girl*, 132.

195. "I have been getting madder and madder": Fosdick, "After the Strike."

195. "They say she could tie up": ibid.

196. She lectured him: Foner, *Women and American Labor Movement*, 212.

196. "You are being advised": Massachusetts Senate, January 19, 1912, Document 870.

196. some people "are worked up": *Lowell Sun*, January 19, 1912.

196. Sweetser told unit commanders: Flynn, *Rebel Girl*, 129.

197. "Nothing could be done": *Lowell Sun*, February 3, 1912.

197. "They rather enjoyed": Pierce, "The Lawrence Strike," 48.

197. "Insolent, well-fed": Cahn, *Pictorial History*, 172.

197. "These soldiers—tin soldiers": Weyl, "Strike at Lawrence."

197. "You may turn your hose": Fosdick, "After the Strike."

198. *The preachers, cops and money-kings:* Joyce L. Kornbluth, *Rebel Voices*.

198. They imported private detectives: Arnold, "A Row of Bricks," 247.

198. "the militia, the special policemen": Massachusetts Senate Document 870.

199.   "any time class consciousness": Hartford, *Where Is Our Responsibility?*, 46.

199.   "Between the American Federation": Weyl, "Strike at Lawrence."

199.   Golden, a Lancashire Irishman: Hartford, *Where Is Our Responsibility?*, 41.

199.   "they are foreign": *Lowell Sun*, January 19, 1912.

199.   "I find them the most intelligent": Hartford, *Where Is Our Responsibility?*, 41.

199.   "Many of those in power": Carol Hymowitz and Michaele Weissman, *A History of Women in America*, 256.

200.   "This is the first time": Mary K. O'Sullivan, "The Labor War at Lawrence."

200.   "Catholics, Jews, Protestants": Yellen, *American Labor Struggles*, 188.

200.   "in the hands": *New York Times*, January 17, 1912.

200.   In Boston, a twenty-four-hour: ibid., January 18, 1912.

201.   "In the spinning room": ibid., February 1, 1912.

201-202.   "I have read": ibid., January 24, 1912.

202.   "It is the historic mission": Haywood, *Big Bill's Book*, 246.

202.   Such pronouncements carried: J. Anthony Lukas, *Big Trouble*, 205.

202.   "In that day": Herbert R. Mayes, *An Editor's Treasury*, Vol. 1, 252.

202.   An "undesirable" citizen: Lukas, *Big Trouble*, 394, 473.

202.   "many feared that Haywood": Cole, *Immigrant City*, 7.

202.   "Take a character like this": Baker, "Revolutionary Strike."

203.   "Do not let them": Arnold, "Row of Bricks," 264.

203.   "The AFL organizes": Flynn, *Rebel Girl*, 131.

203-205.   Flynn and Malone quotations are from Flynn's *Rebel Girl*, 36, 46, 65, 57, 131.

204.   "the excitement of the crowd": Vorse, *Footnote to Folly*, 8.

204.   "In this struggle": Arnold, "A Row of Bricks," 334.

205.   "Many operatives are beginning": *New York Times*, January 26, 1912.

205.   "If the mill men": ibid.

205.   "terrorism, undefined": ibid., March 11, 1912.

205.   "See all who are still": *Lowell Sun*, February 3, 1912.

206.   "Somebody is doing": Roddy, *Mills, Mansions and Mergers*, 71.

206.   Some observers later expressed: Harris, *American Labor*, 321.

207.   "the crisp, short bark": *Lowell Sun*, January 29, 1912.

207.   "awaiting the coming": ibid., January 30, 1912.

207.   "This order is interpreted": ibid.

207.   When the reinforcements arrived: *New York Times*, January 30, 1912.

207.   "treatment of innocent women": Cameron, *Radicals of the Worst Sort*, 176.

207.   Police Chief Sullivan: House hearings, 293.

207.   "the peace of the cemeteries": Arnold, "A Row of Bricks," 234.

208.   "They tell us": Fosdick, "After the Strike."

208.   "Tomorrow will be": *Lawrence Telegram*, January 31, 1912.

208-209.   "In taking the body": ibid., February 1, 1912.

209.   "They have murdered": ibid., January 31, 1912.

209.   "Victory is in sight": ibid., February 1, 1912.

209.   "were very much emaciated": House hearings, 238.

211.   "In a moment": ibid., 196.

211.   "no sooner had": *Lawrence Telegram*, February 24, 1912.

211.   "Both sides went": *New York Times*, February 25, 1912.

211-212. "I was standing there": House hearings, 191, 193.

213.   "It was a day": Flynn, *Rebel Girl*, 138.

213.   "It is an outrage": ibid., 141.

213.   "the attempt to put an embargo": "The Lawrence Strike Children," *Literary Digest*, March 9, 1912, 471-72.

213.   Senator William Borah: Flynn, *Rebel Girl*.

213.   "it is the right": ibid.

213.   "as chuckle-headed an exhibition": "Lawrence Strike Children."

213.   "intended to be only": *Outlook*, February 17, 1912, 358.

213.   "an incipient revolution": *Lawrence Tribune*, February 25, 1912.

213.   "It is now a war": ibid.

214.   He invited a former Socialist: ibid., March 3, 1912.

215.   "stood out there and booed": House hearings, 291.

215.   Joseph Ettor intervened: Cole, *Immigrant City*, 185.

215.   "We did not attack": Flynn, *Rebel Girl*, 132.

215.   Among those joining: Cahn, *Pictorial History*, 236.

216.   "the most unselfish": O'Sullivan, "Labor War."

216.   "This is the first time": *Lawrence Tribune*, March 13, 1912.

216.   "It was a wonderful strike": Haywood, *Big Bill's Book*, 254.

217.   "For these people": Cole, *Immigrant City*, 183.

217.   "To the young American *intelligentsia*": Selig Perlman and Philip Taft, *History of Labor in the United States*, 273.

217.   "When a thoughtful man": Fosdick, "After the Strike."

217.   "The class struggle": "Lawrence Strike from Various Angles," *Outlook*, April 6, 1912, 79-80.

218.   "By temperament and conviction": Harris, *American Labor*, 327.

218.   "Most of us": Flynn, *Rebel Girl*, 150.

218.   Joseph Ettor vanished: Robert D'Atililio, in *Encyclopedia of the American Left*.

218.   "The emancipation of human kind": Dulles, *Labor in America*, 219.

218.   *Aye, think!*: Giovannitti, *Arrows in the Gale*, 29.

219.   She returned to the Washington Mill: Cameron, *Radicals of the Worst Sort*, 163.

219.   Workers who did not strike: Pierce, "Lawrence Strike," 72.

219.   A newspaper recounted: *Lawrence Eagle-Tribune*, November 18, 1990.

219.   His son, William Junior: Roddy, *Mills, Mansions and Mergers*, 75, 116.

219.   "Lawrence lickspittles": Schinto, *Huddle Fever*, 46.

220.   His son helped him: ibid., 166.

220.   William Senior became mentally unbalanced: ibid., 167.

220.   "handled his part tactfully": Donald R. McCoy, *Calvin Coolidge*, 46.

220.   "Arise! Slaves of the World!": Haywood, *Big Bill's Book*, 252.

221.   "A committee in charge": Flynn, *Rebel Girl*, 150-51.

221.   "For God and Country!": Haywood, *Big Bill's Book*.

221.   "The city is waking up": Alice L. Walsh, *A Sketch of the Life and Labor of the Rev. James T. O'Reilly, O.S.A.*, 53.

222. "No bread and roses": *Lawrence Eagle-Tribune*, April 8, 1988.

223. "I think that a corporation": *Portland* (Maine) *Press Herald*, May, 1999.

8. *Last Bells*

225. "The outlook for textiles": Arthur M. Kenison, *Dumaine's Amoskeag*, 82.

225. It employed 17,000: Hareven and Langenbach, *Amoskeag*, 10.

225. Many workers shared: Kenison, *Dumaine's Amoskeag*, 23.

225. A decade earlier: ibid., 1, 82.

226. "We were like family": Hareven and Langenbach, *Amoskeag*, 11.

226. Dumaine invested less: *Dictionary of American Biography*, Supplement 5, 190.

226. "an insult to those": Laurence F. Gross, in *Continuing Revolution*, 289.

226. "Why should the mills": Guignard, *La Foi*, 115.

227. "The city of the dinner pail": Cumbler, *Working-Class Community*, 141.

227. "How are we going to stop it?": Hartford, *Where Is Our Responsibility?*, 53-54.

227. "If it is not": Fairfield, *Sands, Spindles and Steeples*, 101.

228. "I actually saw": Foner, *Factory Girls*, 218.

228. Those gifted with leadership: Evans, *Born for Liberty*, 191.

228. By the 1920s: Foner, *Factory Girls*, 225.

228. Southern towns wooed: George B. Tindall, *The Emergence of the New South*, 75, 319.

229. "By pushing the Northern": Page Smith, *The Rise of Industrial America*, 835.

229. "the terrible years": M.D.C. Crawford, *The Heritage of Cotton*, 168.

229. Towns cast off: ibid., 220.

229-230. Police and mill guards: Nancy MacLean, *Behind the Mask of Chivalry*, 35.

230. When business slowed: Foner, *Factory Girls*, 230.

230. Mattie Hughes, the mother of three: ibid., 231.

230. The Pacific Mills: Hartford, *Where Is Our Responsibility?*, 81, 91.

230. When Elizabeth Glendower Evans: Lord, *Good Years*, 325.

230. "I have never seen": ibid., 322.

230. *The golf links lie*: *Dictionary of American Biography*, Supplement 6, 113.

231. The result was a federal: Hartford, *Where Is Our Responsibility?*, 59.

231. In Georgia, Governor Eugene Talmadge's: Harris, *American Labor*, 340.

231. In Honea Path: ibid., 62.

231. Four New England governors: ibid., 61.

231. During the Depression: Adamic, "Tragic Towns of New England."

232. "If any industry": Wolfbein, *Decline of a Cotton Textile City*, 126.

232. John T. Cumbler described: Cumbler, *Working-Class Community*, 140-141.

233. "I wish you would do something": Wolfbein, *Decline of a Cotton Textile City*, 117.

234. "I went to his assistance": Karen Ahlin, in *Surviving Hard Times*, 141.

234. When Sidney Muskovitz, another dye worker: Blewett, *Last Generation*.

234. "the federal tax code": Hartford, *What Is Our Responsibility?*, 91.

234. Royal Little, a long-time manufacturer: Dunwell, *Run of the Mill*, 161.

235. Events involving the closing of the Nashua mills are from Winship, *A Testing Time*.

236. "hadn't been such a God-awful": Hartford, *What Is Our Responsibility?*, 92.

236.   "We thought the shoe shops": ibid., 169.

236.   "Our roots are deep": ibid., 92.

236.   Mary H. Blewett interviewed: Blewett, *Last Generation*, 42.

237.   John Neild did the same: Wolfbein, *Decline of the Cotton Textile City*, 134.

237.   Greek immigrant workers: Karas, *Greek Immigrants*, 93.

237.   Personnel managers in the mills: Blewett, *Last Generation*, 253.

238.   *I don't hear the bells:* Deschenes, in *Steeples and Smokestacks*, 437.

238.   "Fifty years ago": *Annals of America*, Vol. 17, 89.

239.   John Buckley, a mayor of Lawrence: "Shifting Gears" oral history.

239.   A citizens' group in New Bedford: Neal R. Peirce, *The New England States*, 136.

239.   "one big ghetto": Schinto, *Huddle Fever*, 36.

239.   "ponderous Chartres": Dunwell, *Run of the Mill*, 260.

239.   "working-class revenge": Loretta A. Ryan, in *Continuing Revolution*, 379.

240.   "I regard it": Larcom, *New England Girlhood*, 196, 225.

241.   "I saw my grandparents": *Lawrence Eagle-Tribune*, December 30, 1986.

241.   "No, Mr. Fremmer": ibid., January 26, 1987.

BIBLIOGRAPHY

Abbott, Edith. *Women in Industry*. Appleton, 1910.

Adamic, Louis. "Tragic Towns of New England." *Harpers*, May 1931.

Adler, Mortimer J., editor in chief, *The Annals of America*. Encyclopedia Britannica, 1968.

American Life Histories: Manuscripts from the Federal Writers' Project, 1936-1940.

Amory, Cleveland. *The Proper Bostonians*. Dutton, 1947.

Appleton, Ann Swett. Ann Swett Appleton Letters, 1847-1850. Edited by Priscilla Ordway. Typescript. Manchester Historic Association. Miscellaneous Persons Papers, Box 1, Folder 7.

Appleton, Nathan. *Introduction of the Power Loom and Origin of Lowell*. B. H. Penhallow, 1858.

Arnold, Philip Dexter. *A Row of Bricks: Worker Activism in the Merrimack Valley Textile Industry, 1912-1922*. Ph.D. diss., University of Wisconsin, 1985.

An Authentic History of the Lawrence Calamity. John J. Dyer & Co., 1860.

Baker, Ray Stannard. "The Revolutionary Strike." *American Magazine*, May 1912.

Balch, Emily Greene. *Our Slavic Fellow Citizens*. Charities Publications Committee, 1910.

Barry, Kathleen. *Susan B. Anthony: A Biography*. New York University Press, 1988.

Baxandall, Rosalyn; Linda Gordon, eds., with Susan Reverby. *America's Working Women*. W. W. Norton, 1995.

Beatty, Jack. *The Rascal King: The Life and Times of James Michael Curley*. Perseus, 1992.

Beaupre, Normand R. "Factory Island: Bricks, Mortar and Hope." Oral history. York Institute, Saco, Maine.

Birmingham, Stephen. *Real Lace.* Harper, 1973.

Blewett, Mary H. *The Last Generation: Work and Life in the Textile Mills of Lowell, Massachusetts, 1910-1960.* The University of Massachusetts Press, 1990.

———, ed. *Surviving Hard Times: The Working People of Lowell.* Lowell Museum, 1982.

Brauer, Kinley J. *Conscience versus Cotton: Massachusetts Whig Politics and Southwestern Expansion.* University of Kentucky Press, 1967.

Brault, Gerard J. *The French-Canadian Heritage in New England.* University Press of New England, 1986.

Bridgman, Laura Nichols. Manuscript. Houghton Library, Harvard University, ABC FM Biographical Collection, Box 10.

Brigham, Loriman, ed. "An Independent Voice: A Mill Girl from Vermont Speaks Her Mind." *Vermont History*, 1973.

Brooks, Van Wyck. *The Flowering of New England.* E. P. Dutton, 1936.

Brown, Richard D. *Massachusetts, a History.* W. W. Norton, 1978.

Browne, George Waldo. *Amoskeag Manufacturing Company of Manchester, New Hampshire.* Amoskeag Manufacturing Company, 1915.

Buhle, Paul, ed. *Working Lives: An Oral History of Rhode Island Labor.* Rhode Island Historical Society, 1987.

Buhle, Paul; Scott Molloy; and Gail Sansbury, eds. *A History of Rhode Island Working People.* Regine Printing Co., 1983.

Cahn, Bill. *Mill Town.* Cameron and Cahn, 1954.

Cahn, William. *A Pictorial History of American Labor.* Crown Publishers, 1972.

Cameron, Ardis. *Radicals of the Worst Sort.* University of Illinois Press, 1993.

Carey, John, ed. *Eyewitness to History.* Harvard University Press, 1987.

Cheney, Emiline Burlingame. "The Story of the Life and Work of Oren B. Cheney." Published for Bates College by the Morning Star Publishing House, Boston, 1907.

Coburn, Frederick W. *History of Lowell and Its People.* Lewis Historical Publishing Company, 1920.

Coffey, Michael, ed., Terry Golway, text. *The Irish in America.* Hyperion, 1997.

Cole, Donald B. *Immigrant City.* The University of North Carolina Press, 1963.

Collins, Jennie. *Nature's Aristocracy.* Lee and Shepard, 1871.

Coolidge, John. *Mill and Mansion.* The University of Massachusetts Press, 1993.

BIBLIOGRAPHY

Cooper, James Fenimore. *America and the Americans: Notions Picked Up by a Traveling Bachelor,* *2d ed., Vol. 1.* Lea & Carey, 1828.

Copeland, Lewis, and Lawrence W. Lamm, eds. *The World's Greatest Speeches.* Dover Publications, 1973.

Crawford, M. D. C. *The Heritage of Cotton.* G. P. Putnam's Sons, 1924.

Crockett, Davy. *Davy Crockett's Own Story.* Citadel Press, 1955.

Cumbler, John T. *Working-Class Community in Industrial America: Work, Leisure, and Struggle in Two Industrial Cities, 1880-1930.* Greenwood Press, 1979.

Curtis, Edmund. *A History of Ireland.* Methuen & Co., 1936.

Dalzell, Robert F., Jr. *Enterprising Elite: The Boston Associates and the World They Made.* W. W. Norton, 1993.

Davis, Kenneth C. *Don't Know Much About the Civil War.* William Morrow, 1996.

Dengler, Eartha; Khalife, Katherine; and Skulski, Ken. *Images of America: Lawrence, Massachusetts.* Arcadia Publishing, 1995.

Dickens, Charles. *American Notes for General Circulation.* Penguin Books. n.d.

Diner, Hasia R. *Erin's Daughters in America.* Johns Hopkins University Press, 1983.

Dolan, Sean. *The Polish Americans.* Sandra Stotsky, general editor. Chelsea House, 1997.

Donald, David. *Charles Sumner and the Coming of the Civil War.* Alfred A. Knopf, 1960.

Dorgan, Maurice B. *History of Lawrence, Mass.* The Murray Publishing Co., 1924.

Doty, C. Stewart. *The First Franco-Americans.* University of Maine Press, 1985.

Downing, Paul. *Brunswick, Maine: 250 Years a Town.* Penmor Lithographers, 1989.

Downs, Jacques. *The Cities on the Saco.* The Donning Company, 1985.

Duberman, Martin. *James Russell Lowell.* Houghton Mifflin, 1966.

Dublin, Thomas. *Farm to Factory: Women's Letters, 1830-1860.* Columbia University Press, 1981.

———. *Lowell: The Story of an Industrial City.* Federal Publication Handbook 140.

———. *Transforming Women's Work: New England Lives in the Industrial Revolution.* Cornell University Press, 1994.

Dubnoff, Steven Jan. *The Family and Absence from Work: Irish Workers in a Lowell, Massachusetts Cotton Mill, 1860.* Ph.D. diss., Brandeis University, 1976.

Dulles, Foster Rhea. *Labor in America.* Thomas Y. Crowell, 1949.

Dunwell, Steve. *The Run of the Mill.* David R. Godine, 1978.

Early, Frances H. "The French-Canadian Family Economy and Standard-of-Living in Lowell, Massachusetts, 1870." *Journal of Family History,* Summer 1982.

BIBLIOGRAPHY

Eisler, Benita, ed., *The Lowell Offering, Writings of New England Mill Women.* J. B. Lippincott, 1977.

Emerson, Ralph Waldo. "The Young American." *Nature, Addresses and Lectures.* Riverside Press, 1903.

Evans, Sara M. *Born for Liberty: A History of Women in America.* Free Press, 1989.

Fairfield, Roy P. "Labor Conditions at the Old York: 1831-1900." *New England Quarterly,* June 1957.

. *Sands, Spindles and Steeples, a History of Saco, Maine.* House of Falmouth, 1956.

Fitzgerald, Patricia, and Olive Kennedy. *The Great Famine in Killala.* Mayo County (Ireland) Council, 1996.

Flynn, Elizabeth Gurley. *The Rebel Girl: An Autobiography.* International Publishers, 1973.

Foner, Philip S. *The Factory Girls.* The University of Illinois Press, 1977.

. *Women and the American Labor Movement,* Free Press, 1982.

Fones Wolf, Kenneth, and Martin Kaufman. *Labor in Massachusetts: Selected Essays.* Institute for Massachusetts Studies, Westfield State College, 1990.

Fosdick, Harry Emerson. "After the Strike in Lawrence." *The Outlook,* June 15, 1912.

Fowler, Orin. *An Historical Sketch of Fall River 1841.* Benjamin Earl, Publisher. On file at Maine Historical Society.

Frenette, Yves. "Understanding the French Canadians of Lewiston, 1860-1900: An Alternative Framework." *Maine Historical Society Quarterly,* Spring 1986.

George, Henry. *Progress and Poverty.* Robert Schalkenbach Foundation, 1929.

Gerstle, Carl. "The Mobilization of the Working Class Community: The Independent Textile Union in Woonsocket, 1931-1946." *Radical History Review,* Vol. 17, Spring 1978.

Gersuny, Carl. "A Devil in Petticoats." *Business History Review,* Vol. 50, Summer 1976.

Gibb, George Sweet. *The Saco-Lowell Shops.* Harvard University Press, 1950.

Giovannitti, Arturo. *Arrows in the Gale.* Hillacre Bookhouse, 1914.

Greenslet, Ferris. *The Lowells and Their Seven Worlds.* Houghton Mifflin, 1946.

Gregory, Frances W. *Nathan Appleton: Merchant and Entrepreneur 1779-1861.* University Press of Virginia, 1975.

Gross, Laurence F. *The Course of Industrial Decline.* Johns Hopkins University Press, 1993.

Guignard, Michael J. *La Foi-La Langue-La Culture: The Franco-Americans of Biddeford, Maine.* Privately printed, 1982.

Handlin, Oscar. *Race and Nationality in American Life.* Anchor Books, 1957.

BIBLIOGRAPHY

———. *The Uprooted.* Little, Brown, 1951.

Hareven, Tamara K., and Randolph Langenbach. *Amoskeag, Life and Work in an American Factory City.* Pantheon Books, 1978.

Harris, Herbert. *American Labor.* Yale University Press, 1939.

Hartford, William F. *Where Is Our Responsibility?* University of Massachusetts Press, 1996.

Hartley, Marsden. *Androscoggin.* Falmouth Publishing House, 1940.

Hatch, Alden. *The Lodges of Massachusetts.* Hawthorn Books, 1973.

Hawthorne, Nathaniel. *Mosses from an Old Manse.* Houghton Mifflin, 1882.

Hayden, Tom, ed. *Irish Hunger.* Roberts Rinehart, 1997.

Haywood, William D. *Big Bill's Book: The Autobiography of William D. Haywood.* International Publishers, 1966.

Hemon, Louis. *Maria Chapdelaine.* Macmillan, 1921.

Hendrickson, Dyke. *Quiet Presence.* Guy Gannett Publishing Co., 1980.

Henry David Thoreau. The Library of America, 1985.

Heymann, C. David. *American Aristocracy: The Lives & Times of James Russell, Amy & Robert Lowell.* Dodd, Mead, 1980.

Hilen, Andrew, ed. *The Letters of Henry Wadsworth Longfellow,* Volume 3, 1844-1856. Harvard University Press, 1972.

Hill, Hamilton Andrews. *Memoir of Abbott Lawrence.* Privately printed, 1883.

Holbrook, Stewart H. *The Yankee Exodus.* Macmillan, 1950.

Hubert, Philip G. "The Business of a Factory." *Scribner's,* Vol. 21, no. 3, March 1897.

Hunt, John Gabriel, ed., *The Essential Abraham Lincoln.* Gramercy Books, 1993.

Hymowitz, Carol, and Michaele Weissman. *A History of Women in America.* Bantam, 1978.

An Introduction to Biddeford's History and a Chronological Outline of Events. McArthur Library, Biddeford, Maine, 1944.

James, Edward T., ed. *Notable American Women.* Harvard University Press, 1971.

Jones, Howard Mumford, and Bessie Zaban Jones, eds. *The Many Voices of Boston.* Little, Brown, 1975.

Josephson, Hannah. *Golden Threads.* Duell, Sloan and Pearce, 1949.

Judd, Richard W.; Edwin A. Churchill; and Joel W. Eastman, eds. *Maine, the Pine Tree State from Prehistory to the Present.* University of Maine Press, 1995.

Karabatsos, Louis T., and Martha Mayo. *Communidade.* Lowell Historical Society, 1994.

Karas, Nicholas V. *Greek Immigrants at Work: "A Lowell Odyssey."* Meteora Press, 1986.

Kee, Robert. *The Green Flag.* Penguin Books, 1972.

Keneally, Thomas. *The Great Shame.* Doubleday, 1998.

Kenison, Arthur M. *Dumaine's Amoskeag.* Saint Anselm College Press, 1997.

Kennedy, John F. *Profiles in Courage.* Harper, 1957.

Kennegott, George F. *The Record of a City.* Macmillan, 1912.

Kirkland, Edward Chase. *Brunswick's Golden Age.* C. Parker Loring, 1941.

Kornbluth, Joyce L., ed. *Rebel Voices: An I.W.W. Anthology.* University of Michigan Press, 1964.

Lader, Lawrence. *The Bold Brahmins: New England's War Against Slavery: 1831-1863.* E. P. Dutton, 1961.

Lahne, Herbert J. *Labor in Twentieth Century America: The Cotton Worker.* Farrar & Rinehart, 1944.

Lamont, Lansing. *Breakup: The Coming End of Canada and the Stakes for America.* W. W. Norton, 1994.

Larcom, Lucy. *A New England Girlhood.* Houghton Mifflin, 1889.

Lawrence, William. *Memories of a Happy Life.* Houghton Mifflin, 1926.

Laxton, Edward. *The Famine Ships.* Henry Holt, 1996.

Locke, William N. "The French Colony at Brunswick, Maine: A Historical Sketch." *Archives de Folklore,* Vol. 1, no. 1, 1946.

Lord, Walter. *The Good Years.* Harper, 1960.

Lukas, J. Anthony. *Big Trouble.* Simon & Schuster, 1997.

MacLean, Nancy. *Behind the Mask of Chivalry.* Oxford University Press, 1994.

MacManus, Seumas. *The Story of the Irish Race.* Random House, 1990.

Malone, Dumas, ed. *Dictionary of American Biography.* Scribner, 1961.

Mayes, Herbert., ed. *An Editor's Treasury.* Atheneum, 1968.

McCoy, Donald R. *Calvin Coolidge: The Quiet President.* Macmillan, 1967.

Meltzer, Milton. *Bread and Roses: The Struggle of American Labor 1865-1915.* Facts on File, 1991.

Miles, Henry A. *Lowell As It Was, and As It Is.* Powers and Bagley and N. L. Payton, 1845.

Miller, William Lee. *Arguing About Slavery: The Great Battle in the United States Congress.* Knopf, 1996.

Mitchell, Brian C. *The Paddy Camps: The Irish of Lowell 1821-61.* University of Illinois Press, 1988.

Mofford, Judith Haines. *Talkin' Union: The American Labor Movement*. Discovery Enterprises, 1997.

Montgomery, David. *The Fall of the House of Labor*. Cambridge University Press, 1987.

Mrozowski, Stephen A.; Grace H. Ziesing; and Mary C. Beaudry. *Living on the Boott: Historical Archaeology at the Boott Mills Boardinghouses, Lowell, Massachusetts*. University of Massachusetts Press, 1996.

Mundy, James H. *Hard Times, Hard Men*. Harp Publications, 1990.

Nisonoff, Laurie. "Bread and Roses: The Proletarianization of Women Workers in New England Textile Mills, 1827-1848." *Historical Journal of Massachusetts*, 1981.

O'Connell, William Cardinal. *Recollections of Seventy Years*. Houghton Mifflin Company, 1934.

O'Connor, Richard. *The Irish*. G. P. Putnam's Sons, 1971.

O'Dwyer, George F. *The Irish Catholic Genesis of Lowell*. Lowell Museum Corporation, 1981.

O'Sullivan, Mary K. "The Labor War at Lawrence." *The Outlook*, April 6, 1912.

Parker, James Hill. *Ethnic Identity*. University Press of America, 1983.

Peirce, Neal R. *The New England States*. W. W. Norton, 1976.

Perlman, Selig, and Philip Taft. *History of Labor in the United States*, Vol. 4. Macmillan, 1921-1935.

Phelps, Elizabeth Stuart. *The Silent Partner* and "The Tenth of January". Feminist Press, 1983.

Phillips, Wendell. *Speeches, Lectures, and Letters*. 2d series. Lee and Shepard, 1905.

Pierce, Edward F. *The Lawrence Strike of 1912 and the Role of the Industrial Workers of the World*. Ph.D. diss., Southern Connecticut State College, 1977.

Potter, George. *To the Golden Door*. Little, Brown, 1960.

Priddy, Al. "Controlling the Passions of Men in Lawrence." *The Outlook*, October 1912.

Quintal, Claire, ed. *Steeples and Smokestacks: The Franco-American Experience in New England*. Institut Francais, Assumption College, 1996.

Rand, John A. *The Peoples: Lewiston-Auburn Maine, 1875-1975*. Bond Wheelwright Company, 1975.

Remini, Robert. *Daniel Webster*. W. W. Norton, 1997.

Robinson, Harriet H. *Loom and Spindle*. Press Pacifica, 1976.

Roddy, Edward G. *Mills, Mansions and Mergers: The Life of William M. Wood*. American Textile History Museum, 1982.

Rugoff, Milton. *The Beechers*. Harper, 1981.

Sandburg, Carl. *Abraham Lincoln: The War Years*. Harcourt, Brace, 1939.

BIBLIOGRAPHY

Schinto, Jeanne. *Huddle Fever: Living in the Immigrant City*. Alfred A. Knopf, 1995.

Schlesinger, Arthur M., Jr. *The Age of Jackson*. Little, Brown, 1945.

Scontras, Charles A. *Collective Efforts Among Maine Workers: Beginnings and Foundations, 1820-1880*. Bureau of Labor Education, University of Maine, 1994.

Searles, James W.; Kent Morse; and Stephen Hinchman, eds. *Immigrants from the North*. Pen Mor Printers, 1982.

Secrest, Meryle. *Leonard Bernstein: A Life*. Alfred A. Knopf, 1994.

Selden, Bernice. *The Mill Girls: Lucy Larcom, Harriet Hanson Robinson, Sarah G. Bagley*. Antheneum, 1983.

Semi-Centennial of Lowell. Penhallow Printing, 1876.

Shorey, Eva. *Twenty-second Annual Report of the Bureau of Industrial and Labor Statistics for the State of Maine*, 1908.

Silvia, Philip T., Jr. "The Position of Workers in a Textile Community: Fall River in the Early 1880s." *Labor History*, 1975.

Skulski, Ken. *Images of America: Lawrence, Massachusetts*, Vol. 2, Arcadia Publishing, 1997.

Smith, Paige. *The Rise of Industrial America: A People's History of the Post-Reconstruction Era*, Vol. 6. McGraw-Hill, 1985.

Sochen, June. *Herstory: A Woman's View of American History*. Alfred Publishing Co., 1974.

Stachiw, Myron O. "For the Sake of Commerce: Rhode Island Slavery and the Textile Industry." Museum of Rhode Island History, 1982.

Stampp, Kenneth M. *The Peculiar Institution*. Alfred A. Knopf, 1956.

Steinberg, Theodore. *Nature Incorporated: Industrialization and the Waters of New England*. University of Massachusetts Press, 1991.

The Strike at Lawrence, Mass. Hearings Before the Committee on Rules of the House of Representatives, March 2-7, 1912. Government Printing Office.

Swinford Historical Society. *Famine in the Swinford Union*. Swinford, County Mayo, Republic of Ireland, n.d.

Taft, Philip. *Organized Labor in American History*. Harper, 1964.

Tharp, Louise Hall. *The Appletons of Beacon Hill*. Little, Brown, 1973.

— —. *Mrs. Jack*. Little, Brown, 1965.

Thoreau, Henry David. *The Concord and The Merrimack*. Arranged with Notes by Dudley C. Lunt. College & University Press, 1954.

Tindall, George B. *The Emergence of the New South 1913-1945*. Louisiana State University Press, 1967.

BIBLIOGRAPHY

U.S. Senate. 1910. *Report on Condition of Woman and Child Wage-earners in the United States*. Doc. 645.

Vorse, Mary Heaton. *A Footnote to Folly*. Farrar & Rinehart, 1935.

Walsh, Alice L. *A Sketch of the Life and Labors of the Rev. James T. O'Reilly, O.S.A.* Free Press Printing Co., n.d.

Ware, Caroline F. *The Early New England Cotton Manufacture*. Houghton Mifflin, 1931.

Wayman, Dorothy G. *Cardinal O'Connell of Boston*. Farrar, Straus and Young, 1955.

Weible, Robert, ed. *The Continuing Revolution*. Lowell Historical Society, 1991.

Weisberger, Bernard A. "The Working Ladies of Lowell." *American Heritage Magazine*, February 1961.

Wertheimer, Barbara Mayer. *We Were There: The Story of Working Women in America*. Pantheon, 1977.

Weyl, Walter E. "The Strike at Lawrence." *The Outlook*, February 10, 1912.

Whitehouse, Robert A. *Dover History*. Manuscript, at Dover (New Hampshire) Public Library.

Winship, Stephen. *A Testing Time: Crisis and Revival in Nashua*. Nashua-New Hampshire Foundation, 1989.

Wolfbein, Seymour Louis. *The Decline of a Cotton Textile City*. Columbia University Press, 1944.

Woodham-Smith, Cecil. *The Great Hunger: Ireland 1845-1849*. Penguin Books, 1962.

Wright, Carroll D. "The Factory System as an Element in Civilization." *Journal of Social Science*, no. 16, December 1882.

Yellen, Samuel. *American Labor Struggles*. Harcourt, Brace, 1936.

Yorke, Dane. *The Men and Times of Pepperell*. Pepperell Manufacturing Co., 1945.

INDEX

INDEX